Shakespeare, Trauma and Contemporary Performance

Routledge Studies in Shakespeare

Shakespeare, Trauma and Contemporary Performance

Catherine Silverstone

Routledge
Taylor & Francis Group
New York   London

First published 2011
by Routledge
711 Third Avenue, New York, NY 10016

Simultaneously published in the UK
by Routledge
2 Park Square, Milton Park, Abingdon, Oxon OX14 4RN

Routledge is an imprint of the Taylor & Francis Group, an informa business

Typeset in Sabon by IBT Global.
Printed and bound in the United States of America on acid-free paper by IBT Global.

Library of Congress Cataloging-in-Publication Data

Beyond cognitive metaphor theory : perspectives on literary metaphor / edited by
Monika Fludernik.
   p. cm.—(Routledge studies in rhetoric and stylistics ; 3)
   Includes bibliographical references and index.
 1. Metaphor in literature. 2. Metaphor. 3. Figures of speech in literature
 4. Cognition in literature. 5. Discourse analysis, Literary. I. Fludernik, Monika.
   P302.5.B49 2011
   809'.915—dc22
                                          2010048810

ISBN13: 978-0-415-95645-1(hbk)
ISBN13: 978-0-203-86294-0 (ebk)

Contents

Illustrations

Acknowledgements

Shakespeare, Trauma and Contemporary Performance has been a long time coming and the debts it bears to others are evident on every page. My major gratitude is to those who have read drafts of the book at various stages of its development. I am grateful to Nick Ridout for his comments on the introduction; Nadia Davids and Natasha Distiller for their help with my work on South Africa; and Sarah Annes Brown, Maria Delgado, Jen Harvie, Mark Houlahan and Julie Scanlon for their perceptive comments on drafts of the whole manuscript that have enhanced it significantly. Needless to say, all errors that remain are my own.

I am extremely fortunate to have had excellent teachers and mentors, whose support and advice has been invaluable over many years. I would particularly like to thank Mark Houlahan at the University of Waikato, Margaret Healy at the University of Sussex, Sarah Annes Brown at Anglia Ruskin University and Maria Delgado and Jen Harvie at Queen Mary University of London. I have also benefitted from conversations about Shakespeare, trauma and contemporary performance and related (and unrelated) topics with Pascale Aebischer, Lis Austin, Christian Billing, Gianna Bouchard, Mark Thornton Burnett, Julia Cort, Mark Currie, Bridget Escolme, John Gardner, Joss Hands, Barbara Hodgdon, Peter Holland, Tanya Horeck, Dominic Johnson, Michelle Keown, Brian Lobel, Megan Macdonald, Caoimhe McAvinchey, Michael McKinnie, Gordon McMullan, Jen Mitas, Lindsey Moore, Katy Price, Jim Reynolds, Carol Chillington Rutter, Lara Shalson, Alan Sinfield, Sean Skinner, Cecilia Sosa, Sarah Stanton, Paul Steinberg, Susy Thomas, David Tromans, William Tromans, Lois Weaver, Martin Welton, Ramona Wray, Rowlie Wymer, Tory Young and, most specially, Julie Scanlon. I am grateful for the opportunities I have had to discuss some of the performances considered in this book with my students, particularly those who have taken my Shakespeare after Shakespeare and Performance, Sexuality and Identity courses at Queen Mary. I would also like to thank colleagues in the School of English and Drama at Queen Mary for their encouragement during the writing of the book. I am very grateful to Queen Mary for a sabbatical that enabled me to complete the final stages of this project and for financial support in securing the images. My editors at Routledge—Max Novick, Erica Wetter and, most recently, Liz Levine—have been patient and supportive throughout the duration of the book's production. I am also very appreciative of the reports I received from Routledge's three anonymous reviewers.

This book is stronger for the comments and questions I received on work in progress I presented at the British Shakespeare Association conference (Newcastle, 2005); Quorum, the Department of Drama research seminar at Queen Mary (London, 2008); Scaena: Shakespeare and His Contemporaries in Performance (Cambridge, 2008); the Shakespeare Association of America conference (Washington D.C., 2009); the London Metropolitan Archives' Lesbian, Gay, Bisexual, Transgender History and Archive conference (London, 2009); and "Traces of . . . A Series of Discussions toward an Ethics of Literature, Site and Performance" at King's College London (London, 2010).

I am indebted to the archivists and librarians who curate much of the material on which this book is based. In particular, I would like to thank Claire Brunnen, Gavin Clarke and, especially, Margherita Orlando at the National Theatre Archive; David Ward, Hannah Thomas and, especially, Vicky Holmes at the Archives at Royal Holloway, University of London; Sylvia Morris at the Shakespeare Centre Library and Archive; Rachael Keene and Emma Furderer at the Special Collections of the British Film Institute; John Robson at the New Zealand Collection at the University of Waikato; and Lusanda Zokufa at the Market Theatre.

Material from the Derek Jarman Special Collection held at the British Film Institute is reproduced by permission of the Derek Jarman Estate and Peake Associates. Material from the Gay Sweatshop archive is reproduced by permission of the Archives, Royal Holloway, University of London. Archival material relating to National Theatre productions is reproduced by permission of the National Theatre Archive. I am grateful to Ruphin Coudyzer, Sunil Gupta and Alena Melichar for their permission to reproduce photographs. I am also grateful to Philip Osment and Lois Weaver for taking the time to share their thoughts about Gay Sweatshop with me.

This book could not have been written without the love and support of my friends and family, particularly Anne and Brian Silverstone whose careers are an inspiration to my own.

Earlier versions of parts of the Introduction and Chapter 1 were published as "'Honour the real thing': Shakespeare, Trauma and *Titus Andronicus* in South Africa," in *Shakespeare Survey* 62 (2009): 46–57 and an earlier version of Chapter 2 was published as "Speaking Māori Shakespeare: *The Maori Merchant of Venice* and the Legacy of Colonisation," in *Screening Shakespeare in the Twenty-First Century*, ed. Mark Thornton Burnett and Ramona Wray (Edinburgh: Edinburgh University Press, 2006), 127–45. These chapters are revised and expanded here with permission from Cambridge University Press and Edinburgh University Press, respectively. Every effort has been made to contact copyright holders for the material contained in this book. The publishers would be pleased to hear from copyright holders to rectify any errors or omissions.

Introduction

A domestic interior: a boy plays with toys and food on a red Formica kitchen table, his head covered by a brown paper bag which is pierced by roughly cut holes for his eyes and mouth. His games become increasingly violent as he deluges the toys in ketchup and smashes them. The background noise escalates. The kitchen is bombed and the windows explode. A man carries the boy down a set of stairs and they reappear, as if through a wormhole in the fabric of space-time, in the centre of a colosseum. The man holds the boy aloft. An invisible crowd cheers. A military march: soldiers, victorious from battle, caked in blue war paint, march in unison and perform a tightly choreographed sequence of movements on the floor of the colosseum. A bathhouse: soldiers are bathed in streams of water. Their bodies are washed clean of paint and dirt. Several of the soldiers are missing limbs. A row of empty boots: Titus, dirty from battle, inspects them. As he does so, he lets grains of sand fall from his hand into each boot. Mussolini's Colosseo Quadrato (Square Colosseum) in Rome: black banners tumble down its vertical surfaces.

Lavinia stands on a charred stump in a fire-ravaged swamp: she is dressed in a torn white slip. Her hair is in disarray. Twigs are jammed into her wrists in place of her hands. Chiron and Demetrius torment her and leave the scene, stumbling through the mud. The camera closes in on Lavinia's face to register the blood on her lips, in sharp contrast to the paleness of her skin. The soundtrack registers her distressed groans. Her uncle sees her from afar and the camera discovers her for a second time, tracking toward Lavinia as Marcus moves closer. Lavinia turns toward him and opens her mouth. Blood gushes from it, viscous and crimson. The camera focuses on Marcus's horrified face. Lavinia is invited by her father and uncle to write the names of her attackers in the sand, watched by the "boy" in his guise as Young Lucius. As she scratches the names, the scene is intercut with a densely layered series of images accompanied by heavy guitars and fast beats: Lavinia, a doe, Chiron, Demitrius, tigers, Marilyn Monroe with her dress billowing above a subway grate, silhouettes of tree branches. This sequence—described in the film's production materials as a Penny Arcade Nightmare (P.A.N.)—ends. The names of Lavinia's attackers are etched in the sand with geometric precision.

A banquet with a human pie and four deaths: Lucius force-feeds a long-handled spoon down Saturninus's throat and spits on him; the action freezes so that the globules of spit hang, suspended. While Saturninus remains frozen, Lucius shoots him and at the moment of impact the banquet table is relocated, once again as if through a wormhole, to the floor of the colosseum. This time the colosseum is filled with spectators. They stand, silent, watching, echoing the figure of Young Lucius who has watched a catalogue of violent acts throughout the action of the film. Young Lucius takes Aaron and Tamora's child from a cage and carries the child beyond the exit of the colosseum accompanied by the sound of babies crying, birds squawking and bells tolling. The sun begins to rise and the image of the children is frozen in mid-step as the film cuts to a blackout.

* * *

A consideration of these sequences from Julie Taymor's film *Titus* (1999) identifies, broadly, the territory of this book.[1] *Shakespeare, Trauma and Contemporary Performance* explores relationships between Shakespeare's texts in contemporary performance on stage and screen and violent events and histories through an engagement with critical work on trauma as it has emerged in a range of humanities disciplines. My work in this book is motivated by a desire to account for—but by no means to rationalise—the ongoing and pernicious effects of various forms of violence as they have emerged in selected contemporary performances of Shakespeare's texts, especially as that violence relates to apartheid, racism, colonisation, homophobia and war. In developing this analysis I would argue that critical work on trauma—with its emphasis on repetition, return, avoidance, the unrepresentable and belatedness—provides a productive framework through which to consider violence and its effects. Specifically, I am interested in how contemporary performances of Shakespeare's texts trace (and are traced by) violent events and histories, and in examining how these engagements with acts of violence inform gender, racial and sexual politics and the ethics of representation and spectatorship. The performances of Shakespeare's plays that I consider—*Titus Andronicus, The Merchant of Venice, The Tempest* and *Henry V*—have, over the course of their performance histories, been connected to a wide range of violent events and histories, some of which I will address in this book. Given the prevalence of this performance strategy, which often takes the form of analogy, it is vital to examine what is at stake in the reproduction of the plays' narratives of violence in relation to particular cultures and events. This is particularly important as the reproduction of violence can serve to reinforce its operation, even as it can work to critique it, both of which I will examine in the course of this book.

Archives, which offer the researcher belated access to a performance, are ideally constituted to allow a consideration of the effects of violence.

Just as a performance can be known through its archival traces, which are never quite the "thing itself" of the live event, trauma is known through its after-effects, rather than through the traumatic event itself, as I will explore below. Part of the project of this book is to excavate, through a consideration of performance and its documentary traces, what Ann Cvetkovich describes as an "archive of trauma".[2] For Cvetkovich, an archive of trauma is the field of documentation produced in response to traumatic events and histories; it indexes the effects of violence but also identifies how the "affects associated with trauma" might serve "as the foundation for the formation of public cultures".[3] In Cvetkovich's model trauma might, perhaps perversely, provide the ground for the creation of communities. My critical excavation is concerned to offer an analysis of trauma through a consideration of its documentary traces variously held inside and outside institutional repositories, such as theatre and film archives. I also conceive of "the archive" more broadly to think of how performance might operate, metaphorically, as an archive, accreting or storing traces of traumatic violence within its representational frame and documentary traces. Influenced by Cvetkovich's arguments, I aim to consider the kinds of communities that a performance's engagement with violence calls upon and works to create, without assuming, as Miranda Joseph warns against, that the creation of "community" is a necessary "good".[4] Indeed, performance can work to interpolate spectators such that they are invited to be complicit with violence that they might otherwise abhor, just as it can work to invite spectators to recognise forms of violence and to take action against them.

As contemporary performances of Shakespeare's texts often deploy the plays in order to offer commentaries on contemporary and historical events (and to use these events to comment on Shakespeare's plays), it is crucial that critics continue to examine the cultural politics of these kinds of adaptations and appropriations. It is my hope that an engagement with critical work on trauma provides a way of probing often clichéd understandings of relationships between Shakespeare's texts and violent events that were fuelled by Jan Kott's seminal collection of essays *Shakespeare Our Contemporary* (1965). Shakespeare's texts, (and by extension Shakespeare himself), are thus often cited by theatre makers and reviewers as a "timeless" explanatory mechanism for historical and contemporary violence. These claims are frequently made without adequate consideration of how that mechanism functions, or the violence that this kind of deployment might too perform, for example by de-historicising historical events, generalising violence perpetrated against specific peoples or proposing an "essential" human nature that homogenises difference, often by working to elide minority subject positions.

In thinking through relationships between violent events, histories and performance my goal is not to pose a series of causal relationships or simply to catalogue a series of traumatic intertexts but rather to examine how these catalogues operate or function. In this work I suggest that performances of

Shakespeare's texts and their documentary traces work variously to memorialise, remember and witness violent events and histories, but that these processes are never neutral. Performances offer a *way* of remembering violent events and histories and invite spectators to witness these events; part of my project is to consider what is at stake in the kinds of memorials and memories that performance offers its spectators. An analysis of the catalogue of sequences from *Titus*, which is by no means exhaustive, stands as a brief illustration of the book's central concerns.

Titus bombards its viewers with images of violence that variously represent aspects of the play's narrative as well citing events and histories external to it. What is striking is the way that the film, through visual cues and documentation (interviews, screenplay, publicity materials and so on), works to draw violent events and histories from multiple times and cultures into the cinematic frame, modelling Taymor's goal to "blend and collide time".[5] The returning soldiers with missing limbs are associated with both ancient and contemporary warfare through the temporal jump of the opening sequence; the regimented movements of the soldiers, coupled with the styling of the Square Colosseum and 1930s aesthetic, recall images of Mussolini's Italy but resonate, perhaps more strongly still, with Nazi rallies captured on grainy black and white film by Third Reich filmmaker Leni Riefenstahl in *Triumph of the Will* (1935); and Titus's deposits of sand in the empty boots hint at images of other empty boots in photographs, films and reports of Nazi concentration camps.[6] In its range of references, the film neatly avoids a reductive analogy where the action of the play is deployed as a commentary on specific cultures, only for the analogy to break down under the pressure of the text's narrative requirements, as can so often be the case with contemporary performances of Shakespeare's texts. Yet in its lack of specificity, which attempts to lay claim to a plethora of times and places, *Titus* runs the risk of generalising the operation and effects of violence such that the specific historical and cultural valences of the events it cites are subsumed under a general exegesis of violence. My aim here and throughout the book is not to prescribe particular representational codes or to privilege certain codes over others but rather to take seriously the work of considering the implications of employing particular images and modes of representation. A performance's "archive of trauma" thus bears analysis in terms of what might be at stake in the appropriation of particular images, events and histories, and is a key part of the work of this book.

In addition to events contained within the diegesis, the film's archive of trauma is also produced through the conditions of production and reception, such that events that occur belatedly are sutured to the film's archive. Indeed, two months after the film wrapped, conflict in Kosovo escalated such that Taymor notes that it would have been impossible to film the colosseum scenes, shot on location in Pula, Croatia, with a cast of local extras.[7] The events in the Balkans, coupled with the film's concertina approach to time, enable a reading where the silent witnesses that inhabit the colosseum at the film's end come to stand as witness to local as well as global conflicts. Furthermore, nine days after the attacks on the World Trade Center on 11 September 2001, Taymor was interviewed by Bill Moyers on PBS (Public Broadcasting Service) in response to the question "[w]hat can artists say to us about the tragedy of September 11th?" In this interview Taymor discusses *Titus* and *Titus Andronicus* with respect to revenge, justice, "the enemy" and possible motivations for intercultural, ethnic and religious violence.[8] The play and the film are thus offered as models for understanding the origins of conflict but also as potential solutions. Indeed, the film's comparatively "hopeful" ending is used by Taymor as a commentary on the possibilities that children offer for altering cycles of violence, even as she does not exempt them from responsibility: "[t]he children have to start to question because they're inculcated".[9] By repeatedly positioning the boy as a spectator to acts of violence, Taymor's film works to inculcate him, like the film's spectators, in the acts of violence. While the film posits an ending where responsibility to the other is posited as the only ethical response to violence (a view which has points of contact with Levinasian ethics) and where Shakespeare's narrative is used as the launching pad for an entry into a new (conflict-free?) dawn, the ethics of the film bear further analysis. In particular the ending of the film, which intones hope through its lighting and soundscape, works to elide the problematic racial politics of the paternalistic gesture of the white child leading a biracial child into the future. This tension between the way in which Shakespeare's texts can be co-opted as part of a narrative of healing and reconciliation in response to trauma and how such narratives can work to elide or obscure inequalities—and thereby produce further violence—will inform my analysis at various points in this book.

The film's archive of trauma also invites analysis in terms of spectatorship, witnessing and the possibilities for communicating trauma. As Courtney Lehmann, Bryan Reynolds and Lisa Starks argue, "*Titus* pries our eyes *open*, compelling us to look, and to look further [. . .] in an effort to induce accountability".[10] *Titus* is saturated with acts of watching, framed in such a way that the spectator is invited to bear witness to the events. Here it is helpful to think of witnessing in the sense that Tim Etchells, artistic director of the UK-based experimental theatre company Forced Entertainment, articulates it. For Etchells: "[t]o witness an event is to be present at it in some fundamentally ethical way, to feel the weight of things and one's own place in them, even if that place is simply, for the moment, as an onlooker".[11] Etchells complicates the *Oxford English Dictionary*'s (*OED*) definition of the verb form of witness—"[t]o bear witness to (a fact or statement); to testify to, attest; to furnish oral or written evidence of" (*OED* 1)—in his insistence that the spectator takes an ethical relation to the event. In Etchells's model the act of witnessing is not primarily one where the subject attests or testifies to an event, which implies a relatively strict demarcation between subject and event. Rather it is one where the event solicits a participatory response from the subject such that she is invited to consider her position in relation to it. For Helena Grehan, whose work is indebted to Levinasian ethics, where the focus is on the infinite responsibility to the other, the possibilities for ethical spectatorship occur when performance is able to "challenge spectators in ways that encourage them to probe difficult concepts surrounding their positions in the world and their relationship to others".[12] These concerns with a mode of ethical spectatorship also resonate with Kim Solga's impassioned and articulate call for ethical feminist performance and spectatorship in relation to the staging of early modern acts of violence against women on contemporary stages.[13] Like Etchells, Grehan and Solga, I am interested in how performance might work to solicit or invite this kind of response and/or sense of responsibility, even as I acknowledge that it is not possible to insist (or prove) that all spectators adopt (or even desire) an ethical condition of witnessing.

This invitation to witness is evident in Young Lucius's observation of many of the acts of violence, often from the edge of the cinematic frame, Marcus's discovery of Lavinia following her rape and mutilation, Lavinia's P.A.N. and the final scene in the colosseum where the silent spectators, whom Taymor describes as "us", watch the film's final sequences.[14] These scenes work to interpolate the film's spectators as witnesses to violence through the manipulation of the cinematic gaze. Here it is worth pausing to consider how the spectator is asked to become a witness to violence, such that the act of witnessing is partly constituted through a spectator's participatory, subjective relation to the event. These issues are clearest in sequences concerning the rape and assault of Lavinia. Lavinia is initially offered to the film's spectators as an object, displayed on the stump to be observed. The comparatively more objective nature of this omniscient camera work presents Lavinia as a spectacle for visual consumption, bordering on the voyeuristic. Marcus's discovery affirms and complicates the objectification of Lavinia: spectators are asked to reorientate their initial response to the scene, which was unmediated through the gaze of another character, by looking through Marcus's uncomprehending discovery of his niece. The film here invites the spectator to participate in the discovery of Lavinia by suturing the spectator's gaze to Marcus's. This forces a reorientation of the spectator's gaze such that she is invited to shift from an objective to a subjective relation to the event.

But to bear witness to an act of violence is not, always, to be able to comprehend it. Marcus's long "purple" speech in the play (2.4.11–57) identifies the failure of language to capture or know Lavinia's experience or his response to it; in Taymor's film, Marcus's facial expression of uncomprehending horror stands in for much of this long speech. In *Titus* the opening of Lavinia's mouth at once promises the possibility of communication and negates this possibility as words are replaced with a gush of blood. The film, though, works to investigate the possibility of communicating Lavinia's experience.

In the P.A.N. that follows the invitation for Lavinia to write the names of her attackers, the film offers a visual representation of the trauma of rape: here the objective camera used for the discovery of Lavinia is replaced with a representation of the character's experience, as the film offers a visual and sonic language to describe and communicate the experience of Lavinia's attack. While the diegesis of the film forecloses the possibility of the other characters having access to Lavinia's subjective experience (they see only the effort and result of her writing), the film offers the spectator a privileged position of access to the traumatic experience. My point here is not that the film offers the spectator an unmediated experience of trauma, especially as trauma resists representation as the "thing itself", as I will explore below. Rather, it is to identify how a performance might figure and represent trauma, and the implications this has for spectatorship. By way of further example, Taymor's designation of the crowd in the colosseum as "us", and the description in the screenplay of the crowd as made up "of many nationalities, races, ages", suggests that she imagines some kind of panhuman community, both within the diegesis and in terms of spectatorship.[15] Taymor's drive to produce a community that will bear witness to traumatic events and histories is a phenomenon that recurs in several of the performances discussed in this book. As I will suggest at various points, understandings of "us" and "community" are necessarily marked by inclusions and exclusions, work to collapse difference, and can potentially produce further violence.

As my analysis of *Titus* suggests, this book is located alongside work in which performances of Shakespeare (and other early modern playwrights) are situated in relation to acts of violence and events in contemporary culture more generally. I am thinking here of Barbara Hodgdon's *The Shakespeare Trade* (1998), W. B. Worthen's *Shakespeare and the Force of Modern Performance* (2003), Pascale Aebischer's *Shakespeare's Violated Bodies* (2004), Mark Thornton Burnett's *Filming Shakespeare in the Global Marketplace* (2007) and Kim Solga's *Violence Against Women in Early Modern Performance* (2009), to name but several. Located alongside these projects, this book marks its difference by proposing a reading of Shakespeare in performance that takes as its cue work produced in the rapidly growing field of trauma studies, developing an area that Burnett begins to track in a chapter of *Filming Shakespeare*.[16] It is one of the central claims of *Shakespeare, Trauma and Contemporary Performance* that a critical turn to the traumatic provides a productive framework for analysing Shakespeare in performance. This is because it provides a compelling model for accounting for the ongoing effects of violence and how those effects might be communicated to others, with a view to identifying structural inequalities and oppression. What, then, is this phenomenon called trauma? And how might an engagement with its use—as it has emerged in public and medical discourse and more specifically in a range of humanities disciplines—enable an analysis of Shakespeare in performance?

DELIMITING TRAUMA

Stemming from the popularisation of its clinical usage as Posttraumatic Stress Disorder, trauma is deployed in general, figurative usage to indicate experiences that are distressing or emotionally disturbing (*OED* 2b). This language is pervasive in sports reporting in headlines such as "Chelsea Players Hold Inquest after Trauma of Spurs Defeat" as recorded in *The Independent*, but it also seeps into other areas of the media; for instance *The Guardian* reported that "Alliance & Leicester, which like B&B [Bradford & Bingley] is exposed to the trauma of the UK housing market, fell almost 8.5% this morning".[17] Before trauma came to be used in relation to football matches, the housing market and, crucially, for my purposes, cultural criticism and performance, its usage was primarily confined to medical contexts. Thus, trauma, which derives from the Greek τραῦμα, literally meaning "wound", is a term whose meaning shifts from the physical to the psychological to the public and denotes both an event and a response to an event, as a brief track through the *OED*'s definitions suggests. Originating in the late seventeenth century, trauma is designated in the *OED*'s first definition in pathological terms as "[a] wound, or external bodily injury in general; also the condition caused by this" (*OED* 1). The *OED*'s second definition for trauma, from psychoanalysis and psychiatry, emerges in the late nineteenth century and is given as "[a] psychic injury, esp. one caused by emotional shock the memory of which is repressed and remains unhealed; an internal injury, esp. to the brain, which may result in a behavioural disorder of organic origin. Also, the state or condition so caused" (*OED* 2a). This terminology is repeated in the associated term "traumatic" which derives from the Greek τραυματικός, meaning "of or pertaining to a wound or wounds", and is defined as "[o]f, pertaining to, or caused by a wound, abrasion, or external injury" (*OED* A1) and in psychoanalysis and psychiatry as "[o]f, pertaining to, or caused by a psychic wound or emotional shock, esp. leading to or causing behavioural disturbance" (*OED* A2a).

This sketch of trauma and the traumatic shows how their meanings shift from what appears to be quantifiable and empirical medical discourse of the physical wound to understandings developed in psychoanalysis and psychiatry. But, as Roger Luckhurst notes,

> [t]his is not a straightforward story in which the Victorian physicalist model is displaced by a modern psychogenic one. Rather, there were new biological and neurological resources that were used to reinforce the somatic origins of mental illness, and these arrived at exactly the same time (in the 1870s and 1880s) that different groups of psychological researchers began to argue the radical case for a largely psychodynamic model of mind.[18]

Marking this complex negotiation between the psychological and the physical, trauma's "shift" to the realm of the psychic retains the language of the wound and injury but associates them both with behavioural responses to brain injury and, crucially for this project, to "emotional shock", which registers ongoing psychological effects. These ideas initially came to prominence in attempts to account for nervous shock resulting from accidents, especially those caused by new mechanical developments such as the railways; John Erichsen's *On Railway and Other Injuries of the Nervous System* (1866) and Jean-Martin Charcot's analysis of hysteria in *Clinical Lectures on Diseases of the Nervous System* (1889) stand as markers of this early work. Sigmund Freud offers his two main accounts of trauma in *Beyond the Pleasure Principle* (1920) and *Moses and Monotheism* (1939), one of his final projects to be published; these analyses were influenced by accounts of "traumatic neurosis" produced in response to "severe mechanical concussions, railway disasters and other accidents involving a risk to life",[19] as well as by his work with Josef Breuer on hysteria. In *Beyond the Pleasure Principle* Freud considers trauma with respect to the way in which individual subjects are "pierced" by and respond to external stimuli such as war:

> [w]e describe as "traumatic" any excitations from outside which are powerful enough to break through the protective shield. It seems to me that the concept of trauma necessarily implies a connection of this kind with a breach in an otherwise efficacious barrier against stimuli. Such an event as an external trauma is bound to provoke a disturbance on a large scale in the functioning of the organism's energy and to set in motion every possible defensive measure.[20]

A traumatic response is here coded as a mechanism by which the "pierced" subject attempts to protect itself from assault. Whereas *Beyond the Pleasure Principle* details individual trauma, "Moses, His People and Monotheist Religion" (1938)—the third essay of *Moses and Monotheism*—considers historical trauma in relation to narratives of guilt and repetition, which Freud suggests inhere in the founding and development of Judaism.[21] As Cathy Caruth's lucid reading shows, in this text Freud develops an account of traumatic neurosis as marked by latency, whereby traumatic symptoms do not occur at the moment of injury but rather are delayed or belated.[22] In this schema, trauma operates as a psychic piercing whose effects occur belatedly, even as a subject may appear to escape "some frightful accident [. . .] apparently uninjured."[23] Freud goes on to argue that traumatic incidents can produce polarised responses in subjects whereby they undergo a "compulsion to repeat" an event, an effect which Freud designates as positive, or the opposite, a "negative reaction" where "nothing of the forgotten traumas shall be remembered and nothing repeated", resulting in "defensive reactions" such as "'avoidances', which may be intensified into 'inhibitions' and 'phobias'".[24] As will become apparent, these polarised responses between repetition and avoidance also recur in contemporary clinical definitions of trauma.

In what sounds like a deconstructive paradox, Freud also suggests that traumatic responses entail the possibility of their own "cure". Thus he claims in *Beyond the Pleasure Principle* that in cases of traumatic neuroses, dreams no longer carry the primary function of wish fulfilment but operate instead by "endeavouring to master the stimulus retrospectively, by developing the anxiety whose omission was the cause of the traumatic neurosis".[25] Here dreams, rather than being under the sway of the pleasure principle and its attendant drive toward wish fulfilment, operate as a mode of "cure", assisting the subject to cope with the excess of stimulation before the "dominance of the pleasure principle can even begin".[26] Similarly, in *Moses and Monotheism* Freud claims that the emergence of neuroses following a period of latency might be "looked upon as an attempt at cure—as an effort once more to reconcile with the rest those portions of the ego that have been split off by the influence of the trauma".[27] As Cvetkovich notes in her consideration of *Beyond the Pleasure Principle* and the "pierced" subject, Freud's "meditations on the problem of traumatic repetition, [. . . seem] indistinguishably to constitute both resistance to cure and a form of cure".[28] Like Jacques Derrida's conception of the pharmakon in "Plato's Pharmacy" (1968), to which he attributes the capacity both to heal and to poison, trauma seems at once to indicate injury and to contain the potential for its own cure.[29] This tension between wound and cure recurs in now-obsolete definitions of the term "traumatic". For instance, the *OED* records that in the mid-seventeenth century traumatic balsams or herbs were used to treat injuries, and the word "traumatic" was also used as a noun meaning "[a] vulnerary agent or remedy" (*OED* B) or that which is "[u]seful in healing wounds; having curative properties in respect of external injuries" (*OED* A1). Here the word "traumatic" both names the injury and is associated with its cure. While these particular meanings of traumatic are obsolete, they recur in the twentieth-century discovery of "traumatic acid", a substance produced by some plants in response to damaged tissue and which promotes repair; again a wound, injury or trauma is capable of producing that which entails a cure for the initial intrusion (*OED* A3). More recently, critical writing has also been conceptualised in terms whereby the curative adheres within the traumatic, as I will explore below (18).

Freud's analysis held sway within medical discourses of trauma until the mid- to late twentieth century. However, following the aftermath of the Vietnam War and the experiences of veterans alongside, as Cvetkovich notes, an "increasing attention to rape, sexual abuse, and domestic violence, especially from feminist psychologists", trauma has been most recently codified as Posttraumatic Stress Disorder (PTSD).[30] With this appellation trauma entered the third edition of the *Diagnostic and Statistical Manual* of *Mental Disorders* of the American Psychiatric Association in 1980 and its definition has been developed in the third revised edition in 1987, the fourth edition in 1994, and reprinted with minor amendments in the fourth revised edition in 2000.[31] According to the revised fourth edition, the key criteria for a diagnosis of PTSD include the presence of a traumatic stressor where:

(1) the person experienced, witnessed, or was confronted with an event or events that involved actual or threatened death or serious injury, or a threat to the physical integrity of self or others
(2) the person's response involved intense fear, helplessness, or horror.[32]

In terms of traumatic stressors, the *DSM-IV-TR* identifies events directly experienced by individuals, such as war, terrorism, kidnap, automobile accidents, violent personal assault, including sexual assault and physical attack and the diagnosis of life-threatening illness, among others. A stressor can also include witnessing events such as "observing the serious injury or unnatural death of another person due to violent assault, accident, war, or disaster or unexpectedly witnessing a dead body or body parts" and learning about events experienced by others, such as "violent personal assault".[33] Responses to the traumatic stressor manifest themselves in at least one of the following ways: intrusive recollection which may involve images, thoughts, dreams, flashbacks, psychological distress and reactivity "to internal and external cues that symbolize or resemble an aspect of the traumatic event"; avoidant or numbing behaviours which might involve an avoidance of people, conversations and places associated with the trauma or an inability to recall important aspects of the trauma; and hyper-arousal, such as insomnia.[34] Even though the focus in *DSM-IV-TR* is primarily on the event or threat of physical injury and its psychosomatic responses, this definition offers a more flexible understanding of the traumatic event than that offered in the third edition of the *DSM* (1980, rev. 1987) where the event was defined as "generally outside the range of usual human experience" and where the "stressor producing this syndrome would evoke significant symptoms of distress in most people".[35] As Laura S. Brown suggests, drawing on the work of feminist therapist Maria Root, the *DSM-III-R* definition was not adequate as a description of what she describes as "insidious trauma", or the "traumatogenic effects of oppression that are not necessarily overtly violent or threatening to bodily well-being at the given moment but that do violence to the soul and spirit".[36] The *DSM-IV-TR* definition thus creates the possibility for experiences beyond the catastrophic and extraordinary to be considered within the realm of the traumatic.

Although academic studies of trauma are dominated by the Holocaust and catastrophe is frequently assumed as a necessary condition of trauma, collectively this field of work has moved toward a more flexible understanding as to what might be included within the remit of the traumatic, such as Brown's efforts to consider "insidious trauma". This more flexible understanding of trauma is vital as it works to undo a hierarchy that privileges certain experiences as traumatic over others. This shift toward flexibility certainly informs the work of this project, especially with respect to how the "catastrophic" can impact on the experiences of the everyday, or how trauma can be produced through what might at first appear to be banal events of the everyday. While academic studies often have recourse to the language of PTSD, such work, as is the case with this project, is usually less interested in using the *DSM* definition(s) as a set of symptoms to be checked off with a view to diagnosis, than in how trauma has been conceptualised in response to various cultural pressures. The next section considers the emergence of academic studies of trauma, work which marks its debts to the popular and medical discourses I have tracked above, in order to consider how this work might enable an analysis of Shakespeare in performance.

TRAUMA STUDIES

Since the 1990s, work on trauma has become increasingly prevalent in a wide range of humanities disciplines. Its emergence alongside the increased popular usage of trauma in the wake of the inclusion of PTSD by the American Psychiatric Association suggests that critical articulations of trauma, like the phenomena they seek to analyse, are themselves belated. Such work has included, for example, Cathy Caruth's seminal monograph, *Unclaimed Experience: Trauma, Narrative and History* (1996) and her edited collection *Trauma: Explorations in Memory* (1995), Timothy Murray's *Drama Trauma: Specters of Race and Sexuality in Performance, Video and Art* (1997), Peggy Phelan's *Mourning Sex: Performing Public Memories* (1997), Kirby Farrell's *Post-traumatic Culture: Injury and Interpretation in the Nineties* (1998), Ruth Leys's, *Trauma: A Genealogy* (2000), Dominick LaCapra's *Writing History, Writing Trauma* (2001), Ann Cvetkovich's, *An Archive of Feelings: Trauma, Sexuality, and Lesbian Public Cultures* (2003), Thomas P. Anderson's *Performing Early Modern Trauma from Shakespeare to Milton* (2006), Christina Wald's *Hysteria, Trauma and Melancholia: Performative Maladies in Contemporary Anglophone Drama* (2007), Roger Luckhurst's *The Trauma Question* (2008) and a dossier on trauma in a 2001 issue of the cinema journal *Screen* edited by Susannah Radstone, among others, many of which I will return to in the course of this project. Indeed, this brief survey of titles attests to what might be described as a critical trauma industry which emerges in a variety of humanities disciplines including, but not limited to, American Studies, Cultural Studies, Drama, Theatre and Performance Studies, English, Film Studies, Gay, Lesbian, Bisexual, Transgender and Queer Studies, History, Holocaust Studies, Politics, Sociology and Women's and Gender Studies.

In this broad field of cultural enquiry, Caruth's formulation of trauma stands as a now-classic account of this phenomenon. Caruth writes that "[i]n its most general definition trauma describes an overwhelming experience of sudden or catastrophic events in which the response to the event occurs in the often delayed, uncontrolled repetitive appearance of hallucinations and other intrusive phenomena", such as flashbacks and nightmares.[37] She goes on to argue that this opens a paradox in traumatic experience: "that the most direct seeing of a violent event may occur as an absolute inability to know it; that immediacy, paradoxically, may take the form of belatedness".[38] Key to Caruth's account is the conception of an event that ruptures the subject's psyche to such an extent that the subject is unable to account for or assimilate the event as it occurs. Trauma is, then, a response to the psychic wound, forcing the subject to return again and again to the event. Whereas the direct experience of the event is unknowable by virtue of its magnitude, in the repeated return to the event or wound, the subject might gain, belatedly, some understanding of the event itself, even as it remains unknowable in its entirety: as with the traumatic herbs and acid, the traumatic response entails the possibility of its own "treatment", as the subject engages with and attempts to account for the source of the trauma and assimilate this experience.

In her language of event, flashback, nightmare, repetition, return and knowledge, Caruth's account denotes her debt to Freud, whose texts she explicitly engages with in the course of her analysis, and resonates with the diagnostic language of PTSD which she also cites in both *Unclaimed Experience* and *Trauma: Explorations in Memory*, neatly deploying these discourses as part of her analysis, for example, of Alain Renais and Marguerite Duras's film *Hiroshima Mon Amour* (1959), alongside other texts.[39] In this vein, she reads this film as not so much *"about"* the dropping of an atomic bomb on Hiroshima but as an event that "takes place *at* Hiroshima, a discourse spoken, as it were, *on the site of a catastrophe"* and which, through the "very indirectness of this telling", "explores the possibility of a faithful history" of the event.[40] As part of her discussion of Freud, Caruth also identifies how "trauma seems to be much more than a pathology, or the simple illness of a wounded psyche: it is always the story of a wound that cries out, that addresses us in the attempt to tell us of a reality or truth that is not otherwise available".[41] The repeated return to the crying wound marks the way in which the traumatic response demands that the wound be known, even as it defies the possibility of knowing it fully.

As Caruth notes, the operation of trauma, like the epistemological implications of (post)structural literary and linguistic theory, highlights the problem of reference, or the nature of the relationship between an event and the signifying system used to refer to it, such that there does not appear to be a direct relation: representations of trauma are marked by their indirect relation to the event itself and trauma is known only at a remove through signifiers. For Caruth, the way trauma operates indirectly to produce knowledge of an event which cannot be known in its entirety does not so much eliminate the event, conceived broadly as "history", but rather forces a reconsideration of how knowledge of an event, or history, might "arise where *immediate understanding* may not".[42] Instead of proposing that trauma, conditioned by the impossibility of knowing the event itself, precludes the possibility of knowledge and communication of knowledge, Caruth produces a communicative model of trauma. The departure from the event itself, which characterises trauma, is, as Caruth suggests, "also a means of passing out of the isolation imposed by the event: that the history of trauma, in its inherent belatedness, can only take place through the listening of another".[43] This relation between trauma and communication, coupled with Caruth's formulation of trauma as a belated return to that which cannot be known, will be central to my analysis as performance offers its own forms of knowledge and modes of communication.

To deploy trauma in criticism, as Caruth does, or to name as traumatic a sporting defeat, a collapse in housing markets, an act of terrorism such as the attack on the World Trade Center, or a natural disaster, like the December 2004 Indian Ocean tsunami and earthquake or the 2010 floods in Pakistan, points to how trauma refuses to be contained by medical discourses, working its way into other areas of expression and enquiry. Thus trauma emerges, especially in late twentieth- and early twenty-first-century cultures, as a physical wound, a psychiatric condition and a trope in criticism and in culture more generally. A 2009 BBC Panorama documentary entitled *The Trauma Industry* shown on British television illustrates this "spillover" from the medical to other areas of culture. It identified not only the extent to which the condition of PTSD has become more widespread but, more searchingly, how the medical diagnosis has become entwined in a contemporary culture of personal injury claims. Here, it is claimed, trauma, in economic terms, is an industry and several of the documentary's participants suggested that this association between the medical and the legal had the effect of inhibiting the recovery of the subject.[44]

In its various configurations from the medical to the public to the critical, trauma provides a way of describing and structuring experience. As Kirby Farrell puts it: "[i]t would be hard to overestimate the plasticity and the elemental power of the concept. People use trauma as an enabling fiction, an explanatory tool for managing unquiet minds in an overwhelming world".[45] And in *The Trauma Question*, Luckhurst provides an erudite analysis of how trauma and what might be described as "trauma culture" have come to have a significant shaping influence on Western conceptions of the self.[46] Projects such as Caruth's, Farrell's and Luckhurst's show how criticism utilises some of trauma's key clinical terminology, redeploying it as a way of explaining particular cultural products and their relationships to larger cultural formations and concerns. One way to read these attempts to define trauma is to consider the convergences between psychoanalysis, PTSD and criticism's identification of these phenomena in a range of cultural practices as evidence of the historical longevity of trauma. Here it might be argued that trauma has existed throughout time and cultures, with the language of PTSD the most recent codification of this phenomenon. While a case can be made for this kind of historical longevity, rather than seeking to prove that trauma is always already present, it is perhaps more helpful to think of the various attempts to codify trauma as producing what cultures understand as traumatic. To say that there is no independently existing empirically verifiable phenomenon of trauma that is the same for all times and cultures, is not to deny the lived effects of trauma, constituted variously by subjects and cultures. Rather it is to consider instead how trauma is produced and understood in response to a range of events and cultural pressures, such as those identified in the documentary *The Trauma Industry*. Indeed, Leys claims that "the Holocaust now appears, retroactively so to speak, not only to have been *the* crucial trauma of the century, but also one that can be fully understood only in light of our knowledge of PTSD".[47] Here the shattering event of the Holocaust is understood belatedly in terms of PTSD: trauma becomes the explanatory mechanism by which culture attempts to account for this event and its aftermath and the event, in turn, helps to produce an account of trauma.

This "spillover" from the clinical to the critical certainly provides a powerful framework for the analysis of culture but it also raises important considerations for the work of criticism. In particular, the deployment of trauma's pathological language in relation to particular cultural projects runs the risk of reductively locating such work in terms of diagnosis, treatment and a hierarchical schema of perpetrator and victim. While an absolute escape from the rhetoric of diagnosis is perhaps impossible, it is possible, as Cvetkovich suggests, to focus not only on "texts as representations or narratives of trauma" but also to consider how "cultural production that emerges around trauma enables new practices and publics".[48] As part of this work, Cvetkovich places "moments of extreme trauma alongside moments of everyday emotional distress that are often the only sign that trauma's effects are still being felt".[49] Thus she seeks to engage with "a sense of trauma as connected to the textures of everyday experience" as much as it is to catastrophic collective experiences, such as war and genocide.[50] In Cvetkovich's model, critical and cultural engagement with trauma, from the everyday to the catastrophic, has the potential to become enabling and productive, creating new cultural forms and communities and expanding "the category of the therapeutic beyond the confines of the narrowly medicalized or privatized encounter between clinical professional and client".[51] Cvetkovich's focus on trauma as enabling certainly works to break the grip of a diagnostic approach that orients itself around treatment, but her claim that "trauma cultures are actually doing the work of therapy", although persuasive, tracks straight back into the rhetoric of illness and treatment she seeks to displace.[52] The work of cultural production and criticism is not reducible to individual or group therapy but the notion of a cultural response to trauma outside the strictures of medicalisation is, I think, a useful one, especially when coupled with criticism's development of the tropes of trauma into what Farrell describes as an "interpretative process".[53] Like queer theory which orientates itself around both an object of enquiry and a mode of enquiry, trauma theory both focuses on an object of analysis (which, like the formulation of queer subjects, can be variously constituted) and offers a way of reading.

In this book I am interested in how the key tropes of trauma as they have emerged in criticism inform an analysis of relationships between performances of Shakespeare's texts and various violent events and histories. These events and histories, from the individual to the collective—apartheid, the Holocaust, colonisation, racism, homophobia, war—stand as traumatic wounds in contemporary cultures, repeatedly turned to but not fully accounted for or resolved. Some of the key diagnostic features of trauma in its codification as PTSD appear to invite relatively straightforward structural comparison with particular forms of cultural production, such as the use of flashbacks or dream sequences in film, theatre and literature in which a subject returns to or repeats a traumatic event. Despite this neat similarity, in this project I do not seek to offer clinical diagnoses of individuals (characters, directors, writers, performers) or particular performance projects through an application of PTSD symptoms in an effort to demonstrate that a performance or individual is "traumatised", an activity that would be institutionally misplaced as well as reductive. While I am interested in the deployment of such narrative and formal devices, my interest is less in the diagnostic (where the flashback is, so too is trauma) than in how the deployment of such devices suggests a particular understanding of trauma and its relationship to representation and spectatorship. Thus my analysis of Lavinia's P.A.N. was not aimed at concluding that the character is traumatised but rather was concerned with how the film figures an experience of trauma and its relation to spectatorship. More important, this project locates performances of Shakespeare as part of what might be described as a widespread turn to the traumatic that pervades contemporary culture, a phenomenon that Farrell marks as "post-traumatic culture" whereby trauma is not simply an individual phenomenon but one where "the entire culture is figuratively afflicted".[54] Operating as part of "trauma culture", performance can be read as offering a traumatic response to events, belatedly "working through" that which is not yet fully known or accounted for, returning in manifold ways to the "wound that cries out". Like traumatic acid and Freud's figuration of traumatic neuroses as the subject's attempt at cure, performance's belated "working through" in response to various events and histories is both dependent on a traumatic event and also generative in relation to it: it participates in the articulation of the wound as much as it is made by it.

In my focus on how performance might negotiate or respond to various traumatic wounds or events, I am not privileging either performance or criticism with fully knowing an event, or offering some kind of authentic experience of it, but rather as offering a *way* of knowing such an event: here a traumatic response can be termed, like the work of criticism and psychoanalysis, as a mode of interpretation. In using a model in which performance and criticism are designated as interpretative and generative rather than simply responsive to trauma, I also seek to avoid pathologising the notion of "working through"—freighted as it is with the language of psychoanalysis—as a treatment which, if successful, entails the "end" of trauma and the "cure" of the subject/culture, or one in which a repeated return to the event or "acting out" stands as what LaCapra calls a "melancholic feedback loop" in which the subject fails to resolve the trauma.[55] Rather, I want to consider "working through" as an ongoing negotiation with various traumatic events, predicated on the understanding that there is no unmediated return to an originary moment of trauma or before trauma.

In this work I am interested especially in how performance might offer an articulation of traumatic events either in the moment of performance or in the discourse that surrounds productions. Given the difficulties that attend the relationship between trauma and representation—conventionally figured as one of impossibility—I am concerned to attend to ethical and political implications of attempts to represent trauma in performance. In particular, I am interested in the ethics that surround what Leys, in relation to Walter Benn Michaels's analysis of the Holocaust, describes as the "possibility of 'remembering' someone else's fate".[56] Throughout the book I argue that in this "working through", performances of Shakespeare variously memorialise, remember and witness those events and histories and I seek to account for the politics of this work. In this figuration, performance stands as a storehouse of trauma, archiving the event in the moment of performance and in its material and affective traces. Here my work is situated alongside Burnett's arguments about trauma, Shakespeare and the Holocaust, sketched in a chapter of *Filming Shakespeare*, to which I return in Chapter 2, and develops them in relation to a range of traumatic events and cultures and through the mode of reading outlined in this introduction.

ARCHIVES OF TRAUMA AND PERFORMANCE STUDIES

In many respects, performance criticism stands as an exemplar genre for undertaking an analysis of trauma. Like trauma, which tends to be shadowed by an originary event, performance criticism is shadowed by the originary event of live performance. Criticism works variously in relation to this event, from that which aspires to offer "an illustrated corpse, a pop-up anatomical drawing that stands in for the thing that one most wants to save, the embodied performance" so resisted by Peggy Phelan, to criticism that is aware of the impossibility of such an illustrative project and which works instead in relation to partiality and indeterminacy.[57] Given that the moment of live performance disappears as soon as it occurs, performance criticism might, then, be cast as inherently traumatic, always returning, belatedly, to that which it cannot fully grasp or account for. Indeed, Phelan proposes a model of performance criticism in which she aims "less to describe and preserve performances than to enact and mimic the losses that beat away within them. In this mimicry, loss itself helps transform the repetitive force of trauma and might bring about a way to overcome it".[58] Wary of substituting "interpretations for trauma" where "trauma is tamed by the interpretative frame and peeled away from the raw 'unthought' energy of the body", Phelan instead wants to try "to hear the body" even while admitting that her "hearing is pre-determined by the interpretative frame that limits any encounter with bodies".[59] In these formulations, Phelan locates criticism, or, more specifically, what she terms "performative writing", as possessing what I would term a traumatic participatory force: rather than identifying and interpreting trauma, criticism is located within its very mechanisms and, in turn, is credited with the potential to overcome the loss that inheres within it. Phelan's claims for the transformative power of criticism in relation to trauma simultaneously identify the limits she seeks to counter. Her efforts to enact and mimic loss, though innovative in academic style and form, still entail, like the more conservative modes of criticism she eschews, an act of interpretation which likewise makes and remakes the loss anew in relation to her own and not the other's subjective frame; the voice she seeks to "hear" is always, as she acknowledges, displaced and refigured by the act of criticism. Furthermore, the implied structural equivalence between the mechanics of performance criticism and trauma seems reductive, forcing an equivalence between the material responses to violent events and histories and the act of criticism, even as critical responses, like Phelan's or this project, might too be said to stand as responses to traumatic events. In short, these structural similarities run the risk of generalising traumatic experiences, a risk that occurs in trauma studies more generally and one that can be addressed, at least in part, by specific local analyses of the kind this project seeks to offer.

These structural similarities between trauma and the act of criticism also point to how trauma pervades what Cvetkovich call the "textures of everyday experience", shaping how events from the seemingly banal to the catastrophic are responded to.[60] If performance offers a belated working through of particular events, archiving them in the moment of performance and in a production's material and affective traces, my project at a further remove of belatedness attempts to account for this working through: to see how performance, enmeshed as it is in a structure of repetition and reiteration, might "know" violent events and histories. Rather than the impossible act of recovering the "event itself", performance criticism, like the performances it seeks to analyse, might then stand as a kind of generative archive. My description and discussion of Taymor's *Titus*, for example, does not simply "replay" the film, but rather works to add a further iteration to the performance's field of meaning, specifically in relation to understandings of trauma. As Jacques Derrida succinctly notes: "the technical structure of the *archiving* archive also determines the structure of the *archivable* content even in its very coming into existence and in its relationship to the future. The archivization produces as much as it records the event".[61] In Derrida's formulation, the archive creates the event as much as it documents it, making and remaking it in response to various institutional and technological pressures. By way of illustration, Derrida considers how the development and subsequent understandings of psychoanalysis are profoundly connected to the communication technologies used by its chief proponents, namely the letters written between Freud and his contemporaries, and the technologies available for printing and archiving.[62] The conditions that structure archivable content, including modes of communication, such as letter, email, telephone, and news media, storage media and economic resources, among other factors, thus materially affect how particular events come into being but also how those events might be known in the future. In turn, my reading of such materials in relation to narratives of trauma situates this project as both generative and performative; it produces new iterations of performances that do not seek to recover, stand in for or replicate these events, even as they have a necessary and intimate relationship to performance events. Performance criticism that seeks, as this project does, to engage with the cultural analysis of trauma thus contributes, like the performance event itself, to an archive of trauma. To borrow Cvetkovich's phrase, the chapters of this book "should be understood as working as much to produce an archive as to analyze one".[63]

In addition to conceiving of performance and criticism as working to archive trauma, my work is also engaged, at various points, with what might more conventionally be understood as "archives", or material repositories of documents. The materials from which these archives are produced are various, bearing the traces of the pressures wrought by the Shakespeare performance industry and the cultural institutionalisation of Shakespeare. I have drawn on archival research variously undertaken at a number of specialist libraries and archives, my debts to which will emerge over the following chapters. As has been ably demonstrated by Michael D. Bristol with respect to the Howard Furness Memorial Library and the Folger Shakespeare Library, archiving documents relating to Shakespeare is far from a neutral activity but rather one that is strikingly enmeshed with projects of cultural prestige and power.[64] The archives thus dictate, to a certain extent, the kinds of narratives that I can develop in relation to Shakespeare and trauma. However, in working out of, and in relation to, the archive I also add to it, reshaping the material and making new records or archives of performance. In this work I have made use of a variety of material traces of performance including films, videos, DVDs, play-scripts, programmes, press kits, reviews, diaries, interviews, photographs, post-show discussions, letters, websites and production notes such as prompt books, prop lists, costume sketches, rehearsal notes and stage managers' reports. As the performance event is mediated by its material traces other than the event itself, my reading of these materials is not directed by a desire to reassemble them into a faithful simulation of particular performances. Rather, in reading performance and its documentary traces, I work to identify moments, texts and, on occasion, gaps, in order to explore how performances of Shakespeare might engage with violent events and histories. Archives and other material documents thus provide the ground for much of the analysis in this book, highlighting how trauma is known through its traces but also the ways in which traces privilege some subject positions and exclude others. Collectively, this book models how criticism can operate through a close engagement with performance archives and material documents to generate narratives about trauma, the detail of which I will outline shortly.

SHAKESPEARE AND TRAUMA

Given the extent to which studies of trauma have pervaded the academy it is perhaps surprising that a significant body of work on the convergence between Shakespeare and trauma has yet to develop, especially in relation to productions that directly address traumatic events and histories. To date one of the key strands of work on Shakespeare and trauma, as it has emerged relatively recently, has attempted to historicise trauma in relation to early modern cultural production. This critical practice is exemplified by Thomas P. Anderson's *Performing Early Modern Trauma*, which makes a lucid case for how "significant cultural loss alters normative modes of expression and representation"; Patricia A. Cahill's *Unto the Breach*, which examines "scenes of horrific injury and systematic killing that punctuate Elizabethan performances of martial rationality" to "argue that theater often imagined modern warfare as a phenomenon defined by its traumatic impact—that is, by the fact that it cannot be fully grasped"; Heather Hirschfeld's consideration of *Hamlet*, repetition, trauma and theological precepts; and Deborah Willis's efforts to historicise trauma in order to show how "[h]onor-driven retaliatory practices" in *Titus Andronicus* act "as perverse therapy for traumatic experience".[65] While these projects are concerned with analyses of early modern texts rather than contemporary performances, it is worth drawing attention to some aspects of Willis's argument in particular in order to differentiate further the concerns of my project. Willis mounts a convincing case for how retaliatory practices "allow his [Shakespeare's] characters an alternative way to cope with the overwhelming emotions and shattering of self-structures generated by traumatic events".[66] At the end of her article, she notes some convergences between the representation of trauma in *Titus Andronicus* and the work of trauma theorists but she also suggests "that Shakespeare has his own contribution to make to current conversations about trauma and healing".[67] In particular, Willis argues that "Shakespeare's insight [is] that revenge can provide an emotional container for traumatic loss and humiliation" and that it "may even protect survivors from the many symptoms of PTSD".[68] She also suggests that "Shakespeare lacks the confidence of some trauma theorists that talking about traumatic experience leads to healing", that "in contrast to many trauma theorists, Shakespeare draws attention to the permeable line between victims and perpetrators", and that "Shakespeare's play underscores the limits of healing as a metaphor and a goal for trauma therapy, resisting the optimism and redemptive claims of some trauma theorists".[69] These points concerning what "Shakespeare" (and less frequently, "Shakespeare's play") suggests about trauma are not the domain of this book: that is, I do not seek to identify Shakespeare as an early trauma theorist (even as he might be) nor am I interested in speculating on what his views about trauma and ideas of "treatment" might have been. Here it is also worth distinguishing my project from some of David McCandless's claims about trauma and contemporary performances of *Titus*. McCandless suggests that Titus, as rendered by Julie Taymor in her stage (1994) and screen (1999) productions of the play, "suffers a heightened version of the Vietnam vet's traumatic dislocation" as part of his argument that "the stage production succeeds to a far greater degree in staging trauma and deconstructing violence".[70] Rather than making claims for the characters as traumatised or producing a hierarchy of "successful" instantiations of trauma in performance, I am interested in how performances of Shakespeare's texts enfold and respond to traumatic events and histories and the political and ethical implications of this work.

In terms of work on contemporary performance, the most significant contribution to this debate is Timothy Murray's *Drama Trauma*. In his eclectic and wide-ranging book, Murray seeks to "foreground the cultural manifestation of trauma in its various theatrical guises in theory and in early modern and contemporary performance, television, video, and installation art".[71] Alongside this work he runs an argument about "televisual fear" where he explores the anxieties that attend the use of televisual technologies in the performing arts, especially in relation to discourses of presence. Despite brief considerations of Baz Luhrmann's *William Shakespeare's Romeo + Juliet* (1996) and *All's Well That Ends Well* (1980), directed by Elijah Moshinsky and produced by Jonathan Miller for the BBC, the focus of Murray's analysis is not so much on performance but on analyses of Shakespeare's play texts—*Othello*, *Hamlet*, *King Lear* and *Romeo and Juliet*, in particular—which he puts in "dialogue with feminist, lesbian, and African-American performance".[72] He is concerned, specifically, with "the transformation of genre and gender wrought by Shakespearean spectres of linguistic play, vision gone awry, and well-seeming form".[73] In this work, he argues that "ideology works in Shakespeare as the complex strata of fantasy construction that provides the spectator with a doubled phantasmatic screen of both the pleasure of illusions and the fetishistic preservation of the residues of trauma".[74] Murray's analysis has certainly inflected the way in which I have conceived of performances of Shakespeare as haunted by various traumatic spectres, especially with respect to how performance might be marked with a "residue" of trauma. However, I have sought to develop analyses that, while attuned to the possibilities enabled by Shakespeare's texts for various explorations in trauma as Murray does, are focussed on specific conditions of performance and the narratives of trauma that inhere both in the moment of performance and in the wider field of documentation produced by a particular production.

In the chapters that follow, the book's central propositions are developed through a series of case studies. These encompass performances of Shakespeare's texts, including appropriations, on stage and screen, and consider performances produced, for the most part, in South Africa, the United Kingdom and New Zealand. I am as interested in productions which claim to be "about" various violent events and histories, within or outside the frames of the plays they engage with, as much as those that do not, and I am as interested in examining systemic oppressions as I am in specific acts of physical violence. With these parametres in mind, the project primarily considers apartheid, colonisation, homophobia and war, as well as engaging, at various points, with the Holocaust and various acts of physical violence. As this range suggests, the selected case studies do not pretend a comprehensive coverage of how work in trauma studies might enable a reading of Shakespeare in performance or the kinds of events and histories that might be considered within the realm of the traumatic. Rather they model a way of reading Shakespeare in performance that seeks to be attentive to the complexities of the events to which performance offers its traumatic turns. In exploring these turns, the book aims, on occasions, to offer some perhaps unexpected directions in relation to the dominant thematics by which particular plays have come to be known: for example, *The Merchant of Venice* is considered in relation to colonisation and an appropriation of *The Tempest* is considered in relation to homophobia. While the case studies and my mode of analysis collectively identify some overlaps in how trauma might be figured in performance, my analysis seeks to be attentive to the cultural and historical specificity of trauma. It thus seeks to avoid making equivalences between various traumatic events and histories as the diagnosis of PTSD and work in the humanities, which tend to be based on Western models of psychic and cultural life, can have the effect of doing. As Willis succinctly notes, "[c]ultures also have internal variations: gender, class, and ethnicity introduce other variables that influence the way trauma is experienced".[75] In my attempt to consider how performances of Shakespeare can work to memorialise, remember and witness traumatic events and histories, my efforts to pay close attention to the cultural and historical contexts of the performances I consider stand as a marker of my commitment to avoid universalising these events and histories and the operation of Shakespeare in diverse cultural contexts. As with all selections, there are areas that remain untouched but which offer scope for further work in the terms I have suggested here. I am thinking in particular of the use of Shakespeare's texts in psychiatric hospitals and prisons as part of therapeutic and rehabilitation programmes, such as those documented in Murray Cox's *Shakespeare Comes to Broadmoor* and Amy Scott-Douglass's *Shakespeare Inside.*[76] Although these case studies lend themselves to the kind of analysis I have proposed here, the work of applied theatre and drama therapy falls beyond the scope of this study.

Chapter 1, "Honour the real thing", opens the case studies by returning to *Titus Andronicus*, the text with which I initiated this introduction. My focus in this chapter is Gregory Doran's production of *Titus Andronicus* (1995), a co-production between the National Theatre in London and Johannesburg's Market Theatre. Here I am interested in how Doran's production engaged with the play as a precursor for an exploration of violence in South Africa, among other locales. The production, through its scenography, casting and, most vividly, its rehearsal process, variously raises questions about the ethics of representing violent events and histories in performance and the possibilities for representing and communicating these events and histories. The chapter suggests that the violence demanded by Shakespeare's text was strategically deployed as a way of negotiating historical and contemporary violence but that this deployment worked to produce elisions and marginalisations of its own. Shakespeare's play was employed in Doran's production (and Taymor's film) as a kind of panacea to heal the trauma caused by violence but as the analysis suggests, the wounds continue to seep.

The Holocaust and histories of anti-Semitism tend to be identified as the dominant traumatic frames of reference for considering *The Merchant of Venice*. Chapter 2, "The Legacy of Colonisation", marks its difference from existing scholarship on relationships between *The Merchant* and the trauma of the Holocaust by considering these frames of reference within the context of an analysis of colonisation and its aftermath. This chapter thus extends the discussion of intercultural violence, which dominates much of the previous chapter, through an examination of a New Zealand-made film, *The Maori Merchant of Venice* (2001), in which the performance can be read as an index of the trauma produced through colonisation. In the first full-length feature film to be shot in Māori, the indigenous language of Aotearoa New Zealand, the aim of director Don C. Selwyn was to marry his love for Shakespeare with his passion for the Māori language as a way of showcasing Māori to local and global cinema-going audiences. Selwyn suggests that Pei Te Hurinui Jones's 1945 translation, which uses a classical form of Māori, allows Māori to recover elements of the language that have been lost due to the pressures of colonisation: in effect Shakespeare enables Māori to recapture its linguistic "essence". Strikingly, every Māori sentence is predicated on one written by an icon of the language that displaced Māori and is shadowed, literally, by that language in the form of (modernised) English subtitles. While the publicity surrounding the film tends to represent the meshing of English and Māori as "natural" and seamless, this chapter explores the tensions that surround this intercultural project, especially as they emerge in relation to Aotearoa New Zealand's colonial history and Māori language dispossession. One of the ways in which these tensions manifest themselves most clearly is in the film's citation of the Holocaust as Antonio strikes his bargain with Shylock, exemplifying how productions of the *Merchant* seem always already traced by this event, variously returning it to the field of performance and documentation. This chapter also considers how trauma, perhaps perversely, provides the ground from which communities might mobilise themselves to redress injuries.

Chapter 3, "Sexuality, Trauma and Community", is similarly interested in relationships between trauma and community formation. My focus here is Philip Osment's play *This Island's Mine* (1988) for London's Gay Sweatshop theatre company, which includes the rehearsal of scenes from *The Tempest* as part of its narrative. In this chapter I consider Osment's play in relation to traumatic oppressions on the basis of sexual preference and practices, which variously manifest themselves in verbal, physical and legal violence, and how these intersect with ethnicity. My consideration of Osment's play is contextualised in relation to Dev Virahsawmy's play, *Toufann* (1991), and Derek Jarman's film, *The Tempest* (1979), alongside several of Jarman's other "Renaissance" films. Through an analysis of Osment's text, performance choices, reviews and the Gay Sweatshop archive, an analysis of Osment's play and production is offered with respect to the operation of racism and homophobia, especially in relation to the institution of Section 28 in Britain, which sought to limit the "promotion" of homosexuality by local authority governments. This chapter, as with Chapter 2, also considers how trauma can provide ground for the creation of affective and effective community relationships, but also explores how those communities can work, simultaneously, to marginalise others.

Chapter 4, "Theatres of War", develops the analysis of the trauma produced through cultural conflict through a consideration of the way in which Britain's participation in the invasions of Afghanistan and Iraq have been considered in Nicholas Hytner's production of *Henry V* (2003) for the National Theatre in London. In its synchronicity with contemporary events the production seemed to fold the trauma of war seamlessly into the fabric of its production. Through the mechanisms of representational theatre it promised to offer its performers and spectators access to the realities of contemporary warfare such that they might stand as witnesses to these experiences. As the production moved toward its close, it worked to memorialise and remember the violence of warfare, both onstage and off, as part of a narrative of British victory. An analysis of the production's deployment of the representational modes of realism and a consideration of its documentary traces suggest, however, that the traumatic event of war resists representation as the "thing itself". Under the guise of realism, the production embeds a set of propositions about the experience of war and the behaviour of contemporary British troops. Whereas the production worked to consign the violence of war to the past, both on stage and off via the rhetoric of victory, a consideration of the production's documentary traces, with particular reference to photographs, identifies how trauma refuses to be consigned to the past. It returns "out of time" to call upon spectators to acknowledge the violence and horror of warfare, even as these images, too, can only reveal the hollowed-out quality of representations of trauma. This chapter concludes with a brief recapitulation of the work of *Shakespeare, Trauma and Contemporary Performance* and looks forward to the possibilities it offers for theatre making, criticism and spectatorship.

1 "Honour the real thing"

Gregory Doran's *Titus Andronicus* in South Africa

In John Madden's film *Shakespeare in Love* (1998) one of the historically contingent jokes concerns a young boy with a penchant for rats and violence.[1] Passed over for the lead role of Ethel the Pirate's daughter in Shakespeare's ill-fated new play *Romeo and Ethel the Pirate's Daughter*, the boy is shown playing with rats in an alleyway. In response to Shakespeare's condolences about the part the boy says, "I was in a play. They cut my head off in *Titus Andronicus*. When I write plays, they will be like *Titus*".[2] Grimly nodding in acknowledgement of his admiration for the play, the boy goes on, "I liked it when they cut heads off. And the daughter mutilated with knives" (54). Identifying himself as John Webster, the boy claims that "[p]lenty of blood [. . .] is the only writing" (54). Following the boy's disclosure, Shakespeare *"backs away, unnerved"* (54). The young Webster's interests in violence, blood and *Titus Andronicus* are thus seen as formative influences that led to the writing of his macabre and violent plays such as *The White Devil* (1612) and *The Duchess of Malfi* (c. 1614). *Shakespeare in Love* thus neatly locates violence as the dominant thematic by which *Titus* is known, even as it simultaneously works to distance Shakespeare from this text by having him back away from the boy, mirroring early critical responses to the play, which sought to locate it as apocrypha or juvenilia.[3] As Richard Burt notes, "Shakespeare's bloody tragedy is associated with his juvenilia, and poor Webster is represented as an inferior playwright whose development was arrested at a very young age".[4] No doubt in part due to its status as an "immature" work (the play is cited as an antecedent to *King Lear* and *Othello*), a collaborative work (hence, not quite "Shakespeare"), and the extremities of its acts of violence, *Titus Andronicus* has a relatively minor performance history compared to other of Shakespeare's tragedies. Since Peter Brook's seminal 1955 production for the Royal Shakespeare Company (RSC), with Laurence Olivier as Titus and Vivian Leigh as Lavinia, the play—famous for its scenes of violence, including the rape and mutilation of Lavinia, hand amputations, executions, stabbings, live partial burial and the preparation and consumption of a human pie—has become increasingly popular, engendering a spate of performances on stage and, more recently, on screen, including Christopher Dunne's cult horror adaptation (1999) and Julie Taymor's *Titus* (1999), with which I opened this book. Given the play's growing performance history and its catalogue of horrors which might, in medical and popular discourse, be termed traumatic, it is perhaps unsurprising that it is this play that has attracted the majority of the relatively small body of critical work that has attempted to engage specifically with Shakespeare and trauma, such as work by Anderson, Willis and McCandless that I considered in the introduction.

In this chapter I will explore how contemporary performances of Shakespeare's texts engage with various violent events and histories through a consideration of Gregory Doran's production of *Titus Andronicus* (1995) for the National Theatre in London and Johannesburg's Market Theatre, with expatriate South African Antony Sher in the title role and a South African-based cast.[5] In particular, I am interested in how Doran's production engaged with *Titus Andronicus* as a precursor for an exploration of violence in South Africa, among other locales, through its scenography, casting and, most vividly, its rehearsal process. Doran and Sher used the play's acts of violence as a way of negotiating and attempting to communicate the effects of historical and contemporary violence, especially in South Africa, situating the production as participating in South Africa's newly established project of reconciliation following the 1994 elections. In their attempts to engage with traumatic experiences in rehearsal and performance Doran and Sher's work performs exclusions and marginalisations of its own, and the "trauma work" that they propose for South Africa is, for the most part, resisted by local audiences.

SETTING THE STAGE FOR TRAUMA

Stimulated by a series of workshops run in Johannesburg by the Studio, the developmental arm of the National Theatre (NT), Doran's production of *Titus Andronicus* was a joint venture between the NT Studio and Johannesburg's Market Theatre. Taking place in the wake of South Africa's first democratic post-apartheid elections, this collaboration is an example of the kind of artistic exchange made possible since 1991 when the United Nations lifted the cultural boycott on South Africa, sanctioned by its 1968 Resolution which requested that "all States and organizations [. . .] suspend cultural, educational, sporting and other exchanges with the racist régime and with organizations or institutions in South Africa which practice *apartheid*".[6] The Resolution of 1991, in contrast, "[c]alls upon the international community, in view of the progress made in overcoming obstacles to negotiations, to resume academic, scientific and cultural links with democratic anti-apartheid organizations and the individuals in these fields, to resume sports links with unified non-racial sporting organizations of South Africa".[7] Sanctioned by the call of this resolution, the production was developed through auditions in Johannesburg, two weeks of workshops in London followed by a rehearsal period in Johannesburg, before opening for an eight-week run at the Market Theatre in March 1995, with the first anniversary of the April 1994 post-apartheid democratic elections falling during the run. *Titus Andronicus* was subsequently performed at the West Yorkshire Playhouse's Courtyard Theatre in Leeds, the National's Cottesloe Theatre in London and at the Almagro festival in Spain during July 1995.

Since it was founded by Barney Simon and Mannie Manim in 1974, the Market Theatre has sought, as noted in the programme for *Titus Andronicus*, to present its "audiences [with] a reflection of the world in which they lived", mainly through "the development of indigenous work that reflects our aspirations and our lives".[8] One of the most striking examples of this ethos is Percy Mtwa, Mbongeni Ngema and Simon's hugely successful *Woza Albert!* (1981), which offered a satirical critique of apartheid via a "fantasy of a Second Coming to South Africa by Morena, the Saviour".[9] The Market also has a history of staging Shakespeare's plays and adaptations, including, for example, *Romeo and Juliet* (1982), *Othello* (1987), directed by Janet Suzman, and Yael Farber's *SeZaR* (2002), a production that mixes the text of *Julius Caesar* with several African languages as part of a narrative about war and corruption in a fictional African state.[10] As Martin Orkin and David Johnson have shown, Shakespeare has been used for conservative pedagogical and pro-apartheid ends in South Africa as well as co-opted for the kind of anti-apartheid work that Orkin considers.[11] However, Natasha Distiller trenchantly notes that Orkin's project to use Shakespeare as a weapon against apartheid "reinscribes exactly the all-knowing, universal genius he says is invoked by the state to silence and control".[12] Knowledge of this "universal genius" can, though, provide access to cultural capital and, depending on the ideologies at work, it can also provide access to an imagined "universal humanity". A conception of universal humanity can in turn be mobilised against racist ideologies that work to dehumanise certain groups and communities, even as it can also work to elide difference and cultural specificity and to uphold dominant cultural formations.

Given the complexities of the history of Shakespeare in South Africa, especially with respect to the production of cultural capital (and exclusion from that capital) through the education system, to which Orkin's, Johnson's and Distiller's work, among others, speaks, what, then, is at stake in a performance of *Titus Andronicus* in post-apartheid South Africa? In particular, how might a play that stages a series of violent acts and racial tensions be performed in a theatre that promises, as the programme notes, "a commitment to our community in a time in need of healing, understanding, sharing and reconciliation"? *Titus Andronicus* is a play that stages a resolution where power is purchased, to some extent, through the incorporation and expulsion of those that are perceived as "other", acts that are primarily located on the bodies of a Moor and a woman. What, then, are the implications of its performance in a theatre that is actively engaged in projects of reconciliation and healing and in a culture in which "black" and "coloured" populations have been systemically oppressed, where the rape rate is extremely high and where violence against women is described as "endemic" by the South Africa Law Commission?[13] As will become apparent, Doran and Sher's production is traced by the traumatic spectre of apartheid and its ongoing effects, but it also encodes a range of other traumas that, collectively, raise questions about the possibility of representing trauma and the ethical implications of rehearsal and performance. I am interested especially in how the performance of *Titus Andronicus* was used as a precursor for exploring a series of violent events and histories. I am also concerned with how this exploration worked, on occasion, to reiterate or recycle stereotypes about race without sufficient critique and to occlude and conflate the voices of others that it sought to acknowledge.

Perhaps wary of forcing a relationship between the play's narrative and South Africa's apartheid-era racial politics, Doran has claimed that the production was "not presenting allegory".[14] And indeed, the production did not offer a sustained allegorical reading in which the action of the play was deployed as a straightforward analogy between the narrative of Shakespeare's text and apartheid-era South Africa. Yet the production simultaneously instituted a South African frame of reference for engaging with the play, repeatedly turning to iconic South African images and sounds, many of which worked to make associations between aspects of the play and South Africa's history of racial conflict, especially as it was codified during apartheid. One of the notable features of the production, and certainly one that received resistance from some members of the cast and also several negative reviews, was the decision to have the actors perform in South African rather than assumed English accents, as part of Doran and Sher's commitment to finding a "South African way" of performing Shakespeare (45). Distiller notes, though, that the accents used by the actors, such as Dorothy Ann Gould's production of a "poor-white accent" (124) for the Goth Queen Tamora, were as produced "as much as they would be if they reverted to the English accents Sher and Doran decry as inauthentic".[15] Here Distiller identifies how the production's claims to have found an authentically "South African" way of playing Shakespeare relied on reproducing "apartheid-inflected identities at a time when South Africans were uncertainly adjusting to what it meant to be post-apartheid".[16] Rather than giving space for this kind of adjustment, or engaging with how "post-apartheid" identities are enmeshed in a history of apartheid identities, Doran and Sher's "authentic" South African Shakespeare instead reproduced a collection of racial and cultural stereotypes marked by accent.

The decision to use South African accents to locate the play in South Africa was developed further through a series of ethnic parallels with

Figure 1.1 Antony Sher as Titus in Gregory Doran's 1995 production of *Titus Andronicus*, co-produced by the National Theatre and the Market Theatre, Johannesburg. Photograph © Ruphin Coudyzer, FPPSA, www.ruphin.com, reproduced with his permission.

respect to casting. Here the production's concerns with South African culture more broadly, through song and accent, became entangled with a history of colonisation and, more specifically, apartheid-era racial politics. Early in the audition process, Doran noted an interest in representing the Andronici as Afrikaners. As Doran asserts, "[l]ike the Afrikaner nation, they are God-fearing and pure-bred" (48). Distiller astutely notes that Doran's claim recycles an "historical inaccuracy, and [is] a repetition of the apartheid ideology used to underwrite the policy of separatism".[17] Sher appears to overlook the racist implications of the designation of "pure-bred", focussing instead on aesthetic concerns, noting that he wanted "the facial look of all the Andronici to be very old-style Afrikaner", citing the Voortrekkers and the images in the Anglo-Boer War book *To The Bitter End,* as examples (120). To achieve this effect he grew his beard and had it square cut, and cropped his hair in a military crew cut; in addition he developed a series of gestures and movements that suggested a military bearing (Figure 1.1). Consequently, reviewers read Titus as Afrikaner in both South Africa and the United Kingdom: it was noted that "Titus resembles nobody so much as the Afrikaner Weerstandsbeweging's [Afrikaner Resistance Movement] farcical leader" Eugène Terre'Blanche, and Sher was further described, for example, as a "barrel-chested Afrikaner" and a "weary battle-scarred Afrikaner".[18] Sher imagined an older historical precedent for his Afrikaner-Andronici, informed by heroic images of war. In practice the reception of the images was also refracted through more recent history, especially in relation to pro-apartheid and separatist movements, which Terre'Blanche and his party's campaigns for an independent Boer state embody; public responses to his murder in April 2010 exemplify the racial tensions that have continued to coalesce around Terre'Blanche's politics and actions in post-apartheid South Africa. Reporting for the South African press, Digby Ricci made a direct comparison between Sher and Terre'Blanche, an association that recurred in reviews by Mark Gevisser and Robert Greig and also by reviewers in the British press.[19] Sher's old-style Afrikaaner, which speaks to a history of colonisation, was thus read primarily as a signifier of contemporary racism, ensuring that the violence of separatist politics was repeatedly returned to the field of performance. The disjunction between Sher's conception of Titus as "old-style Afrikaner" and the way he was read as Terre'Blanche speaks also to Sher's apparent dislocation from contemporary South African politics. To reproduce, even unwittingly, the image of Terre'Blanche in the context of a play that reifies Titus's grief in terms of heroic suffering implicates the production in racial politics that work against Doran and Sher's project of reconciliation, to which I will return below.

As a counterpoint to Sher's Afrikaner Titus, the images of Aaron, played by Sello Maake ka Ncube (Figure 1.2), invited spectators to read his plight in the context of the oppression of black people in South Africa and more widely, reinforced by the speeches in which Aaron asserts his subjectivity and identifies the inequalities that attend being black. Doran makes his desire for these connections explicit in his assertion that South African audiences "can feel the weight of oppression and subjugation on his [Aaron's] shoulders".[20] The association between black people and servitude was reinforced by casting black actor Daphney Hlomuka as the nurse and, more pointedly still, by casting black actor Paulus Kuoape as the boy, Young Lucius: in the play text Titus's grandson is referred to as "boy" and in the context of the casting decision, the name "boy" worked to recast Young Lucius as Titus's boy, or servant. As Christopher Thurman notes in his discussion of the Nurse and Young Lucius, "a black actor was cast in a role that implied a weak black character, undermining the production's attempt to avoid past stereotypes".[21] Here the production tracked straight back into a reiteration of racial stereotypes and inequalities that post-apartheid South Africa seeks to redress. The question of how to figure the Goths in relation to this black/Afrikaner dichotomy was explained during a National Theatre Platform post-show discussion. Thus the "Afrikaner rigidity in the Romans" was contrasted with "elasticity in the Goths" who, in a catch-all ethnic category, "could be everything else including black", "poor white" or "mixed race and that mixed race could come from Cape Malay, from Indians".[22] Here the specificity of "other" South African identities was negated in favour of a generalised "otherness", which worked to collapse difference. Similarly, the production's representation of the Andronici, Aaron, the Nurse and the Boy, which, as I have suggested, relied on stereotypes in terms of accent and characterisation, did not create sufficient space to acknowledge the diversity of black and white cultures in South Africa.

These casting decisions, which worked to give the play a South African frame of reference, were reinforced further by the scenography. The set, designed by Nadya Cohen, was split apart at the interval to reveal a gash of red Johannesburg earth, literally bringing the land of South Africa into the frame of Shakespeare's play. The symbolic importance of incorporating the land of South Africa was made clear before the first performance at the Courtyard Theatre in Leeds as Doran sprinkled red Johannesburg earth, collected by Sher from the Market set, on the new set, a ritual that was repeated in London at the Cottesloe (261, 273). From the point in the action at which the set was split, Doran figured the space as an "encroaching dump", peopled by "an underclass of drop-outs, runaways and homeless tramps" (125) who later became Titus's army of helpers. The characterisation of these individuals was based on an observation exercise conducted under Sher's guidance by four of the actors in Hillbrow, a densely populated area of central Johannesburg. Hillbrow was once inhabited primarily by white South Africans but its ethnic demographic changed significantly following the movement of black South Africans from the townships to the central city in the early 1980s and the immigration of black populations from other African nations, particularly Nigeria and the Democratic

Figure 1.2   Sello Maake ka Ncube (left) as Aaron and Martin Le Maitre (right) as Lucius in Gregory Doran's 1995 production of *Titus Andronicus*, co-produced by the National Theatre and the Market Theatre, Johannesburg. Photograph © Ruphin Coudyzer, FPPSA, www.ruphin.com, reproduced with his permission.

Republic of Congo in the mid-1990s. As Tomlinson *et al.* report, this movement "accelerated rapidly" such that "by 1993, 85% of the inner city residential population was black [. . .] and by 1996 only 5% was white", a demographic shift that Doran also notes (125).[23] In the actors' observation work and the use of scenography, the production sought to bring local South African sites into the space of performance. This work does, however, raise questions about the ethics of appropriation and representation of the experiences of others. Specifically, the observations and subsequent representations drew on stereotypical and selective images of Hillbrow such as substance abuse and homelessness, thereby offering a reductive set of images of this area and its inhabitants. Furthermore, the inhabitants of Hillbrow were, in effect, treated as objects of anthropological inquiry to be used as material for generating performance. This exemplifies an asymmetric power relationship where the "other" is objectified, and, in the course of the exercise and its subsequent use, exploited for economic gain through the economy of theatrical production. These South African visual signifiers were reinforced with the use of objects, such as masks and the scimitar-shaped panga, or machete, that Aaron uses to murder the nurse, and the butterfly knives and *okapi* (folding knife) used by Chiron (Oscar Petersen) and Demitrius (Charlton George). According to the explanation offered in the National's Platform discussion, the knives were intended to allude to the culture of the Cape Flats, an area to the south-east of central Cape Town where "non-white" people were forced to relocate as a result of the 1950 Group Areas Act. Again the production resorted to racial stereotypes, recycling them without critique in performance.

Although the production did not offer a seamless analogy between the text and South Africa, the South African frame of reference offered by these images does invite allegorical readings of the kind Doran claims to be resistant to: Titus is identified as Afrikaner, and, on occasions with an explicitly white-separatist Afrikaner, Aaron carries the weight of racial oppression in South Africa, the fall of Rome is linked to the fall of the Andronici-Afrikaners and this shadows the end of apartheid; disturbingly, given the contemporary political situation of the play's production, this regime is reinstituted in modified form at the close of the play following the expulsion of Aaron and Tamora. These associations recurred in rehearsal with Doran reporting that a member of the company observed that what "happens in Rome is just what all the whities feared would happen after the Elections here" (113). The parallels that the production invites with respect to its characterisation of South Africa's past and present are not politically benign and the creation of what Thurman describes as some "awkward anachronisms" serves to reinforce a dynamic of fear and to misrepresent aspects of South Africa's recent history.[24] As Thurman notes, the potential for the play's opening elections to plunge Rome into a state of chaos, which Doran and Sher place in relation to the 1994 election (112), runs contrary to the "months and years following the elections [that] were comparatively peaceful"; Thurman goes on to argue, "[w]ith this in mind, the mood suggested by the production's opening was inappropriate to the historical actuality to which it claimed relevance".[25]

The histories of violence in South Africa to which the performance turned, aided by scenography, casting and the mission statement of the Market Theatre, among other factors, were thus placed in dialogue with a play text that deals with at least two additional temporalities—Ancient Rome and Elizabethan England. Images of South Africa, especially its history of racial segregation, were in effect spliced into Shakespeare's text, forcing equivalences between the text and aspects of South Africa's culture and history, even as the analogies broke apart under the narrative requirements of the text and developments in post-apartheid South Africa. The colonial and apartheid-era images to which the production had recourse thus operated as traumatic fragments, piercing the play's narrative concerns with racial power struggles in Ancient Rome, and turning the spectator repeatedly to traumatic aspects of South Africa's history, traumas that are reinforced in the fate of Aaron. The performance thus registers a history of colonisation and apartheid but it was in the audition, workshop and rehearsal processes that the production's engagements with the traumatic effects of violence were most explicitly developed. I am now concerned to identify the various traumatic histories and events that were brought to bear in the preparation phase and the implications of this work for performance.

In the course of this exploration I will draw extensively on *Woza Shakespeare! "Titus Andronicus" in South Africa*, the text of which is based on diaries Doran and Sher kept throughout the duration of the production, marking both their personal and professional relationships; some elements of *Woza Shakespeare!* were also published by Sher in *The Times* following the workshop period.[26] The title *Woza Shakespeare!* cannily references *Woza Albert!* This works implicitly to claim an anti-apartheid authenticity for the project, locating the production alongside the protest work of *Woza Albert!* even as it recycled racial stereotypes without embedding a sustained critique, as I have suggested above. *Woza Shakespeare!* is, of course, a partial and selective document and one that works both to represent and occlude the voices of others as well as offering a necessarily selective view of Doran's and Sher's concerns. With this partiality in mind, I want to read this text as a document, which like the production it seeks to account for, offers a "working through" of a series of violent events and histories. As will become clear, in Doran and Sher's "working through", they tend to romanticise the rehearsal process and make assumptions about how the process works for others, without problematising their working methods or the kinds of assumptions upon which these methods rest. While they seek to identify the traumatic aftermath of violence and how performance might, belatedly, engage with these lingering after-effects, Doran and Sher often reproduce clichés and stereotypes about violence and Shakespeare, elide cultural specificity and appropriate the experiences of others, as will emerge in the following section.

REHEARSING TRAUMA

One of the most striking aspects of the audition, workshop and rehearsal processes as they are documented by Doran and Sher is the extent to which various activities were structured in order to create an archive of trauma, which is variously composed of stories and documents, for members of the cast to draw upon in performance. These activities included autobiographical storytelling, watching films, listening to visiting speakers and individual research work. This kind of work is indebted to various Method acting systems of training, originating from Konstantin Stanislavsky's work at the Moscow Art Theatre, codified in acting manuals such as *An Actor Prepares* (1936), *Building a Character* (1949) and *Creating a Role* (1961), and popularised by Lee Strasberg at the New York Actors Studio in the 1950s and in his book *A Dream of Passion* (1987). These training methods emphasise an actor's use of her memory and the creation of sense impressions such that she will be able to recall these in performance and hence play the role "truthfully". As Peter Brook summarises in *The Empty Space* (1968), the Method actor is "trained to reject cliché imitations of reality and to search for something more real in himself".[27] But, as Lauren Love notes in her feminist critique of Method acting, "[p]sychological realism as a genre in theatre and the Method acting approach which is designed to serve its principles, rehearse liberal humanist ideals that privilege dominant ideologies as 'natural'".[28]

Sher mentions his interest in Method acting, especially the idea of using "emotional recall to make the moments of sorrow, joy, fear, etc., completely real" (164) and his performance work certainly shows evidence of this kind of emotional memory work. Indeed, Doran notes that in Sher's performance of Shylock for the RSC's production of *The Merchant of Venice* (1987) he "explored his own experience of prejudice, as a Jew, as a gay man, as a South African, and lent Shylock the voice of his own anger" (27). In this account, Doran suggests that Sher's personal identifications are deployed as a way of exploring and developing the character of Shylock. An engagement with "real" experience similarly pervaded the preparation of *Titus Andronicus*; as Sher puts it in an interview: "[w]e were concerned with studying people with real examples of violence".[29] For Love, though, the construction of "a believable character" which the Method "purport[s] [. . .] flow[s] logically from the empirical 'truth of lived experience' [. . .] helps to secure the actor's complicity with its principles and by extension with dominant cultural modalities".[30] Although Doran and Sher attempted to engage with selected minority and oppressed subject positions, the difference between these positions was often collapsed in the service of a generalised understanding of violence in relation to (South) Africa, other cultural contexts and the play. Furthermore, the exercises used to focus this concern with "truth"—many of which aimed to create an archive of traumatic memories resulting from real experiences to be capitalised on in the moment of performance—in turn raise questions about the ethical engagement with such material, especially in relation to the "use" and representation of such experiences in performance. In this production the act of performance became about more than playing the role; it was simultaneously characterised as about honouring (and I use the word advisedly as will become clear below) the experiences that were shared and encountered in the audition, workshop and rehearsal periods.

The production's drive to utilise personal experiences of trauma was evident from the outset of the audition process. As Sher recalls, in casting Lavinia, Doran used an exercise where he asked the actors to place socks over their fists to represent Lavinia's amputated hands and "communicate [without speech] the story of some traumatic event in her life" (50). In this work, it was Jennifer Woodburne who made her case most convincingly: "[h]er sock-fisted, dumb-tongued story—about an intruder breaking into her flat one night—is very upsetting" (50). In this exercise Woodburne was asked to draw on her own experience of a violent event and communicate it through performance. Here the task stages a communicative model of trauma and makes a claim for the efficacy of performance in carrying out the work of communication. That is, the exercise is predicated on the notion that performance has the capacity not only to represent a traumatic event, but in so doing it is able to communicate or transmit something of the emotional affect of that event, registered in Sher's comment that the performance is "very upsetting". The use of performance as a mode of transmitting what Cathy Caruth would call "simple knowledge" of a traumatic event is antithetical to an understanding of trauma in which the action of trauma hollows out the point of traumatic reference and resists literal representation.[31] However, Caruth's Freudian-inflected model shares with Doran's a similar belief in the communicative power of trauma or "the historical and personal truths it transmits", where it is the responsibility of the spectating subject to listen to the "wound that cries out".[32] In Doran's model, the performance of trauma is credited with the capacity to transmit such personal truths, the success of which is registered at the level of content (Sher was able to understand easily the situation that Woodburne performed) and affect (Sher found the performance upsetting).

Work on the transmission of trauma also recurred in the workshop phase of the preparation process in London, but here the work of communication was also figured in terms of the production of emotional resources. Early in this process, which comprised a series of activities and research rather than work on the play text, an activity that was reserved for the rehearsal period in Johannesburg, Sher records that, as "part of our work on violence, we've asked each member of the group to recount a personal experience of it" (73). Here the workshop space was modelled as a kind of therapeutic space where members of the group were invited to talk through various experiences. These are acts that were also repeated in therapeutic contexts in South Africa. For example, a newspaper advertisement, contemporaneous with the production, advises that "The Trauma Clinic offers one to one counselling to victims of violence and group debriefings", noting that this is a "service provided by the Centre for the Study of Violence and Reconciliation".[33] Furthermore, the documentation of the Truth and Reconciliation Commission (TRC) records a series of individual testimonies of experiences of violence and oppression, from 1995 until the Commission closed early in 2002, identifying how South Africans were invited to share publicly their experiences in the aftermath of apartheid.[34] These acts of sharing were not, of course, ideologically neutral. As Ashley Dawson argues, the Commission's "emphasis on reconciliation imposed a narrative of healing and nation building that threatened to promote a kind of amnesia among South Africans [. . .] eliding the suffering of average South Africans caught up in the quotidian forms of state and civilian injustice that characterized apartheid".[35]

The workshop, the therapy session and the state-sanctioned site of testimony are not, of course, reducible to one another. They do, though, share an interest in the enactment and elucidation of emotional states in the service of larger projects, such as nation building in the case of the TRC and a successful performance in the case of the rehearsals. The rehearsal exercises, as I will show, are also positioned such that individual testimony was placed in the service of working through wider cultural concerns, especially in relation to apartheid. In the workshop, this interest can be framed in terms of affective labour, or that which is designed to produce emotional affects in others and/or the self. Here the individual experiences of violent events, while still retaining their primary relationship to the teller, take on the status of commodities, available for consumption as material for performance. Subsequently Sher records that one member of the group recounted the rape and murder of a family member, including details of how another member of the narrator's family was given police photographs of the crime scene, depicting a bed with blood where the head and genitals would have been; the narrator explained that the family member kept the photos because "[t]hey were part of *us* . . . my family . . . part of our history" (73, Sher's emphasis and ellipsis). Just as the photographs function as mementos, signs to be incorporated into the family's history, the individual experience of violence was offered as a memento to the cast, something for them to hold, return to and incorporate within their own performances. The narrative also offered the group specifically South African contexts for violence as it touched on the difficult topics of interracial violence and its relation to the operation of the law during apartheid and attempts to redress wrongful imprisonment in its aftermath. As Sher reports, the murdered woman was white; one of the men convicted for her death was black and was subsequently pardoned as part of the amnesty that followed Nelson Mandela's release. Sher notes that in his role as chair of the session it is his "job now to draw comparisons, to fit this personal story into the scheme of our work—but it's difficult to speak" (73). Here he imagines how the personal experience of violence will somehow be able to be deployed in relation to work on Shakespeare's play. But he also notes that the group sat in silence and that he found it difficult to speak, thinking of how he would respond to the event and photographic evidence if it pertained to a member of his own family, such as his mother or sister (73).

In this episode, the individual experience of violence was reiterated and narrativised and thus made available as an emotional resource in the workshop process for future use by other performers. Caught up in the emotionally profound effect that the story has on the group, and on himself in particular, Sher does not seem to acknowledge the kinds of emotional risks that members of the group are being asked to take in sharing personal stories. As Method actor and instructor Doug Moston notes, the creation of affective memory, especially where a teacher has suggested "an event for a student to use [. . .] can be dangerous because the student may not be psychologically ready to deal with some of the stimuli touched upon".[36] While I am not convinced by Moston's conception of psychological readiness, which seems to be predicated on normative emotional states, his comment points to the potential risks a performer is asked to take in divulging personal information in the rehearsal process. What seems to matter in Sher's account is less the potential risk to the individual concerned and more the production of affect for use in performance. What also emerges is that the emotional resource produced through the labour of the workshop process threatened the process itself: Sher was unable to assimilate easily the experience into the work of the production and Doran finished the session early in response to further silence from the group. Here the traumatic narrative thus operates as a remainder, a surplus; it was both desired as part of the workshop process, doing the work of producing emotional affects that can be redeployed in performance, and simultaneously threatened this process. Here the narrative, not yet fully comprehended, forced participants, at least in Sher's account, to return to traumatic events—real and hypothetical—that he was unable to incorporate seamlessly into an understanding of the play.

Whereas the foregoing episode suggests that traumatic narratives resist a straightforward application to the play and the business of the workshops, the rehearsal process also models the opposite position, most clearly in relation to ka Ncube's rehearsal of the moment in which Aaron encounters his child and considers Tamora's injunction to kill it, with the line "is black so base a hue?" (4.2.71). Doran says that he encouraged ka Ncube "to honour that thought" (161), which denotes the moment in the play where Aaron begins to assert his subjectivity. Doran goes on to note that this line "releases something. And suddenly we're blasted with his anger. A lifetime of the humiliations of apartheid, decades of his people's struggle, centuries of his race's oppression, howl up through Sello now" (161). Here Doran envisages a rehearsal model where the lived experiences of the actor (in this case with respect to apartheid) can be welded to the character through the work of rehearsal. The resulting traumatic force of this archive of personal and cultural history provides the means through which to perform Aaron. Once again, there is no apparent acknowledgement of the emotional risks that the actor is asked to take in engaging with the trauma of racial oppression. Furthermore, Doran unquestioningly designates ka Ncube as a synecdoche for that oppression; his reference to "centuries of his race's oppression" also extends well beyond the apartheid policies of the National Party, codified in 1948, thereby conflating different histories in the figure of ka Ncube. Doran and Sher's work with ka Ncube thus models, at the micro level, how their rehearsal techniques work to appropriate and, potentially exploit, the experiences of others for the purposes of performance.[37]

The way in which ka Ncube's experiences under apartheid were bonded to the act of playing Aaron recurred subsequently in Doran's 2004 production of *Othello* for the RSC in which Sher was cast as Iago and ka Ncube as Othello; this subsequent pairing of the actors hints at how the business of "working through" evident in the rehearsals for *Titus* is subject to a process of repetition, recurring in the preparation for *Othello*, albeit in a more marginal position. In a conversation between the two actors, published in *The Guardian*, ka Ncube says,

> we've found a certain way of playing with each other, which in a film you would see in the eyes. There's a look I would know as a black person. And I guess there's a look you [Sher] would know [. . .] And I have seen situations when things become dangerous—there is a look a white person will give you that means you can't get all charged up.[38]

Sher responds by saying,

> [w]hen you have me on the floor, the look of you above me does touch something deep. I mean, we as white kids, the horror story we were always told was that "they" will murder us in our beds—"they" being the word for black people. I suppose it comes back when you're on top of me like that.

Here their personal experiences of growing up under apartheid seem necessarily to imprint the relationship between Othello and Iago with this traumatic legacy, racial stereotypes and violence, played out through a racially freighted interchange of looks. Sher goes on to say that there is a moment in the cellar scene that he finds "South African" when ka Ncube as Othello takes off his cap and starts to bow to Brabantio which "reminds [him] so much of black behaviour under apartheid". ka Ncube responds by noting that in rehearsals he felt he "was trying too hard" and then realised that he didn't have to because, as Sher puts it, "it was just your life". For ka Ncube, playing Othello was partly a matter of allowing his life "to filter through". As with the earlier pairing of the actors in *Titus Andronicus*, individual experience, especially with respect to racial oppression, is again signalled as one of the primary means through which to act. In a performance that was not otherwise especially concerned with a specifically South African frame of reference, the lived experiences of apartheid are cited as integral to the performance.

As the examples from the *Titus* workshops and their subsequent manifestation in *Othello* suggest, experiences under apartheid are a crucial element of these performances. In addition to producing an archive or storehouse of traumatic personal memories for the performance of *Titus*, the experiences of others were also co-opted for this work. This is in keeping with research-based exercises that often formed part of workshop and rehearsal processes, even as the material generated by these processes sometimes proved difficult to use in relation to the play, as I have discussed above. As part of this work, Sher recalls that the cast watched a documentary about the My Lai massacre, which offers testaments from both Vietnamese women and American Vietnam veterans. In his observation that the My Lai massacre is a "useful model for the Roman-Goth war" (91), and that the experiences of the Vietnam veteran are "a good example of how real life confounds the clichés about violence" (91), Sher highlights how the violent events were offered as a way of understanding aspects of *Titus*: here events and experiences were given utility value, available to be used and deployed as part of the workshop process. Sher goes on to observe that the South African cast "are curiously unmoved" by the veteran and the film (91). He accounts for this reaction by suggesting that "having grown up with violence, they view it in a more cynical, less sentimental way than Greg and I", and that they "often find aspects of violence *funny*" (91, Sher's emphasis). Here Sher locates the South African cast as having a culturally determined response to violence, and one that Sher believes works well in relation to the play: as Sher notes earlier in *Woza Shakespeare!*, the "rhythms of Elizabethan and African society are strangely compatible: the violence and beauty and *humour* in both" (19, Sher's emphasis).[39]

Sher does not, though, interrogate the equivalence he makes between Elizabethan and African society. He generalises "Africa"—a continent made up of some 64 countries and territories—as a homogeneous entity and unproblematically aligns this with Elizabethan culture. His effacement of difference is underpinned by the rhetoric of relevance and universalism, exemplified by Jan Kott's claim that "[b]y discovering in Shakespeare's plays problems that are relevant to our own time, modern audiences often, unexpectedly, find themselves near to the Elizabethans".[40] As Alan Sinfield succinctly notes, Kott's claims are "predicated on the ideas of an essential human nature", and I would suggest that Doran's production is also inculcated with this kind of essentialising strategy in order to legitimate the production through a romanticised kinship between "Africa" and the Elizabethans (and, by association, Shakespeare).[41] As Jonathan Holmes summarises, both Suzman and Doran in their respective "South African" productions of Shakespeare, "work to expunge all otherness and difference from their writing in favour of a universal humanist sameness which in reality is the province of a few western Europeans".[42]

Alongside Sher's apparent collapse of historical, geographical and cultural difference in his comparison between "Elizabethan and African society", what emerges most clearly from the My Lai massacre documentary episode is how the attempted loading of the traumatic experiences of Vietnam onto those of contemporary South Africa and *Titus Andronicus* seemed to fail. That is, despite Sher's designation of the material as having a utility value for understanding the play, it left the cast apparently "unmoved". By contrast, Sher credits the specificity of local experiences with offering possibilities for the kind of traumatic cultural work that the production engages with. As Gys de Villiers, who played Saturninus, recorded in his newspaper diary, video footage of pre-election violence in 1986 "affects us far more than the Vietnam video".[43] Indeed, Sher records how the cast's reactions changed when they watched Michael Buerk's 1987 report on South Africa for the BBC, which contained images of violence, including a scene where a man is knifed to death by a group of people. For Sher, this footage once again provides a model for the action of the play: "without this kind of research, actors wouldn't think of playing them [the play's several stabbings] as happens here" (93). Sher notes how the cast "watch it in shocked silence—some weeping—these are images from their own nightmare. Like photos of a loved one raped and murdered, this *belongs* to them" (93, Sher's emphasis). Here Sher credits the research work, which he claims shows the cast "images of themselves" (91), with providing access to their own history, which, in turn, will feed directly into the practicalities of enacting *Titus*'s scenes of violence. As with the effects produced through the individual narratives of violence, the workshop was once again recoded as space where traumatic incidents are turned to and where the work of mourning can take place. The grief that Sher reports in relation to the experiences of watching acts of violence was once again appropriated and deployed as a resource to be recycled in the act of playing *Titus*.

The work of mourning thus functioned to produce a practical and emotional archive for use in performance. As with the other exercises, Doran and Sher do not seem to acknowledge the potential risks of this kind of emotional/therapeutic performance work and how the generalised assessments of the cast's (and by default South Africans') responses to violence work to elide difference. For Sher, the act of performance does, though, entail a responsibility to the images they have watched and the stories the cast have shared: "[o]ur exploration of violence has been hard going, but worthwhile. When we come to reproduce it, we will be compelled, as Greg puts it, 'to honour the real thing' [. . .] The South Africans have a very intense, *personal* attitude to violence" (91, Sher's emphasis). Once again, Sher makes generalisations about the character of his ex-compatriots, but here he also acknowledges a responsibility to the subjects whose stories have been turned into resources in the process of the workshop, just as he also reaffirms that one of the key drivers for the production is to institute a South African frame of reference for the violence.

The exercises I have discussed thus far identify how Doran and Sher worked to create an archive of trauma for use in performance. This work is predicated on a feedback loop where the production of Shakespeare's play becomes the trigger for examining the trauma of "real" violence and where the exploration of these narratives of violence will, in turn, imbue the performance of the play with "the real". This feedback loop is sustained by rhetoric concerning the "relevance" of Shakespeare to historical and contemporary situations, a belief in the capacity of performance to communicate trauma, an apparent elision of the risk involved in this kind of memory and emotional work, and generalisations about the nature of violence and its effects on individuals and communities. What also emerges is that the smooth operation of this feedback loop is threatened by certain traumatic narratives, such as the story of rape and murder and the recollections of the My Lai massacre. The after-effects of violence that trauma registers are thus more resistant to the kind of straightforward application of "real" trauma to the space of performance than Doran and Sher's presentation of the exercises tend to suggest. I want, now, to push Sher's sense of ethical responsibility to the experiences of others and the implications for exercising this responsibility in the act of performance further through a consideration of Jennifer Woodburne's preparation for the role of Lavinia, as it is recorded by Doran and Sher.

Woodburne's commitment to engaging with traumatic events was evident throughout the audition, workshop and rehearsal processes. In this work she drew on the research material provided by Doran and Sher, and her own research, as the following sketch reveals. Woodburne thus used the image of the man who was stabbed in Buerk's documentary as a point of comparison for the moment in the play when Tamora sanctions her sons' rape of Lavinia (125). She attended a talk Doran and Sher arranged to be given to the cast in London by Lindy Wootton from the North Westminster Victim Support Scheme, and drew on Wootton's experiences with rape victims as a context for her work on Lavinia. In addition, Woodburne also conducted her own medical research, using her mother's connections as a medical technologist at Groote Schuur Hospital to research Lavinia's hand and tongue amputations. On Woodburne's behalf, her mother questioned colleagues about the effects of Lavinia's injuries and Woodburne was also given access to medical textbooks which depict images of severed hands and facial gunshot wounds, photocopies of which she brought to rehearsals (81). In the course of her research Woodburne also met a cancer patient with no tongue for an insight into managing saliva (143–44) and spoke to a doctor about the difficulty of eating with Lavinia's injuries, employing this knowledge to explain the scene where Titus has to cajole Lavinia into eating (144). The results of Woodburne's research are revealed in the video of the production made by the South African Broadcasting Corporation

in association with the Market and the National at the end of the production's run in South Africa, during which Woodburne is shown with
streams of saliva running from her mouth.⁴⁴ This work is also captured in
a still from the production in which saliva runs from Lavinia's mouth during Marcus's discovery of her (Figure 1.3). Woodburne also used medical
expertise regarding the shock and regression effects of mutilation in order
to explain Lavinia's response to Titus's efforts to comfort her in Act 3,
Scene 1. Sher notes further that Woodburne extended her interest in the
pragmatic effects of Lavinia's injuries such that she developed a theory that
Lavinia might have both a sexually transmitted disease and a miscarriage
following the double rape (144–45), an idea that was quashed by Doran
and Sher. Woodburne's use of research materials was also evident from
her dressing room mirror. Sher notes that the mirror was covered with
a mass of research materials that had been collected on the cast's notice
board, including topical images of violence such as a picture of a girl in
Grozny, covered in white dust and splashes of blood, in close proximity to
an exploded shell, and that of Ambrose Sibiya, a Zulu man who had his
hand cut off with a *panga* (machete) in an attack, and subsequently had it
sewn back on in a Durban hospital (199).

Woodburne's development of her character rested, at least in part, on the
appropriation of the experiences of others. Indeed, this drive toward appropriation—where images are treated as material to be utilised in performance—is registered sharply in her response to an image of a girl wounded
by the shell in Grozny, an image Sher says Woodburne wonders if she
"could use [. . .] for Lavinia's make-up [. . . .] The way her lips are outlined
in red, her eyes too" (81). Here the image of suffering is read primarily in
terms of its potential for generating theatrical effect through makeup such
that the image seems to become shorn from the particularity of the violence
it depicts. This drive toward appropriation is, though, also traced in Doran
and Sher's narrative by Woodburne's sense of responsibility to her research
subjects in which her performance is cast as a kind of testimony to these
individuals. Thus, when the production was under threat of cancellation
because of funding problems, Sher says that Woodburne was concerned
about the people she had worked with in the course of her research and
he remembers her saying: "I felt such responsibility to them. If we didn't
do the play, I would've sort of cheated them" (143). This sense of responsibility also recurs in Sher's record of Woodburne's response to her image-
covered mirror. Sher recalls Woodburne giggling and saying "I can hardly
see myself", before going on to ask, "without the smile [. . .] 'How am I
going to do justice to all these people?'" (199). Woodburne's image-covered
mirror literally inscribes the suffering of others over her own image. The
mirror's function—to verify the existence and appearance of the subject of
the gaze—has been refigured such that the subject sees in the mirror the
experiences of others, not a confirmation of the self. To look at the mirror of images, plastered with the images and stories of others, thus offers

Figure 1.3 Jennifer Woodburne (foreground) as Lavinia and Dale Cutts (background) as Marcus in Gregory Doran's 1995 production of *Titus Andronicus*, co-produced by the National Theatre and the Market Theatre, Johannesburg. Photograph © Ruphin Coudyzer, FPPSA, www.ruphin.com, reproduced with his permission.

a challenge to the subject's conception of the self: here the reflected self is, in part, constituted by the experience of others. In her comments Woodburne is represented as reading herself into the trauma of others, envisaging herself as a surrogate for their suffering. In identifying the extent to which her own image has been partially occluded by the images of others, Sher depicts Woodburne as offering an image of herself as all but erased by the experiences of others. For Woodburne performance is designated as the mode by which she seeks to honour the experiences of the others with whom she has engaged. These kinds of sentiments are echoed by Sher who comments: "I believe we are achieving what Greg urged . . . we're 'honouring' the personal stories we heard, those films we watched, Jennifer's research" (156, Sher's ellipsis).

In considering the performers' attempts to honour the experience of others, it is worth considering Ronald J. Pelias's suggestion that "[e]ven when performers attempt to enact others with care and sensitivity, they are increasingly confronted with the idea that speaking for others is a problematic act [. . ..] Actors who attempt to speak for others, silence them in some important ways".[45] In order to counter this difficulty, Pelias suggests that performers should "engage in a dialogic encounter" such that they "attempt to isolate and inhabit at least one voice and body beyond their own".[46] For Pelias, such work is "an act of giving without abandoning or surrendering oneself" where performers "are engaged in a shared conversation in which they speak, not for, but with, the community".[47] The drive to "honour" the experiences of others in the production might be conceived as an attempt at just such a community conversation and seems informed, as Pelias's claims are, by a utopian conception of a unified "human community".[48] What is less clear is whether the performance of *Titus* made this conversation legible to others or whether those concerned consented to the use of their testimony in this performance. This is largely because the modes of performance did not make sufficient space for the acknowledgement of the voices of others. For example, in the framing of the offstage rape, which depicted Chiron and Demetrius "raping" and stabbing a shop mannequin while Lavinia carried out a numbed, trance-like dance, the production, as Pascale Aebischer notes, "slips from a realistic mode of representation that is in tune with Woodburne's performance choices to a symbolic mode".[49] In both the movement score of the dance and in Woodburne's creation of a nonverbal sound score, which Aebischer notes consisted of "groans, sobs, giggles and shrieks", Woodburne worked to create a space in which to insert the experiences she researched into the field of performance.[50] However, I would suggest that the specificity of the other stories was likely illegible to spectators, reduced to a series of conventional gestures and actions to represent pain and mutilation. The disjunction between the performance modes also highlights how both realistic and symbolic modes of performance "stand in" for rather than instantiate the "real" thing. In Woodburne's efforts to represent trauma through both these modes, the production highlighted the difficulties (or, indeed, the impossibility) that attend any such attempts at traumatic instantiation.

In her attempts to honour the experiences of others, Woodburne's performance operates less like the "community conversation" that Pelias imagines and more as a kind of Kristevian "transposition", refiguring both the experiences she has engaged with and her own position as an acting subject whose performance is marked and changed by the experiences she has encountered. As Julia Kristeva notes, transposition "specifies that the passage from one signifying system to another demands a new articulation of the thetic—of enunciative and denotative positionality".[51] Woodburne's intertextual or transpositional performance, which presses the experiences she has encountered into a new signifying system of the acting subject, also raises questions about the ethics of the process of transposition. Woodburne sought to do justice to the people whose experiences she has engaged with. Her polysemic performance, which deployed cancer and other medical narratives alongside documentaries, personal narratives, medical advice and the experiences of those working with victims of violence, did, however, run the risk of conflating, or forcing an equivalence between, various kinds of traumatic experiences. It brought them to bear in a performance context that had little relation to their original contexts, and thus risked the occlusion of the specificity of their narratives. This kind of conflation is not only evident in Woodburne's performance as the production collectively drew on South African contexts alongside images of grief, war, violence and justice from other cultures. Images of Ayatollah Khomeni (112), Vietnam (124) and experiences of self-harm (176) and therapy sessions (75–77) were thus deployed alongside newspaper clippings of state-sanctioned surgical hand amputations in Iraq, the Grozny girl and Ambrose Sibiya, and various dramatic and filmic references, such as *Tamburlaine* (*c.* 1587), *Henry V* (1599), *Patton* (1970) and *La Strada* (1954). In this series of references the production's concern with relationships between South Africa and Shakespeare's text were spliced with other cultures, events and (auto) biographical narratives.

The production thus invites a consideration of the ethical implications of the deployment of these images and narratives variously in rehearsal and in the moment of performance. This invites questioning with respect to the extent to which the production is able to realise its sense of responsibility toward its research subjects in performance, such that that responsibility might be communicated to others. Even though an utterance is, as M. M. Bakhtin suggests, subject to centrifugal forces which posit its potential for multiple meanings, the meaning(s) of an utterance are also shaped and determined by centripetal forces that shift according to the context of the utterance, which work to unify its meaning(s).[52] In the case of the performance, the various voices that Woodburne and the production sought to honour were at least partially occluded, or sacrificed, in the moment of performance, subsumed under the narrative requirements of Shakespeare's play and the production decisions made by Doran and Sher. Given the partial and selective nature of Doran and Sher's text, it is perhaps ironic that Woodburne's archive of trauma and her narrative of responsibility to her research subjects emerge perhaps most directly not in performance but belatedly in *Woza Shakespeare!*

MOURNING AND RECONCILIATION

Despite the difficulties that attend making the various violent acts and personal histories of trauma legible in the moment of performance, Shakespeare's play and the workshop and rehearsal activities that attended its production, were, as I have suggested, appealed to as ground for working through violent events and histories. In the repeated traumatic returns to acts of violence—personal, historical, contemporary, South African, global—performance comes to be conceived as a mode of mourning by Doran and Sher, even as it also comes to stand as what Distiller describes as a "vehicle for expressing Sher's personal journey" in his return to South Africa.[53] This relationship between the play's action and mourning is articulated in Doran's director's note in the programme where he asserts that the play's "acts of brutality, rather than appearing gratuitous or extreme, seemed only too familiar, and our attention turned instead to how people deal with that violence, to the impact of grief, and man's capacity for survival." His comment here identifies how the performance was conceived as a way of exploring violence and grief; as I have suggested, this took place both in terms of the narrative arc of the play and also at the level of the performer and the company. But once again Doran's assertion betrays the assumptions about "relevance" and an essential human nature upon which it rests, working to generalise the specific details of the play and its production context.

Alongside the exploration of grief and the designation of performance and its preparation as a mode of mourning, the production was explicitly linked to South Africa's programme of reconciliation when Ben Ngubane, the Minister for Arts and Culture, addressed the audience at the end of the production's opening night. He pledged three million rand to the Market Theatre and Mark Gevisser reports Ngubane as saying: "[i]f there is one message to be got from this [the play . . .] it is that violence begets violence and that reconciliation is the only answer", a comment Gevisser reads as symptomatic of the new South Africa's capacity to "squeeze reconciliation out of any stone—even one as dense and bleak as Titus Andronicus."[54] Here reconciliation is presented as the dominant mode of engagement in relation to violence both in the play and in culture. Similarly, Doran worked to offer the conclusion of the production as an act of reconciliation and healing, resonating with the rhetoric that surrounds post-apartheid South Africa which was formalised in the order to establish the Truth and Reconciliation Commission, shortly after the end of the play's South African run. In his director's note to the programme, Doran explains how in working through the play in a South African context, it "took on new meaning for us, as a struggle to discover the nature of Justice, and ultimately as an appeal for reconciliation and healing". In this vein, the play's concluding speeches, which focus on the punishment of Tamora and Aaron, were tempered by shifting Marcus's speech to the end of the play. The last lines of the production, reprinted in the programme, thus became: "O, let me teach you how to knit again/ This scattered corn into one mutual sheaf,/ These broken limbs again into one body" (5.3.69–71). Doran argues that:

> [t]hese words hold such resonance in South Africa, where the new political orthodoxy is reconciliation. But in order for this unifying idea to be meaningful, justice must be done, and be seen to be done.
> We want Marcus's words to resonate with the audience, for them to hear the echo. (179)

Distiller neatly identifies the assumptions upon which this proposition rests, arguing "[t]hat Sher and Doran thought it apposite to use *Titus* to comment on reconciliation points to their assumptions about the meaning of 'Shakespeare' as an iconic figure of universal humanity, whose lessons about life will always soothe and resolve".[55] For Doran and Sher, "Shakespeare" and Shakespeare's text act as traumatic balsam, able to soothe and resolve the effects of violence. But this restorative vision requires first a manipulation of Shakespeare's text, such that the play's bleak declarations of punishments are somewhat mitigated by Marcus's words; here Shakespeare is "cleaned up" so that his text might more effectively participate in the essentialising project of articulating "man's capacity for survival". Second, the plea for reconciliation was synchronised with one of the production's final images of Aaron chained and threatened by Martin Le Maitre's Lucius, a member of the Afrikaaner-identified Goths (Figure 1.2). While Doran does not claim a one-to-one correspondence between the end of the play and contemporary South Africa, his desire for the production to resonate with the call for justice and reconciliation is also traced by a history of racial oppression in South Africa, chillingly visualised in this image of a white man threatening a chained black man. Shakespeare's play is employed as a kind of panacea to heal a fractured culture but as this analysis suggests, the wounds continue to seep and were far from contained by the narrative of the play, its performance and reception. *Woza Shakespeare!* and comments made by Doran and Sher elsewhere present the cultural work of the performance as an unequivocal "good", providing a way of coming to terms with violent events and histories. But the production offers a much less optimistic vision of the capacity of performance to heal and reconcile; instead it unwittingly works to reiterate images of racial oppression that it no doubt sought to challenge.

AUDIENCES FOR TRAUMA

One of the crucial requirements for the successful operation of a transmission model of trauma that informed much of the workshop and rehearsal work—spectators—was largely absent in South Africa. Despite the attempts to locate the project in South African contexts and appeals to the contemporary political situation, the production received mixed reviews in South Africa, with the use of South African accents and references the subjects of particular comment.[56] In Johannesburg the production played to what Doran describes as "poor houses" (222), in contrast to high-capacity performances in the United Kingdom. Sher seemed at once baffled by this response—"how can the people of Johannesburg not be interested in our experiment with Shakespeare?"—but also at pains to account for this phenomenon.[57] In addition to the section of *Woza Shakespeare!* that deals with responses to the production (205–43), Sher also addressed these issues during the National Theatre Platform post-show discussion, in the London *Evening Standard*, the UK *Sunday Times* and in a letter to the Johannesburg *Star*.[58] The letter to the *Star* was published in the paper's opinion section, correcting the "half-full houses" identified by Barry Ronge in his opinion piece in the *Star Tonight*; indeed Sher went further saying "[w]e're lucky if the house is a quarter-full, and last Tuesday [we] played to only 50 people!"[59]

Sher offers four possibilities for the poor houses in his letter to the *Star*.[60] First he wonders if they are "because of people's fear about security at the Market", an explanation he dismisses even as he suggests that there could have been more security officers and lighting in the car park. In a follow-up letter to the *Star*, Sher cites a letter he received from a woman who asked him not to be "hard on those no longer wishing to venture into the centre of town . . . it's a disgusting experience".[61] This kind of response is symptomatic of how the shift in the area's ethnic demographic, as André P. Czeglédy notes, "gave pretext for well-to-do city center residents and businesses to quickly move from the urban core", re-establishing themselves in the northern suburbs of the city, a move that worked to establish the "CBD as a virtual 'no go' zone".[62] Perhaps in an effort to address anxieties of this kind, an advertisement announcing the forthcoming production in the *Star Tonight* included the phrase "Safe parking protected by Spot On Security", and this advertising ploy was repeated in advertisements in the *Star* throughout the run.[63] Second, Sher suggested that poor transport links may have prevented black audiences from Soweto or Alexandra attending but he discounts this argument in his observation that Hugh Masekala's performance at Kipples, the bar next to the Market, attracted a predominantly black audience, although he does not identify where these spectators are resident. Third, he queries whether the "mixed reviews" may have dissuaded potential spectators but again dismisses this view on the grounds that some of the reviews were good and that another production at the Market, got "a rave review from the Weekly Mail yet suffered the same fate as us". After mooting and negating these possible explanations, Sher mounts his fourth, and key, argument that the aftermath of the cultural boycott may be to blame. In outlining this proposition he notes his debt to Janet Suzman whom he credits with suggesting that the boycott reduced people's range of artistic experiences. Sher thus suggests that "[p]eople's sense of curiosity has been whittled away, and curiosity is at the heart of all artistic activity, both for those who make art, and for those that watch it" culminating in what he describes as a state of "cultural indifference". Sher's claim that the cultural boycott dampened the curiosity of potential spectators provides a convenient explanation for the poor houses and allows the production's value (and values) to go unchallenged. Furthermore, Sher does not seem to notice that any possible ambivalence toward his production does not necessarily equate with an antipathy or lack of curiosity toward other forms of theatre or cultural production. Indeed, in her survey of the Market Theatre through apartheid to post-apartheid cultures, Hilary Burns notes that John Kani, the Market's Executive Director at the time of Doran's production, argued that the cultural boycott had positive effects by encouraging black artists to examine their own practice and that this assisted the development of South African theatre and a wider audience demographic.[64]

Sher's letter to the *Star* prompted a series of letters in response and the debate was played out over a week and a half in the paper's opinion pages, concluded by a second letter from Sher. Collectively, these letters suggest that the poor houses were the result of a number of factors, including the fears about security, particularly with respect to the central city location of the theatre, ticket prices, especially in relation to high levels of unemployment, inadequate transport links, performance times, the emigration of middle-class citizens who form the basis of audiences of theatres such as the Market, a resistance to Shakespeare and fleeting visits by celebrity actors and directors, apathy, antipathy of the reviewers, the violent content of the play and the cultural boycott (and Sher's support of it).[65] Many of the factors cited are likely to play into an individual spectator's decision—shaped variously by economics, education and ethnicity among other factors—to attend, or not to attend, *Titus Andronicus*. However, the failure of the production to attract audiences also speaks to the failure of the Market Theatre—through programming and prices—to develop, on this occasion, an audience out of the changing demographic of central Johannesburg, which is characterised by the influx of black residents to the central city after the 1980s, a movement that increased with the repeal of the Group Areas Act in 1991. Indeed, Joyce Ozynski, a former member of the board of the Market Theatre, suggests in her response to Sher's first letter that the "dynamics of political change have landed a potential audience of thousands virtually on the doorstep of the Civil, Windybrow, the Wits Theatre and the Market".[66]

The production also alienated a group of spectators who, on the basis of the reviews and letters Sher and the Market received, appear to have been resistant to a production of Shakespeare in South African accents and setting. Indeed, Sher cites again from a letter from a woman who says that she did not attend the production because she "could not abide the excruciating experience of the ugly accents of southern Africa abusing some of the most beautiful language ever written", a comment which bespeaks a desire for "proper" Shakespeare (read: RSC, NT, RP (Received Pronunciation), English).[67] In contrast, for Israel Motlhabane, "to the theatre lover in the townships, Shakespeare is sawdust", and the production is symptomatic of the failure in both apartheid and post-apartheid South Africa to address black audiences, writers and performers.[68] In his formulation of Shakespeare as sawdust, or worthless imperial detritus, Motlhabane highlights the failure of performances of Shakespeare's texts, such as Doran and Sher's, to communicate in a meaningful way with township communities, thus subverting Doran and Sher's claims for the production's relevance and importance in South Africa. The implication of Motlhabane's comment is that the performance of Shakespeare's texts and productions such as Doran and Sher's do further cultural violence by failing to address adequately black audiences, writers and performers. Motlhabane identifies how theatre in the townships has been systematically marginalised and the poor houses of *Titus* thus come to seem insignificant in relation to "all the scripts and theatrical productions that have never had proper theatres in which they could be produced or performed". To redress this situation he calls for adequate theatre facilities to be built in the townships. During the National's Platform discussion, ka Ncube also highlights this lack, and Sher called for theatres to be built in Soweto and Alexandra. While the Anglican Church Society of Soweto booked out the performance for one night (212), the production did not attract substantial black audiences from the townships to the Market. This may, in part, identify a resistance to the kind of cultural product offered by Sher and Doran, and/or to obstacles to access resulting from pricing or geographic proximity. Sher describes how ka Ncube attempted to arrange a performance of the play in Soweto as a means of making the production more accessible in terms of location and ticket prices to a predominantly black audience (Sher estimates that the audiences at the Market were 90% white [215]). Sher notes, though, that the performance was cancelled due to a series of miscommunications between ka Ncube, John Kani, and the editor of the *Sowetan*, who was to provide advertising (231–32).

These responses go some way toward identifying the material conditions, born of economics, geography, ethnicity, education and culture, that resulted in low-capacity audiences. But this is not, simply, a one-way process whereby the production was foisted on a wholly unsuspecting South Africa that sought to reject it summarily. The production was supported and made possible by the South Africans involved in the project, which speaks in part, as I suggested earlier, to a complicated relationship between Shakespeare, South Africa and cultural capital; the low turnouts suggest, though, that the currency of that capital may not be quite as strong as it was in apartheid-era South Africa. Doran and Sher's gesture, which might be described as paternalistic in their efforts to help South Africans understand their relationships with violence through Shakespeare, coupled with the lived experiences of the trauma of apartheid offer yet another, and more searching, reason for the apparent rejection of this particular traumatic "working through": perhaps the performance of a violent Shakespeare play in a production which attempted to offer specifically South African contexts for violence in the wake of the first democratic elections and the lead-up to the establishment of the Truth and Reconciliation Commission in July 1995 was too reductive, too inadequate, in the face of the ongoing legacy of apartheid, even as those same acts proved popular at a remove in the United Kingdom and in Spain. Here the wound cries out but the acts of listening to and witnessing these particular theatrical instantiations of trauma were resisted in marked contrast to the public "performances" of the Truth and Reconciliation Commission.

The auditions, workshops, rehearsals, production and responses in relation to Doran and Sher's *Titus Andronicus* thus negotiate a complex set of relations between trauma and performance. In this work Shakespeare's text was used as a kind of *aide-mémoire* for remembering and engaging with a range of traumatic experiences, especially in relation to those wrought by apartheid. The production simultaneously used those experiences as a means through which to engage with the play. What I have tried to show is that this is not a linear relation, whereby experience can be neatly mapped onto the action of the play and vice versa. Rather, the production and its documentation highlight the difficulties that attend traumatic representation, especially in relation to the way in which the production sutured Shakespeare's narrative to particular violent events and histories. Furthermore, the "turn to" apartheid and the other violent and painful events and histories, medical and otherwise, that the cast used as part of their preparation processes, identify the difficulties that surround the appropriation of the experiences of others in performance, especially in relation to acts of responsibility and the possibility for making that sense of responsibility legible in performance and its documentation. While the production worked to acknowledge the traumatic effects of violent events and histories, it often failed to acknowledge the terms of its engagement, instead resorting to clichés about Shakespeare's relevance. In so doing the production and its documentation performed its own marginalisations and exclusions, working to generalise the experiences of South Africans in relation to violence, especially that perpetrated by apartheid. The attempt to participate in post-apartheid South Africa's project of reconciliation via the performance of a violent Shakespeare play, which finishes with a black man chained and sentenced to death by live partial burial, comes to stand, then, as a kind of misfire. Its traumatic working through, which promises a therapeutic resolution of sorts through the rhetoric of reconciliation, is, largely, resisted by local audiences. I want now to turn to *The Maori Merchant of Venice*, which in its engagement with the after-effects of colonisation models, among other concerns, how trauma might, in contrast to Doran and Sher's *Titus*, provide the basis for productive community responses to the violent legacy of colonisation.

2 The Legacy of Colonisation
Don C. Selwyn's *The Maori Merchant of Venice* and Aotearoa New Zealand

"After the horrors of the twentieth century, there can be no imaginative realization of Shakespeare's play that is not shaped by the Holocaust. Like the commemorations dedicated to the liberation of Auschwitz, [Michael Radford's] *The Merchant of Venice* functions as a memorial: its construction of a Shakespearean past is tunnelled through a more immediate legacy, with the inevitable result that its pre-images are also after-images", writes Mark Thornton Burnett in his analysis of Radford's 2004 film, *The Merchant of Venice*.[1] Burnett neatly identifies how the film embodies a contradictory logic whereby it at once works to institute memories and images of the Holocaust within the field of the film's production and works to distance itself from this material. This contradictory logic can be extended more widely to identify how productions of *The Merchant of Venice* after the Holocaust are, to some extent, haunted by this traumatic legacy, such that this event is variously avoided, embraced, memorialised and returned to the field of performance. Thus the Holocaust "returns" in direct references and images, such as the red hat Shylock is forced to wear outside the confines of the ghetto in Radford's film, which as Burnett argues "resonates less with an audience's awareness of sixteenth-century practice as with a knowledge of the insignia thrust on Jews during the Third Reich", namely white armbands and blue Jewish stars.[2]

The play's performance history is enfolded in a history of anti-Semitism marked most strikingly by its popularity in Nazi Germany and also in Austria where it was used as anti-Semitic propaganda. For example, in Lothar Müthel's 1943 production of the play at the Burgtheater in Vienna, Werner Krauss played Shylock by drawing on an extensive range of anti-Semitic images and stereotypes.[3] Conversely, the play has also been used to critique anti-Semitism and Jewish stereotypes, such as Arnold Wesker's adaptation *Shylock* (1989)—formerly *The Merchant* (1976)—in which a benevolent Shylock and Antonio "are old friends".[4] In this play Shylock does not want to make a contract with Antonio, preferring instead for him to "[t]ake the ducats" (212). Forced by the law to make a bond, they make what Shylock refers to as a "lovely, loving nonsense bond" so that they might "mock the law" (213). When the bond is proved unenforceable, Shylock is delighted and embraces Antonio (256). However, the Doge confiscates Shylock's books and possessions and he *"moves away, a bitter man"* (259). Even as Wesker's play offers a more benevolent interpretation of Shylock, this does not excise the cruelty of the punishment or the anti-Semitism that is directed toward him. Recalling the uses of the play in Nazi Germany, Hanan Snir's 1995 production of the play at the Deutsches Nationaltheater in Weimar, Germany—50 years after the liberation of the Buchenwald concentration camp—is framed by a narrative where Jewish prisoners are brought onstage and forced to perform *The Merchant of Venice* for the entertainment of the SS officers.[5] These instances of the play's relationship with the Holocaust and anti-Semitism are far from isolated and their multiple instantiations are the subject of a wide-ranging reception study at the Freie Universität Berlin, which argues that "[t]he changes in the perception of the Jewish money-lender Shylock since 1945 are understood as conflict-ridden attempts at coming to terms with the German past: the Shoah, guilt and remembrance and German anti-Semitism".[6]

As well as performances' direct negotiations with the Holocaust and histories of anti-Semitism, these references also occur indirectly where that which is not offered space in a performance's diegesis nevertheless shadows performance as a kind of supplement, working to return that which is refused or elided to the frame of performance. Gregory Doran's comment on his 1997 production of the play for the RSC exemplifies this dynamic: "[t]he play has been hijacked by history. We are putting it back in to the world of renaissance trade. We've started with the title: Shylock was a merchant of Venice. I wanted to take the swastikas and stars of David out of the play".[7] Notwithstanding the fact that the merchant of the play's title is usually understood as referring to Antonio, Doran's intentions for his production at once cast history as that which has usurped a properly historical reading of the play and rehabilitate history as that which will ground his interpretation in relation to Renaissance mercantilism. While images of the star of David and swastikas might have been excised from the visual field of his production, the excision is not total as the signifiers work their way in to Doran's language, demanding to be acknowledged; his refusal thus bears the trace of that which he seeks to banish. Similarly, Michael Billington, in his response to Loveday Ingram's 2001 RSC production, notes: "one hoped for slightly more [. . .] than a romantic reading that treats the play as a fairytale in Edwardian dress: in a post-Holocaust world, let alone one where differing concepts of global justice confront us daily, it is difficult to return to such blithe innocence".[8] Here Billington returns the Holocaust to the frame of Ingram's performance, even as its visual images and documentation, like Doran's production, worked to elide such associations. Here, then, I am suggesting, as Burnett and others have done, that performances of *The Merchant* are unable to escape the accretions of history, where the anti-Semitic discourse of the type the play offers (even as it works, on occasions, to complicate it) invokes a relation with the historical consequences of this discourse.

I begin with these relationships between *The Merchant of Venice*, the Holocaust and histories of anti-Semitism in order to acknowledge how performances of *The Merchant of Venice* after 1945, perhaps inevitably given the cataclysmic nature of the Holocaust, fold the trauma of this event into their frame of reference, regardless of the political and cultural imperatives of the production. In so doing I seek to draw attention to an aspect of the territory covered by this chapter, which focuses on Don C. Selwyn's 2001 film, *The Maori Merchant of Venice*, produced in Aotearoa New Zealand and released in February 2002.[9] I also want to mark a difference to criticism concerned with *The Merchant* and discourses of trauma, which tend to coalesce around anti-Semitism and the Holocaust, as Burnett's work does, and also a difference to work which examines the play's refusal to endorse homoerotic desire in its resolution, especially with respect to the treatment of the eponymous Merchant (I will return to the trauma of homophobia in the next chapter).[10] In contrast, I am concerned to consider Selwyn's film in relation to the trauma of colonisation, identifying how this traumatic working through also folds the trauma of the Holocaust into its iterations. Like Radford's film, Selwyn's tracks a series of what Burnett describes as pre- and afterimages which here work to memorialise Aotearoa New Zealand's history of colonisation and which also offer possibilities for a future-to-come, even as this future is traced by past trauma, of which the Holocaust is deployed as a central marker.[11]

AOTEAROA NEW ZEALAND AND TRADITIONS OF PERFORMANCE

Settled by the Māori from their ancestral homeland in the Pacific approximately 1,000 years ago, New Zealand was first discovered by Europeans as part of Abel Tasman's 1642 voyage to the southern hemisphere.[12] But it was not until after James Cook's landfall in 1769 that the European presence in Aotearoa New Zealand increased with the arrival of sealers, whalers, traders and missionaries and in 1840 a treaty was signed between the British Crown and the Māori. Although promised the benefits and rights of British citizenship and, hence, equality, in the 170 years since the signing of the Treaty of Waitangi/Te Tiriti o Waitangi, Māori have been affected, often adversely, by the European settlement of Aotearoa New Zealand. These effects—which have been present to a greater or lesser extent over the last century and a half—include the dispossession of land, a lower life expectancy and poorer health record than *Pākehā* (white New Zealanders of predominantly British and Irish origin), lower educational achievement and a higher rate of offending and imprisonment. Since the 1970s there have been significant efforts by both Māori and the Government to redress some of the systematic inequities that have been perpetuated since the signing of the Treaty/Tiriti, particularly with respect to the Crown's promise that Māori would maintain possession and authority over their *taonga* (treasures), such as lands, fisheries and, also, *te reo* (Māori language). While recent census results and the 2001 *Survey of the Health of the Māori Language* suggest that the situation is, in some respects, improving for Māori, Aotearoa New Zealand still bears the difficult legacy of its colonial history, especially with respect to land, language and cultural dispossession of the Māori people.[13]

As with this book's other chapters, I am interested here in how performances of Shakespeare can be analysed in terms of how they "work through" traumatic cultural histories and events. In identifying colonisation as one such traumatic history, my intention is not to posit a simplistic one-way process whereby indigenous peoples have been uniformly and unequivocally wounded and oppressed by colonising nations and settler cultures. Indeed, as critics such as Homi K. Bhabha have shown, encounters between colonisers and colonised peoples are significantly more complex and multifarious than such an analysis would allow, and Daiva Stasiulis and Nira Yuval-Davis make a case, with specific reference to settler cultures such as Australia, Canada and Aotearoa New Zealand, for considering "the histories of indigenous and migrant peoples as interdependent".[14] Rather, in denoting colonisation as traumatic I seek to acknowledge how histories of colonisation are often marked by violence, both physical and cultural, as well as how the ongoing legacy of the ensuing trauma can be measured in the specific material effects on indigenous peoples. I am thinking in particular of how indigenous peoples have been socially and economically disadvantaged and disenfranchised from their culture and language (and often that of the colonising culture), while recognising that intercultural encounters can also produce nonviolent possibilities for ethical exchange and the creation of new intercultural forms. My work here is informed by recent analyses of intercultural performances of Shakespeare, such as Ania Loomba and Phillip B. Zarrilli's subtle reading of Kathakali productions of *Othello* and *King Lear,* respectively, and W. B. Worthen's wide-ranging analysis of the phenomenon, which have sought to explore what Rustom Bharucha describes as the "ethics of representation underlying any cross-cultural exchange" and the "space in between" cultural polarities.[15] My analysis of *The Maori Merchant* thus seeks to stress how performance is engaged in processes of cultural exchange and to explore the material conditions that have shaped this performance and on which the performance acts. I aim to show that the film both memorialises and witnesses the trauma of colonisation and also has the capacity to create affirmative and productive community responses to this trauma.

At first glance *The Maori Merchant* invites consumption as a celebratory exemplar of what Bharucha calls the "space in between". The first feature film to be shot in Māori, the indigenous language of Aotearoa New Zealand, and the first feature-length film of a Shakespeare play to be made in Aotearoa New Zealand, it might thus be termed an intercultural hybrid which works to locate Shakespeare's narrative in the context of Aotearoa

New Zealand, meshing Western and Māori performance traditions into a singular cultural product. Drawing on the production strategies of Western cinema, the lush *mise-en-scène* oscillates between Venice/Weniti, shot at various Italian-inflected locations throughout Auckland, and Belmont/Peremona. The scenes in Venice/Weniti, where the actors wear ruffs and britches, stand as homage to the play's early modern origins. Simultaneously, the images of bustling traders and visiting ships allude to Aotearoa New Zealand's colonial period and work to draw attention to the country's landscape; these scenes also reference Māori culture in the inclusion of *poi* dancers and flax artefacts. Peremona extends Venice/Weniti's range of references to Māori culture in the inclusion of the *tūrehu* (mist children) who are seen flying in the bush, the *tukutuku* panels (flax lattice) and *taiaha* (spears) that adorn the walls, the carving of Portia/Pohia's *tipuna* (ancestors), *moko* (facial tattoos), feather cloaks and *koru* (spirals).[16] Peremona is also home to Māori performance traditions, most clearly seen in the *karanga* (call of welcome) and *wero* (challenge) that are issued to the Prince of Morocco. In its visual signifiers which allude to a specifically New Zealand landscape, the film offers a neat counterpoint to the way in which the landscape has been used by internationally funded film and television projects, encouraged by Aotearoa New Zealand's relatively low production costs, to stand variously for J. R. R. Tolkien's Middle Earth in Peter Jackson's *Lord of the Rings* trilogy (2001, 2002, 2003) and Japan in Tom Cruise's epic *The Last Samurai* (2003), not to mention the faux-ancient worlds depicted in the television series *Xena: Warrior Princess* (1995–2001) and *Hercules: The Legendary Journeys* (1995–1999). As an aural accompaniment to the visual, the soundtrack merges Clive Cockburn's soaring orchestral compositions, performed by the New Zealand Symphony Orchestra, with Hirini Melbourne's compositions for traditional Māori instruments, which he and other musicians perform within the diegesis.

The film employs a range of cultural signifiers to produce a world that combines Māori cultural artefacts, clothing and performance with Shakespeare, opera and Renaissance costumes. Filmed in *te reo* (Māori language) with an (almost entirely) Māori cast and director and a multicultural crew, *The Maori Merchant* seems to exemplify Māori self-determination and the resulting film offers a challenge to some of the dominant stereotypes by which Māori tend to be identified, both in Aotearoa New Zealand and internationally. A media release notes that "[c]ontrary to what some expect, there are no piupius [traditional clothing] and no mokos [facial tattoos] in this vision of cross-cultural fertilisation".[17] Producer Ruth Kaupua Panapa also notes that "[i]n this movie there are no tattoos, no leather jackets and no men in blue uniforms"; in other words, there are no references to gang culture or the police.[18] Instead *The Maori Merchant*, with its representation of Māori actors in Renaissance costumes, counterpoised against more familiar signifiers of Māori culture, seems to play with or parody the notion of cultural authenticity and "exoticism". Although, as Emma Cox notes, the film's "unashamedly exoticised and fantastical representation of Peremona might be criticised for promulgating particular mythologies and stereotypes of Maori culture", such as the Victorian conception of "Maoriland", this kind of critique "may ultimately end up circumscribing Maori creative expression" by insisting on particular modes of originality and authenticity.[19] Instead, through its recycling and mixing of images of Māori and *Pākehā* cultures and histories, the film offers an alternative to representations of colonial-era Māori culture, exemplified in films such as Jane Campion's representation of traditional Māori tribal life which functions as a backdrop to a Western narrative of colonial romance in *The Piano* (1993). The film also stands as an alternative to films such as Niki Caro's *Whale Rider* (2002) which, as Claire Murdoch argues, is "fostered from an indigenous myth, washed (intentionally or not) in the gloss of its national and international arts-export ideology" in which cultural authenticity becomes "one, totemic and inherently 'meaningful' part of an appealing package".[20] *The Maori Merchant* also offers a challenge to the pervasive association between Māori and violence propagated by Lee Tamahori's internationally successful *Once Were Warriors* (1994). As Kaupua Panapa comments, "[w]e were sick and tired of seeing so much [Māori] violence in films. There is conflict in this film but it is not highlighted in a violent way".[21] The film also offers an additional challenge to the representational practices of Hollywood where Māori actors have variously played Iraqis, Colombians, Easter Islanders, and the entire clone army in *Star Wars*, episodes two, *Attack of the Clones* (2002) and three, *Revenge of the Sith* (2005). In these films it is as if Māori are able to function in the global filmic marketplace as blank ethnic signifiers, able to be substituted for any non-European nationality, almost invariably playing roles with negative character trajectories. The phenomenon of "cross-ethnic" casting is not, of course, unique and Hollywood has a long history of this kind of casting practice where actors are asked to play roles at odds with their ethnic identifications, often without consideration to the ethical and cultural implications of these decisions.

Unlike many indigenous films, which are read as an analogue of the "real" (which may or may not be the intention of the filmmakers), *The Maori Merchant* refuses this collapse. As Valerie Wayne suggests, the film's "derivative narrative in a sense shields it from being taken as a direct representation of contemporary Māori experience".[22] Instead it proposes an alternative vision that celebrates images of Māori in a fantastical filmic diegesis. The modes of presentation and reception of this *mise-en-scène* are certainly celebratory: a press release included in the Media Kit asserts that the "design, costumes and music interweave Shakespearean elements with Maori arts in a rich, textured and modern way", reviewer Sam Edwards praises the film for "knitting different and often conflicting cultures and histories into a remarkable whole" and Mark Houlahan describes the film as a "luminous example" of "New Zealand Shakespeare" in his article on the film for Sonia Massai's collection of essays, *World-Wide Shakespeares*.[23]

Without wanting to deny the efficacy of this celebratory mode for participants and spectators of the film, in this chapter, as with this book as a whole, I am interested in an excavation of the film with respect to trauma. My work here is not to "diagnose" the film, its participants and spectators as "traumatised", but rather to consider how the film, produced at the turn of the millennium, is enmeshed in the traumatic effects of colonisation, especially in relation to *te reo* and Māori culture more broadly, even as aspects of this traumatic history also enable the creation and development of affective and effective communities and new cultural forms. Through a reading of the film, a consideration of its representation in reviews, interviews and publicity materials and an analysis of its relationships to political and cultural discourses, I want to examine how *The Maori Merchant* remembers, responds to and, paradoxically, on occasions elides aspects of Aotearoa New Zealand's colonial history and ongoing effects. The film thus comes to stand as a monument to this history and traumatic aspects of its colonial legacy, operating alongside other Shakespeare productions in Aotearoa New Zealand in which the performance of Shakespeare creates a charged site for enabling an engagement with aspects of this history.

While one strain of Shakespeare performance in Aotearoa New Zealand does not seek to draw attention to its cultural contexts as a site of production or a potential source for adaptation, there is another strain, emergent primarily over the last 15 years, which has sought to perform Shakespeare's texts with particular reference to Aotearoa New Zealand's cultural politics, especially with respect to race relations. Theatre at Large's controversial production *Manawa Taua/Savage Hearts* (1994), which utilised a range of performance styles and texts including Shakespeare, music hall routines, melodrama, Māori performance arts and French-influenced improvisational theatre, is one such striking example.[24] Set on the eve of the 1860s New Zealand land wars between Māori and British colonial settlers, *Manawa Taua* detailed the fictional story of Tupou, a Māori chief who journeys to London to meet Queen Victoria to gain her protection for his people. Victoria promises to help him, provided he agrees to play the part of Othello in a touring Shakespeare troupe that is about to embark on an expedition to the colonies. By charting the changes in Tupou as he rehearses *Othello*, falls in love with Lottie (the production's Desdemona) and returns to New Zealand, the performance used his body to register his colonisation and attendant alienation from his culture, a process in which Shakespeare played a central part. Thus Tupou's clothes changed from a traditional Māori cloak to European garb. More tellingly, he lost his capacity to speak Māori; instead all he could do was speak "Shakespeare". Despite the comic "happy" ending, in which a member of the theatre company was punished for appropriating Māori land, the performance dramatised issues concerning Māori cultural alienation as a result of the process of British colonisation of New Zealand through Tupou's corporeal transformations while playing Shakespeare. The discourse surrounding the production, which I have written about elsewhere, also identifies how this colonial fable is implicated in contemporary race relations and debates about how aspects of Aotearoa New Zealand's history might (or should) be represented.[25]

Another apposite example of the way in which the performance of Shakespeare has been deployed in relation to contemporary race relations is evident in a plotline of the New Zealand soap opera *Shortland Street* (1997).[26] Over several episodes, the rehearsal of *Othello* by a group of secondary school students engaged with questions of race, ethnicity and the ethics of affirmative action in a settler culture. This critique, however, eventually gave way to a liberal humanist understanding of acting and casting and Bradleyan notions of character, where characters are treated as psychologically complex "real" people, which works to disregard cultural specificity under the rubric of "universal" emotional states.[27] In contrast, the short film, *God and Shakespeare* (2001), which deploys the codes of the Western (pistols, Stetsons, cowboy boots and a shoot-out), depicts a sparring match between Shakespeare and God on one of Aotearoa New Zealand's black sand beaches.[28] Shakespeare, played by a young Māori man, and God, played by an older *Pākehā* man, duel both with "pistols" in the shape of hand-held power-tools, and words from their respective texts. Here the film pays homage to three colonial imports: Shakespeare, the Bible and firearms. In Shakespeare's chunky red-heart ring and the ribbons that are used to symbolise the wounds inflicted by the power-tools, it also includes allusions to Baz Luhrmann's *William Shakespeare's Romeo + Juliet* (1996) and Peter Brook's *Titus Andronicus* (1955), respectively. After a series of verbal and power-tool passes, God and Shakespeare eventually kill each other; a woman clad in a wetsuit, identified in the credits as Venus, subsequently discovers their bodies, which lie head to head on the beach. As the film closes, the camera pulls back to an aerial shot and pans over the bodies such that the closing shot consists of the black sand beach with Venus's footprints emerging from the water, neatly erasing Shakespeare and God from the frame of the Aotearoa New Zealand's beachscape.

These adaptations can be set alongside Cathy Downes's *Othello* (2001), Toi Whakaari's (New Zealand Drama School) *Troilus and Cressida* (2003), directed by Annie Ruth and Rangimoana Taylor, and Jonathon Hendry's *Othello* (2007), all of which set the play in the context of Aotearoa New Zealand's mid-nineteenth-century land wars as a means for exploring historical race relations. Other striking engagements with Shakespeare in relation to contemporary and historical contexts include Oscar Kightley and Erolia Ifopo's production *Romeo and Tusi* (1997–2000) for Pacific Underground, which set a rehearsal of *Romeo and Juliet* in the context of conflict between Samoan and Māori families living in Auckland, and Samoan artist Lemi Ponifasio's *Tempest: Without a Body* (2007), created with his Auckland-based company, Mau.[29] Mau, named after a nonviolent Samoan independence movement of the early twentieth century that resisted German and

New Zealand colonisation, makes work that engages specifically with Oceanic cultures. *Tempest: Without a Body*, employed dance, theatre, oratory and video images and utilised elements of Shakespeare's play, Paul Klee's "Angelus Novus", and the philosophical work of Giorgio Agamben, in an exploration of an apocalyptic post-9/11 world. It also included an appearance by Māori activist Tame Iti, who was arrested in an anti-terrorist raid in New Zealand, along with 16 other activists, in 2007. As the media release for the 2009 Sydney Festival notes, the production offered "Iti a ceremonial platform to present his case for social change and his vision for his own people, the Tūhoe iwi [tribe]".[30] Such productions can, as Houlahan suggests in his discussion of *Romeo and Tusi*, be seen as "driven by a desire to settle with Shakespeare on specific and highly localised terms".[31] These are terms that I would suggest lend themselves to consideration with respect to how these performances might negotiate difficult aspects of Aotearoa New Zealand's past, present and future. In my work on *The Maori Merchant* my aim is to trace the various spectres of colonial violence which haunt the film and enable it to function, suggestively, as a repository of traumatic historical memories, contemporary cultural initiatives which work to redress past injustices and also, of imagined futures. In the present time of the film's production and its imagined futures, the film models how trauma might, paradoxically, provide a means through which communities might mobilise themselves and others to redress acts of violence. I want, now, to begin my excavation of the film with respect to its hybrid conceit *par excellence*: the translation of *The Merchant of Venice* into *te reo*.

SPEAKING (MĀORI) SHAKESPEARE

The Maori Merchant is an adaptation of Pei Te Hurinui Jones's 1946 translation of Shakespeare's play into Māori, *Te Tangata Whai-Rawa O Weniti*.[32] Jones has been widely acclaimed as a bicultural pioneer, who sought to foster closer relations between Māori and *Pākehā*. In particular, he recorded the history of the Tainui *iwi* (tribe), translated Māori *waiata* (songs) into English, contributed to a Māori translation of the Bible (1949), and translated Shakespeare into Māori (in addition to *The Merchant of Venice* he also translated *Othello* as *Owhiro: Te Mua o Weneti* [1944] and *Julius Caesar* as *Huria Hiha* [1959]).[33] After a gap of some 50 years, Jones's mid-century translation projects have been joined by Merimeri Penfold's translation of nine of Shakespeare's sonnets into Māori, published in a limited edition of 200 copies on the occasion of the 6th Biennial Conference of the Australia and New Zealand Shakespeare Association in 2000.[34] Sonnet 147 is not included in Penfold's collection but it was the subject of *Te Po Uriuri (The Enveloping Night)*, a short film made in *te reo* in 2001 that set the sonnet in Aotearoa in 1592.[35] The sonnet was used as the pretext to develop a story of obsessive desire and enforced marriage in context of a pre-European contact *iwi*, and it played also with contested and sensitive historical narratives about Māori cannibalism.³⁶ Produced in the same year as *Te Po Uriuri*, the *Maori Merchant*'s dialogue is delivered in *te reo* and accompanied by English subtitles which mix elements of Shakespeare's language with modern English, in sharp contrast to *Te Po Uriuri*'s reproduction of Shakespeare's text in the film's subtitles. With the action unfolding over 158 minutes, *The Maori Merchant* does, however, offer a "faithful" adaptation of Shakespeare's narrative through its rendering of the plot and the characters.³⁷ The translation might thus be posited as one, in Jacques Derrida's words, "that performs its mission, honours its debt and does its job or its duty while inscribing in the receiving language the most *relevant* equivalent for an original, the language that is *the most* right, appropriate, pertinent, adequate, opportune, pointed, univocal, idiomatic, and so on".³⁸ In the film's Media Kit and reviews, the project is framed repeatedly as honouring a twin debt by marrying Selwyn's "passion for Shakespeare with his lifelong commitment to the revitalisation of the Maori language".³⁹ Here the debt is to be paid not only to the "original" language of Shakespeare's English, but also (and primarily) to the "target" language of *te reo*. Indeed, the focus of Selwyn's long career was to promote *te reo* and to create training opportunities for Māori in Aotearoa New Zealand's film and theatre industries. As part of this programme he ran He Taonga I Tawhiti (Gifts from Afar) from 1984 until 1990, a film and television training course for Māori and Pacific Islanders; in 1992 Selwyn and Ruth Kaupua Panapa created He Taonga Films, *The Maori Merchant*'s production company, which has provided a platform for creating Māori film and television dramas.

Given He Taonga Films's focus on training Māori with the skills to tell stories about themselves, Selwyn acknowledges the apparent difficulty that producing a Shakespeare play creates in relation to this remit and suggests that "Shakespeare in Maori is enough to turn most people off".⁴⁰ However, the media discourse surrounding the production works to naturalise this choice and to package it as part of a programme of both cultural recovery and development in the face of dispossession. The focus of this discourse is Jones's translation, which uses a poetic, rhetorical style of Māori known as *te reo kohatu* where *kohatu* (stone) represents the language's ancient and enduring nature. This is in contrast to contemporary Māori language, which has undergone considerable change since the arrival of the British. Indeed, the language literally registers a history of colonisation through the number of slightly modified English words that have entered *te reo*, such as tiriti for treaty. As Scott Morrison, the film's Antonio/Anatonio, who also works as a Māori newsreader and part-time lecturer in Māori Education, elaborates, Jones's translation is:

> a different kind of language. It's a language you don't hear that often. I believe our language initially belonged to the environment. It developed from the call of birds and the rustling of trees and so when our

ancestors spoke they used imagery and metaphor and simile and other devices in conjunction with the environment to describe their feelings. That kind of expertise is lost in the language now, where a lot of Maori speakers are just using the language to translate their English thought processes and that metaphoric language is lost.[41]

Morrison continues, "you can see by the way Shakespeare wrote and the way Pei Te Hurinui translated it, that the poetical element is back inside it, so I believe this film will really lift our language and people will get a lot out of it".[42] Morrison also posits Jones's translation as a return to pre-colonial times, suggesting that the film "captures the essence of how Maori language would have been spoken before the arrival of Europeans".[43]

In an ironic paradox, Shakespeare—the emblem of the language which has linguistically colonised aspects of *te reo*—is the vehicle by which Māori are able to reclaim and develop their language. In effect, Shakespeare becomes the means by which Māori are "given" back their language, enabling a return to a prelapsarian world before an encounter with European colonisation. In this process it is as if Shakespeare emerges somehow unscathed as the saviour of the Māori and *te reo*, sheered from associations with a well-documented history of colonisation. But, by the same token, it is asserted in the Media Kit that the film works by "enhancing" Shakespeare's plot, characters and setting by, as Selwyn notes, "using Maori language and cultural elements as a vehicle to be able to express the dynamics that Shakespeare came up with".[44] Here, Māori is credited with improving Shakespeare and releasing "his" meanings. The film might thus be said to embody Walter Benjamin's claim in "The Task of the Translator" (1923) that "[i]n translation the original rises into a higher and purer linguistic air" even if "[i]t cannot live there permanently"; for Benjamin "[i]t is the task of the translator to release in his own language that pure language which is under the spell of another, to liberate the language imprisoned in a work in his re-creation of that work".[45] The discourse surrounding the film thus works to blend *te reo* and Shakespeare's English into a seamless hybrid product which improves both languages, eliding any negative associations with a history of colonisation which Shakespeare might be seen to mark. Instead it seems to propose what Derrida, drawing on Benjamin, might describe as that "rare and notable event", or a translation "that manages to promise reconciliation", both of languages and, by association, cultures.[46] Indeed Waihoroi Shortland, the film's Shylock/Hairoka, seems to suggest a kind of cultural reconciliation in his claim that Shakespeare's language is "actually quite synonymous with whaikorero [traditional Māori oratory]". Furthermore, Selwyn reports Jones as saying that he only worked on his translations when he felt that he was "in tune with what Shakespeare was doing".[47] Here Jones is cast as a surrogate of sorts for Shakespeare and Shortland posits sameness between Shakespeare and *whaikorero*. In claims such as these the film participates in a discourse that works to elide cultural difference and any potentially negative effects produced through colonisation, especially with respect to language.

The Maori Merchant—through its title and subtitles—also works to undo this seamlessness, playing out a set of hierarchical power relationships between English and Māori, speech and writing, which hint at historical grievances stemming from translation between English and Māori and which simultaneously offer a response to this history. As Lawrence Venuti remarks, "asymmetries, inequities, relations of domination and dependence exist in every act of translating".[48] In Aotearoa New Zealand these issues can be traced to the inequities produced by the mismatch in meaning between the English and Māori versions of the Treaty/Tiriti; in particular, Māori understood that they ceded *kāwanatanga* (governance), rather than sovereignty, as the English version demanded. *The Maori Merchant* might, then, be seen as an attempt to displace the historical dominance of English instated with the signing of the Treaty/Tiriti. A consideration of the various translations that have led to the finished film helps to clarify these issues. First, Shakespeare's play was translated into classical Māori by Jones; second, Jones's translation was adapted into the screenplay by Selwyn; and third, the Māori voice-track was then translated into "modern" English subtitles, also by Selwyn. The finished product thus privileges Māori over English, with Shakespeare's text positioned at several relations of difference to the text of *The Maori Merchant*. For Selwyn the "cryptic and very simple" subtitles were integral in ensuring that non-Māori speakers might "follow the story, get a feel for the reo, and a feel for the emotional element [. . . .] they'll hear the beauty of the Maori language, and their understanding will be cryptically in their own particular language".[49] Selwyn suggests that the cryptic subtitles, necessarily incomplete and brief, will have the effect of forcing a closer spectatorial and auditory engagement with Māori from non-native speakers. The subtitles thus work to pose Māori as the dominant language and to situate the language of translation as an inadequate supplement. Here the language of translation does not look capable of functioning as what Derrida would call a "dangerous supplement", or that which threatens to intervene in and replace the dominant discourse of Māori.[50]

The title reinforces this effort to instate the primacy of Māori, especially in relation to Shakespeare's text. In the majority of the media discourse, including He Taonga Films's website, the film is known primarily as *The Maori Merchant of Venice* rather that its Māori title *Te Tangata Whai Rawa O Weniti*. The twin titles here flag the inability of translation to produce analogues, especially of names. Whereas the Māori title offers a translation of *The Merchant of Venice*, in the English title the word Maori is used to modify the title of Shakespeare's play *The Merchant of Venice*. If a title, as Derrida suggests, "names and guarantees the identity, the unity and the boundaries of the original work which it entitles", the reconfiguration of the title, both in Māori and as a modified English title, shifts the frame of reference for interpreting the film.[51] The use of the word Māori, which refers both to the Māori people and to *te reo*, effectively displaces the "original" title of *The Merchant of Venice*. It also offers a succinct way of cannily differentiating the film from other *Merchant*s in the Shakespeare on screen marketplace by signalling its ethnic origins. Whereas Baz Luhrmann sought to exploit Shakespeare's cultural authority by naming his film *William Shakespeare's Romeo + Juliet* (1996), the use of the word Māori to supplement the English title partially displaces the primacy of Shakespeare from the enterprise: the promise of the title is that Shakespeare's *Merchant* will be remade by Māori and in Māori. This process of displacement of English by Māori is further promised through the renaming of Shakespeare's characters with Māori names: Hairoka for Shylock, Pohia for Portia, Anatonio for Antonio, and Patanio for Bassanio. This reassignment is fractured by the use of the more familiar (for me, at least) Shakespearean names in the subtitles, while the actors speak the Māori names.

This effect of fracture, or unravelling of the alleged seamlessness between spoken Māori and written English, occurs throughout the subtitles with respect to more than the title and the characters' names. Specifically, the brief prosaic, or "cryptic", as Selwyn puts it, nature of the subtitles, in contrast to the lengthy rhetorical speeches in Māori, exposes a series of differences between English and Māori. In this way the film, as the viewer might expect, privileges speakers of *te reo*, excluding nonspeakers from a "fuller" account of the play's narrative. Furthermore, the film contains moments where the camera tracks over the inscriptions of the caskets, the scrolls they contain and various written messages; these are expressed in Māori, denying comprehension to the nonspeaker, except in cases where the text is reproduced as part of the dialogue and, hence, "cryptically" in the subtitles. Here, the film works to counter language dispossession and to displace the primacy of English. The film, however, uses a canonical English text and provides English subtitles, which, as supplements to the alleged "fullness" of speech, always add to and threaten to exceed that to which they refer. In this respect the film cannot help but be traced, graphically, by the language of colonisation that litters the screen. The film is caught in a kind of traumatic feedback loop: it operates as a celebratory response to linguistic and cultural disenfranchisement but that response is enabled in part by elements of the colonial machinery (English, Shakespeare) which worked to produce the conditions of disenfranchisement and alienation in the first place.

TE REO AND THE FUTURE-TO-COME

Although Selwyn was aware of Jones's translation in the 1950s, it was not until 1990 that he staged the play as part of Auckland's Te Koanga Spring Festival of Maori Arts and it took another 10 years before funding was secured to produce it as a film. These temporal gaps sustain exploration as they offer a gloss on the history of language dispossession and cultural alienation, and also speak to a relative absence of "Māori Shakespeare" of the kind that Jones's and Selwyn's projects imagine. Following European contact the oral language of the Māori began to be expressed in written form and by 1820 the orthographic foundations of the language were articulated in Thomas Kendall's *A Grammar and Vocabulary of the Language of New Zealand*, produced by the Church Missionary Society. As Samuel Lee notes in the preface to Kendall's text, this work was carried out with the aim "of reducing the language itself of New Zealand to the rules of Grammar, with a view to the furtherance of the Mission sent out to that country", which facilitated "the double purpose of civilizing and evangelizing the Natives".[52] The word "reducing" identifies how *te reo* was to be articulated as a written sign system; as "reducing" also entails the possibility of "diminishing", Lee's preface hints at how this act of translation of committing an oral language to written form performs a violence on the language. Furthermore, the word "civilizing" embeds a value judgement that Māori are, conversely, not civilized, where "civilized" can be read as primarily symbolising Western values and behaviours. In the work of the Church Missionary Society *te reo* was codified partly for the purposes of religious conversion and "civilization", key apparatuses of colonisation, and also subjected to the rules of English grammar. Not only was *te reo* linguistically colonised as part of missionary work, it was further subjected through colonial systems of education. As has been carefully documented by Gauri Viswanathan with respect to the development of literary studies in India, education is one of the key means by which colonisation operates in the service of converting and containing indigenous cultures. This is strikingly evident in the 1835 Indian Education Act, which stated that Indians would be educated in English and in Western arts and sciences at the expense of classical Indian languages and subjects. Thomas Babington Macaulay makes the aims of this project clear in his 1835 minute on "Indian Education" where he proposed that an English education would produce "a class of persons, Indian in blood and colour, but English in taste, in opinions, in morals, and in intellect".[53] The effect of this education programme was to produce an educated Indian elite who would assist the British in governing the rest of the indigenous population.

Māori were not the subject of a Macaulay-style minute but they were identified as subjects for education in specifically British terms, which was partially responsible for large-scale language and cultural dispossession; as the British settlement of Aotearoa New Zealand expanded, *te reo* suffered a series of setbacks. Although the Native Schools Act 1867 enabled the establishment of primary schools in Māori communities, the language of instruction tended to be in English. This can be read as part of a process of cultural domination on behalf of the new settlers, whereby English was established as the primary mode of communication. This pattern was to continue; even under the more inclusive education policies of the 1930s Labour Government, the use of Māori continued to decline. This situation was compounded further by the "urban drift" of Māori into the cities during the 1950s and 1960s; consequently Māori were further alienated from their language and culture, as highlighted in the 1960 Hunn Report.

In considering the possibility of staging the play in Māori, Selwyn remembers Jones saying, "Kua tae mai te waa—the time will come".[54] In a sense Jones proposed a "future-to-come", a future in which there would be sufficient numbers of Māori speakers to mount such a production. *The Maori Merchant*, spoken entirely in *te reo*, stands as testament to this future-present of cultural recovery. In part this future has been produced as a response to Māori urban protest movements of the 1970s and what is commonly termed the Māori cultural Renaissance. This saw a renewed interest in traditional Māori arts such as weaving and carving and also the creation of works that employed Western cultural forms, such as Witi Ihimaera's short story collection *Pounamu Pounamu* (1972) and his novel *Tangi* (1973). Furthermore, the Government sought to address its responsibilities under the Treaty/Tiriti, especially its obligation to allow Māori to protect their *taonga* (treasures), of which *te reo* is one. As such, *kōhanga reo* (language nests) were established in 1982, offering Māori language immersion environments for preschool children, *kura kaupapa* (schools) were created in 1985 and Māori was designated an official language of Aotearoa New Zealand in 1987. As a *Pākehā*, or white New Zealander (and both are terms that I feel uncomfortable laying claim to as they speak to a history of colonisation and racial inequality), my own education in Aotearoa New Zealand in the 1980s and 1990s certainly benefitted from these developments in the 1970s. Compared to many children and teenagers educated before the 1980s I gained a comparatively increased awareness of Māori culture and language and also some understanding of the acts of violence—linguistic, cultural and physical—that led to the formation of Aotearoa New Zealand and continue to inform its history, even though that education felt partial and incomplete. As this chapter suggests, there is, however, still significant work to be done in increasing knowledge of Māori language and culture in Aotearoa New Zealand.

The actors' biographies included in the film's Media Kit stand as witness to past dispossession but also register the possibilities for a future where *te reo* has been encouraged to develop. Andy Sarich's (Tubal/Tupara) biography notes that he "grew up speaking the Maori language and was of the generation which was punished for speaking Maori at school and punished for speaking English at home, but he retained his Maori language".[55] Charting a shift from Sarich's experience, several of the younger members of the cast noted that they grew up in families fluent in *te reo*, attended *kōhanga reo* and *kura kaupapa* or learned Māori at university. That said, some members of the cast noted that they were not fluent in *te reo* or that they did not grow up learning Māori, instead having to learn it as part of an intensive language-learning programme before the filming began. This suggests that the utopian future-to-come is, as the phrase suggests, yet to come. In this respect it is interesting to note that the Government's Māori Language Strategy consultation document, produced by Te Puni Kōkiri (Ministry of Māori Development), *He Reo E Kōrerotia Ana—He Reo Ka Ora* [A Spoken Language Is a Living Language], *A Shared Vision for the Future of Te Reo Māori*, proposes 2028 as a target date by which:

> the Māori language will be widely spoken among Māori throughout New Zealand. In particular, the Māori language will be in common usage within Māori homes and communities. By 2028, non-Māori New Zealanders will have opportunities to learn and use the Māori language if they choose to. New Zealanders will recognise and appreciate the value of the Māori language within New Zealand society.[56]

The Maori Merchant, positioned halfway between the language initiatives that began in the 1970s and the future-to-come of 2028, can thus be read as a cultural project that indexes—and contributes to—the progress of the revival of *te reo* at the cusp of the millennium.

MEMORIALS AND RESPONSIBILITIES

But just as the proposed utopian future-to-come will be shadowed by the traces of colonisation, so too is the present. In this way *The Maori Merchant* stands as an emblem of the future/past, condensing both what has gone before and what might be into the event of performance. Writing of justice in relation to accretions of the past and the future, Derrida argues that:

> no justice [. . .] seems possible or thinkable without the principle of some *responsibility*, beyond all living present, within that which disjoins the living present, before the ghosts of those who are not yet born or who are already dead, be they victims of wars, political or other kinds of violence, nationalist, racist, colonialist, sexist, or other kinds of exterminations, victims of the oppressions of capitalist imperialism or any of the forms of totalitarianism.[57]

He goes on to suggest that it is not possible to ask questions of the future-to-come "without this responsibility and this respect for justice concerning those who *are not there*, of those who are no longer or who are not yet *present and living*".[58] Indeed Selwyn notes that "young people are the most important thing . . . In Maori we have a saying (that) we are but a moment between two eternities, the past and the future. Whatever time is occurring now, to help young people is what you are here for".[59] Here the time of the present is hinged to the past and is also marked as the site from which a responsibility to the future must issue; it is as if the events of the past, be those traumatic or pleasurable, are condensed into the now-time of the present where it is the responsibility of those living now to shape time-past and time-present for those who are to come. *The Maori Merchant* might be said to model such a sense of responsibility to what has gone before and what might come in the context of justice for violations of the Treaty/Tiriti. This is most obviously borne out by an allegorical reading of Shakespeare's play in the context of Aotearoa New Zealand's race relations.

If one strand of *The Merchant of Venice* concerns the violation of a written bond that is then debated in court, an analogy might be made with the interpretation of the Treaty/Tiriti, especially following the Government's creation of the Waitangi Tribunal in 1975 to investigate and redress land claims. The Tribunal initially had the power to consider breaches of the Treaty/Tiriti from 1975 but the Treaty Amendment Act 1985 gave it the power to consider all breaches of the Treaty/Tiriti since it was signed in 1840. This has led to a number of high-profile compensation claims that have resulted in reparations being made to various *iwi*. The film's website and Media Kit certainly work to locate *The Merchant of Venice* in the context of Aotearoa New Zealand's cultural politics. Shylock's quest for justice is expressed as a desire for *utu*, which is translated as both "revenge" and the less emotive "payment", which it also entails. As such, Shylock's efforts to gain redress for the violation of his bond through the courts might be read as neatly referring to the processes administered by the Tribunal. Shakespeare's plot resonates further in relation to Tahupotiki Wiremu Ratana's successful spiritual and political mission, which was established in the 1920s. The Ratana movement located the Māori as God's "Chosen People" in place of the Jews and interpreted the Old Testament as a parable for the displacement and suffering of the Māori. Shortland makes this connection between Māori and Judaism explicit when he says:

> playing Shylock from a Maori perspective is the easiest role because you know something of what it is to hang onto your identity and to deal with prejudice, some of it overt, some of it not so overt, in the New Zealand sense anyway [. . . .]
> I see him as acting on behalf of his people.[60]

Selwyn makes the connection between the anti-Semitic prejudice examined in the play and race relations in the context of Aotearoa New Zealand, claiming:

> New Zealand is very conscious of its history, we're continually debating the misunderstandings and lack of a cohesive relationship. Prejudice is prejudice, and it's something that we have to address, and my feeling is that anything that is going to allow us to understand or face

up to our own history is going to be for the better, because then we can get on with it.[61]

Here the narrative work of the play is cited as a mechanism by which Aotearoa New Zealand might engage with or "face up to" its past, even as the historical specificities of prejudice are collapsed into the tautological "prejudice is prejudice". Again, a Shakespeare play, as with Sher and Doran's work with *Titus Andronicus* in South Africa, is deployed as a means through which to confront difficult aspects of cultural history. Furthermore, in the possibility of "get[ting] on with it", Selwyn seems to mark a moment whereby Aotearoa New Zealand might engage with the future more directly in relation to the difficulties wrought by the past. Aspects of the film certainly work to elide traumatic aspects of this colonial history, such as the part that the English language played in cultural dispossession, even as the use of Shakespeare has enabled, subsequently, a project of cultural reclamation. Other parts of the film are, however, more equivocal about the traumatic events of the past and the ongoing inequalities produced through colonisation and its aftermath. Specifically, the analogy between Shakespeare's play and the history of the Māori warp under the weight of further analysis to reinforce the oppression of the Māori, coded in specifically Shakespearean terms. Indeed, the film's "one-liner" tag, "Revenge is not so sweet", coupled with Shylock's failure to attain *utu* in the court, might be read symbolically as a bleak view of the possibility of honouring the "bond" of the Treaty/Tiriti through the processes of the legal system. The film's courtroom scene resonates in the context of Aotearoa New Zealand in the ways I have suggested. It is, though, through extra-textual referents that the film most clearly references a sense of responsibility to the traumatic violence of the past and the future-to-come. This is most sharply articulated in the film's representation of 1.3, where Antonio/Anatonio makes his bond with Shylock/Hairoka.

As Bassanio/Patanio and Shylock/Hairoka begin their negotiations, the camera tracks their journey through a Venetian marketplace before Bassanio/Patanio introduces Antonio/Anatonio to Shylock/Hairoka in an artist's studio. As the scene progresses, through a sequence of slow-moving shots, which highlight the division between the Christians and the Jew, the camera also captures scenes from the paintings that hug the perimeter of the studio. These images, painted by Māori artist and the film's co-producer Selwyn Muru, who is present as a painter in the diegesis, offer yet another instance of intercultural production. Here Muru uses the medium of painting to depict Māori history, which traditionally was recorded orally and through carving. More tellingly, the paintings offer a visual record of conflict over land between Māori and *Pākehā* at Parihaka in the 1880s; coincidentally in 2000–2001 Wellington's City Gallery/Te Whare Toi housed an exhibition entitled "Parihaka: The Art of Passive Resistance", which explored the legacy of Parihaka in New Zealand art. While the Treaty/Tiriti gave the

Crown first option of buying land, the history of land purchase in Aotearoa New Zealand is enmeshed in narratives of land confiscation. The *pa* (village) at Parihaka, situated near Mount Taranaki, whose imposing shape is registered in Muru's paintings, attracted Māori who were drawn to the teachings of the prophets Te Whiti-o-Rongomai and Toho Kakahi. These prophets are remembered primarily for their campaigns of pacifism and passive resistance against *Pākehā* attempts to survey land. These programmes met, however, with an invasion of 644 troops and 1,000 settler volunteers on 5 November 1881, which resulted in the destruction of the *pa* and the arrest of the prophets. In the inclusion of paintings that depict this event, *The Maori Merchant* reiterates the memory of this traumatic event, emblematic of more widespread land dispossession and violence. It is, though, in the closing moments of this scene that the film works, most pointedly, to stand as witness to past events.

As Antonio/Anatonio and Bassanio/Patanio leave the studio, the paintings, which have occupied a peripheral position throughout most of the foregoing scene, are brought to the centre of the filmic gaze. Focussing on one painting the camera pans up. At the bottom of the painting the spectator sees the word "holocaust" broken up along the painting's vertical and horizontal axes to read "HO/LO/CA/UST". As the camera reaches the top of the painting, the phonemes are again shown, rearranged horizontally to spell "HOLOCAUST". In this double iteration, the word "holocaust" registers multiple meanings that the spectator is invited to witness, their responses shaped by the particular circumstances of their cultural backgrounds. The dominant meaning that "holocaust" carries is, of course, the genocide of six million Jews under the instruction of Hitler's Nazi Germany. The insertion of the word thus provides a reminder of the way in which productions of *The Merchant of Venice* after the Holocaust are, perhaps inevitably, traced by this traumatic history, exemplified by the productions with which I opened this chapter. In a film which has resolutely insisted on the primacy of *te reo*, the insertion of an English word into the diegesis provides a sharp reminder of the linguistic colonisation which has created the need for the film in the first instance: literally, a linguistic holocaust is referenced. The dual iteration also signifies at the level of contemporary national politics.

In 1996 the Waitangi Tribunal released a report on land claims in the Taranaki region. Buried near the end of the lengthy report Chapter 12.3.3 states:

[a]s to quantum, the gravamen of our report has been to say that the Taranaki claims are likely to be the largest in the country. The graphic muru [confiscation] of most of Taranaki and the raupatu [conquest and marginalisation] without ending describe the holocaust of Taranaki history and the denigration of the founding peoples in a continuum from 1840 to the present.[62]

The report thus makes a connection between the effects of colonisation on the Māori and the term's more common association with Hitler's programme of genocide. The term "holocaust" was to resurface amid much public controversy in 2000. In an address to the New Zealand Psychological Society Conference, Tariana Turia, an Associate Minister of Te Puni Kōkiri, claimed that while Post-Traumatic Stress Disorder was readily considered in relation to Holocaust survivors and Vietnam veterans "[w]hat seems to not have received similar attention is the holocaust suffered by indigenous people including Maori as a result of colonial contact and behaviour".[63] Turia's comments here, alongside her assertion that Māori child abuse and domestic violence could be linked to the effects of colonisation, were attacked. The New Zealand First leader Winston Peters dismissed Turia's claims as "psychobabble" and National MP Roger Sowry asserted that it was "the most off-the-planet speech by a politician in living memory".[64] Following the outcry, Turia made a speech in Parliament; while she apologised for any offence caused, she did not offer an official retraction of the term holocaust.[65] In response to Turia's speech, Helen Clark, the Labour Prime Minister at the time, issued the following edict: "I know the [Waitangi] tribunal used it [holocaust] with respect to Taranaki. I do not agree with that and I do not want to see ministers using the term and causing offence again".[66] She went on to say: "I don't accept that the word holocaust can be validly used about the New Zealand experience [. . .] I would not use that particular term, which has a specific and very tragic meaning".[67] Furthermore, Wendy Ross, a member of the Auckland Jewish Council, commented that it was "a pity" that Turia "reinforced the Waitangi Tribunal's use of the word".[68]

The scene in the artist's studio was shot after Turia had been castigated and Selwyn says that "[t]hey couldn't resist" referring to it in the film.[69] The inclusion of this textual referent, coupled with the images of Parihaka, offers a graphic (in a literal sense) representation of the dispossession of the Māori in the context of other histories of dispossession; indeed the term has been used in relation to other indigenous peoples, such as David E. Stannard's analysis of the effects of colonisation on indigenous cultures in the Americas.[70] In attempting to ban the word (for Government ministers at least), Clark limited the vocabulary available to account for Aotearoa New Zealand's cultural history, highlighting how language can be used both to articulate and limit self-representation. In referencing the word "holocaust", *The Maori Merchant* unshackled the term from its "ban" and makes a case for the right to self-representation through denoting aspects of Aotearoa New Zealand's colonial history as violent and painful for Māori.

As the scene in the artist's studio works to acknowledge traumatic historical events and their figuration in contemporary politics, the film's distribution process, alongside the way in which it fostered Māori language, actors and filmmakers, also works to redress some of the damage created by colonisation. The film, like the production of *This Island's Mine* which I will explore in the next chapter, thus identifies how traumatic events and histories can also offer acts of resistance and the capacity to produce and sustain communities, even as these communities, as Miranda Joseph notes, are still yet caught in (and maintain) capitalist systems of production and consumption, here denoted through the operation and labour of the film industry.[71] *The Maori Merchant* was made primarily for an audience fluent in *te reo*, with the aim of recovering lost aspects of the Māori language, encouraging Māori to learn *te reo* and, in the longer term, to become an educational resource. The film, a 2004 Ministry of Education resource kit, which included a video of the film, a book and a teachers' guide, and the 2008 Ministry of Education reprint of Jones's 1946 text, thus offer an early twenty-first-century reprise of Jones's mid-century efforts to create Māori Shakespeare and Selwyn's 1990 staging of the translation.[72] As Selwyn notes, "[i]t's a long-term educational resource and an opportunity to celebrate the artists and people who are learning the language. But it's also a catalyst for the broader community thing—such a wide range of artists are employed on it".[73] Here Selwyn imagines how the film will galvanise communities of Māori speakers, now and in the future, but also the way in which the film is seen as a means of creating a community based on affiliations in addition to speaking Māori. The film's participation in narratives of community creation also recurs in the release strategy. Using a slow-release strategy, the film toured around Aotearoa New Zealand and was screened at a series of charity premieres to benefit the Pei Te Hurinui Jones Trust, formed to fund creative writing in *te reo*. In this way He Taonga Films located *The Maori Merchant* as a performance event, designed to showcase it to maximum cultural effect and to raise money to benefit Māori education. The film also screened on the then newly launched Māori Television channel in 2004. This channel is the latest addition to Māori broadcasting which, like the cast biographies in the Media Kit note, has included *Te Karere*, the Māori language news programme, Ruia Mai, a Māori language radio production company and *Marae*, a Māori magazine programme. The biographies and network screening stand as testament to the development of Māori (language) broadcasting, which has benefited from Government support as it has worked to meet its obligations, set out by the Waitangi Tribunal, to support Māori language. Indeed the film was primarily funded (NZ\$2.4 million) by Te Māngai Pāho, the Crown entity, established in 1993 "to make funding available to the national network of Māori radio stations and for the production of Māori language television programmes, radio programmes and music CDs".[74] The film also screened as part of the inaugural Wairoa Maori Film Festival (2005). It can thus be seen as an integral part of the development of Māori filmmaking that this festival marked, and continues to mark, as the 2010 festival screened several new short films by Māori filmmakers.[75]

Māori filmmaking still makes up a relatively small percentage of Aotearoa New Zealand's film industry and no other feature film in *te reo* has yet, at the time of writing, been produced. A consideration of the New Zealand Film Commission/Te Tumu Whakaata Taonga's list of 294 feature films made since 1939 and catalogue of short films in relation to Te Māngai Pāho's funding decisions suggests that significantly more work is made by Māori artists and in *te reo* for radio, music and television than for the cinema.[76] Indeed, the production company Whenua Films was started by Cliff Curtis and Ainsley Gardiner in 2004, partly in response to Curtis's sense that the "Maori Film Industry" was not "flourishing with a diverse range of characters for him to play" on his return to Aotearoa New Zealand from Hollywood; "[t]he reality inspired him to start a company devoted to creating a home for indigenous storytelling, that would in turn encourage an aspect of the industry informed by tikanga Maori".[77] Although Selwyn's project did not initiate a wave of feature films in Māori, its success in promoting Māori filmmaking and *te reo* is perhaps better measured in the proliferation of smaller scale projects, such as short films and documentaries of the kind that the Wairoa Festival showcases, and Māori involvement in Aotearoa New Zealand's film industry more broadly. This work has largely been made possible by projects such as Selwyn's He Taonga I Tawhiti and He Taonga Films, representative bodies for Māori working in film, video and television such as Nga Aho Whakaari, and government funding for Māori broadcasting.[78]

In addition to this local development agenda, Selwyn also sought to tap international markets to gain exposure for *te reo*. Indeed it was Selwyn's intention "to introduce the Maori language through Shakespeare to the world through this".[79] Alongside positive reviews in Aotearoa New Zealand and the Award of Best Actor for Shortland at the 2003 New Zealand Film Awards, the film won the Blockbuster Audience Award for Best Feature Film at the 2002 Louis Vuitton Hawaii International Film Festival and screened at the second Denver Indigenous Film and Arts Festival in 2005. Outside the festival circuit, screenings of the film at the 2003 meeting of the Shakespeare Association of America in Victoria, British Columbia, and at a 2004 seminar on Māori Shakespeare at the International Center for Writing and Translation at the University of California, Irvine, proved popular; chapters on the film have also been included in Sonia Massai's collection *World-Wide Shakespeares*, Mark Thornton Burnett and Ramona Wray's collection *Screening Shakespeare in the Twenty-first Century* and in the postcolonial journal *Kunapipi*.[80] As such it would seem that the film has, indeed, managed to acquire a place in the niche (film and academic) markets of metropolitan centres. However, given the niche nature of these markets, the film was positioned in such a way that its potential audience outside Aotearoa New Zealand was limited primarily to communities of spectators interested specifically in indigenous filmmaking and Shakespeare films. This prevented the development of broader audience demographics, of the kind that screenings at Sundance and Cannes and an international release would have enabled.

The film can be seen as contributing to various communities as I have suggested above but it also marks the work still to be done in developing and raising the profile of *te reo* Māori both inside and outside Aotearoa New Zealand. In particular, given that *The Maori Merchant* has received only limited international festival play and the much awaited multi-language-subtitled DVD has yet to be released, Selwyn's dream of taking "Maori language to the world" has yet to come to pass outside the relatively small arenas of academic and independent film markets. Furthermore, in the wake of Selwyn's death on 13 April 2007, the obituaries and news reports of his death cited *The Maori Merchant of Venice* as an exemplar of the significant contribution he has made to regenerating *te reo* and developing opportunities in the film industry for Māori, even as several commentators acknowledged that the film has not been as commercially successful as it might have been. For example, in a series of memorials to Selwyn in *Onfilm* magazine, Judith McCann asserts that "Don's own acclaimed directorial achievement [was] with the stunning Maori Merchant of Venice. Sadly, his Merchant stands as a magnificent inspiration to many, but remains under-exposed here and overseas as an audacious and culturally unique expression of Aotearoa New Zealand".[81] Similarly, speaking at Selwyn's funeral, the high-profile Māori entertainer Howard Morrison was reported by Denise Irvine as saying said that "the movie [for Morrison] was Selwyn's 'greatest triumph' and had not had the accolades it deserved"; for Morrison "[i]t should have had a premiere not only in Taumarunui, but also in London".[82] Although responses such as these acknowledge that the film's impact might have been greater, several commentators, such as the Acting Minister for the Arts, Judith Tizard, and the co-leader of the Māori Party, Pita Sharples, identified *The Maori Merchant* as Selwyn's "masterpiece".[83] In the reification of the film as Selwyn's masterpiece, it comes to stand not only as a legacy to the traumatic effects of colonisation and the possibility for development in the face of cultural dispossession but also as a legacy to Selwyn and his extensive career in developing *te reo* and Māori participation in theatre, film and television industries, even though this work is not yet over. In a sense the film operates as a synecdoche for Selwyn's career and works to memorialise his significant contribution to Māori cultural development.

SPEAKING MĀORI (SHAKESPEARE)

The Maori Merchant might thus be situated alongside productions of Shakespeare in Aotearoa New Zealand, such as those I mentioned at the outset of this chapter, which have drawn attention to the politics of their location, particularly with respect to race relations and the trauma of colonisation (61–63). Taken together, these productions make a mockery of New Zealand actor and director Ian Mune's dismissal of the concept of

"New Zealand Shakespeare" with "not yet" at a 2000 panel discussion on "Shakespeare in the Pacific".[84] In the scenes set in Belmont/Peremona and in the artist's studio, coupled with a large cast of actors performing in the once profoundly endangered *te reo* and the celebratory mode in which the film was produced and received, *The Maori Merchant* offers a striking example of just such a New Zealand Shakespeare. In considering *The Maori Merchant* I have suggested that this Māori Shakespeare film from Aotearoa New Zealand, while promoting an apparently seamless relation between Shakespeare and Māori, is also traced by the effects of colonisation, which it works to redress. *The Maori Merchant* might, then, be seen as Janus-like, always already reaching back and looking forward. As such, it stands as a monument to the trauma and ongoing effects of what has gone before. It is subject to and materially affects the conditions of the present through the creation of a large-scale Māori language and staffed project; in its potential life as an educational resource and voice of *te reo* on national and global markets it also offers a glimpse of the future-to-come. In keeping with Selwyn's goals to revitalise the Māori language, this might be a future in which *te reo* is secure and, perhaps, one in which Shakespeare is secondary, rather than positioned as pivotal, to that security. This chapter's concerns with Shakespeare, trauma and the potential for the creation of productive community relationships are developed further in the next chapter with respect to Philip Osment's appropriation of *The Tempest* for Gay Sweatshop theatre company.

3 Sexuality, Trauma and Community
The Tempest, Philip Osment's This Island's Mine and Gay Sweatshop

The dominant strands in critical and performance histories of *The Tempest* have been concerned primarily with the play's position as a "late" play and its relation to the end of Shakespeare's career, its relation to English colonial expansion in the sixteenth and seventeenth centuries, and its deployment in twentieth- and early twenty-first-century (post)colonial and settler cultures.[1] Strikingly, the play has been used as the basis for trenchant critique of the mechanisms of colonisation and its aftermath, exemplified by George Lamming's collection of essays, *The Pleasures of Exile* (1960), Aimé Césaire's play, *Une Tempête [A Tempest]* (1969) and Roberto Fernández Retamar's essay "Caliban: Notes toward a Discussion of Culture in Our Americas" (1971). *The Tempest*'s (anti-)colonial performance strand certainly lends itself to an analysis in relation to a consideration of relationships between Shakespeare, trauma and performance. In particular, performances which situate the play in relation to narratives of colonisation, especially with respect to the effects on indigenous populations, offer an apposite engagement with the trauma associated with colonisation, issues that I considered further in my discussion in Chapter 2 on *The Maori Merchant of Venice* with respect to Aotearoa New Zealand. However, in researching this book, I became interested in what might be described as unexpected turns to the traumatic, especially in relation to dominant performance and critical histories, such as that between *The Tempest* and colonisation. In this chapter I am concerned to offer an excavation of a *Tempest*-inflected narrative—Philip Osment's *This Island's Mine* (1988) for the London-based theatre company Gay Sweatshop—in relation to sexuality, especially with respect to the trauma of homophobia. I want to consider this performance in relation to traumatic oppressions on the basis of sexual preferences and practices, which manifest themselves in verbal, physical and legal violence, and the ways in which these oppressions variously intersect with those based on ethnic difference.

Although my focus in this chapter will be *This Island's Mine*, it is worth noting that the trauma of homophobia also traces other performances and adaptations of *The Tempest*, even if not to the same degree that narratives of colonisation have saturated the play's late twentieth- and early twenty-first-century performances. Dev Virahsawmy's play *Toufann* (1991), which deploys characters from *The Tempest, King Lear* and *Hamlet* and elements of Mauritian folklore, engages primarily with the circulations of power in relation to colonisation in Mauritius. While Virahsawmy's play suggests the possibility of relationships outside heteronormative dynastic couplings, exemplified in *The Tempest* by the marriage of Miranda and Ferdinand, these relationships are shadowed by homophobia. In this play, Aryel, who is characterised as "[a] robot, but almost a human" and Ferdjinan are identified as having a relationship with each other.[2] Although Aryel is "not programmed to express [. . . his] feelings" (33) he suggests to Ferdjinan that "you and I could work together [. . . .] we could make a life together [. . . .] I'm feeling that I like you very much" (32). Ferdjinan codes his delight in Aryel as one of brotherly love, whereas Aryel presents it in more sexual terms; when Ferdjinan "*throws his arms round Aryel's neck*" (33) Aryel responds by saying "[i]f you continue to touch me, I shall lose control" (33). Ferdjinan replies by saying "[t]hen lose control! [. . . .] Forget about convention! You and I can live happily together, wherever we are!" (33). Toward the end of the play Ferdjinan refuses to marry Kordelia (the play's Miranda character) in favour of a life with Aryel, whom he describes as his "genuine partner" (49). He claims that his father will "call it perverted, but to me this is what's normal" (49). Here the play challenges an association between "perversion" and relationships outside a heterosexual matrix. The relationship between Aryel and Ferdjinan not only refigures *The Tempest*'s sexual politics, but in proposing that Kordelia and Kalibann should marry and that Kalibann should become King (50–54), it also realigns *The Tempest*'s class and racial politics. In *Toufann*, Kalibann—the oppressed inhabitant of Prospero's island in Shakespeare's play—is to become King and permitted to marry Miranda, who actively chooses him as her husband. This action, though, is shadowed by racist insults as Prospero describes Kalibann as a "half-bred bat" (50), and objections from the clowns Kaspalto and Dammarro and the sailors (53) to the prospect of Kalibann's rule. Furthermore, the relationship between Ferdjinan and the apparently sexless robot Aryel is also subject to an association between homosexuality and impotence, crystallised in Ferdjinan's revelation of his impotence (acquired following a car accident) to his father (49). Here the homoeroticism of the interplay between Aryel and Ferdjinan and the promise of an alternative partnership structure seems to be offered, at least in part, as the only viable alternative to a failure to participate in reproductive heterosexuality.

Michael Walling, one of the play's co-translators from Mauritian Creole to English, suggests in an interview that the representation of homosexuality in the play is:

> probably a question of censorship or self-censorship. The attitude to homosexuality on the island [Mauritius] is deeply repressed. So this is

a way of doing it without doing it and I think if you look at it like that it becomes quite clever and in a strange way really rather radical. The problem is that we're not doing the play in that context and I am aware of that as a problem.[3]

Walling's comment succinctly identifies how particular forms of oppression, in this case in relation to sexuality, may determine the kinds of narratives that can be told in a culture. He also tries to recuperate a representation that might be understood as homophobic as the inverse, indicating how the efficacy and legibility of particular images are intimately tied to cultural context. That is, Walling reads a potentially homophobic representation as transgressive within the cultural context of Mauritius, even as it might signify as homophobic outside this context. In noting that the "problem" with this reading is that the production was performed outside Mauritius, his comments bespeak an anxiety about the potentially homophobic nature of the representations. In her interview with Michael Walling, Jane Wilkinson notes that the relationship between Aryel and Ferdjinan was enacted in more obviously physical terms in Walling's production of the play with his co-translator Nisha Walling at the Africa Centre in London in 1999.[4] This physicalisation worked to highlight a gap between the textual narrative, which stands as witness to the oppression of homosexuality in Mauritius (homosexuality is illegal), and the (comparatively) more permissive culture of the play's production in London.

Predating Virahsawmy and Osment's plays by some 10 years, Derek Jarman's 1979 film *The Tempest*, which he started developing in 1974, can be located as part of his long-term project to critique what he describes as "heterosoc" or the hegemony of heterosexual culture and its attendant mechanisms of repression, especially in relation to prohibitions on same-sex desire and practices.[5] As Niall Richardson notes, "[r]epresenting same-sex passion in an historical setting is not simply the political exercise of showing that there were famous 'queers' in the cultural/historical landscape. Instead, Jarman's films offer the altogether more queer potential of exposing the institionalized repression of dissident sexual desire throughout history".[6] Notable for their homoeroticism, painterly aesthetic, innovative use of video and film technologies and interest in the Renaissance, Jarman's films work to queer the past and present, without producing what he refers to in a notebook for *The Angelic Conversation* (1985) as "the so called gay cinema of realism".[7] In *The Tempest*, Jarman manipulates the cinematic gaze so that men become, on occasions, both the subjects and objects of the gaze; in contrast to the dominant heteroerotic scopic mode of mainstream cinema, this works to create homoerotic relations of looking, such as the sequence where Ferdinand stumbles, naked from the surf, watched by Ariel from the sand dunes. Furthermore, Jarman designs and directs the wedding celebration to include a spectacular display of dancing sailors punctuated by the appearance of Elizabeth Welch who gives a performance of "Stormy

Weather", clad in gold with cornstalks in her hair as a glittering twenties' chanteuse. Here the film deploys codes of gay cultures (the sailors allude to a history of associations between homosexuality and sailors, indentified in music, visual arts, poetry and theatre, which includes, for example, The Village People, Tom of Finland, and writing by Federico Garcìa Lorca and Jean Genet, among others) and camp (or what Susan Sontag in her seminal 1964 essay "Notes on 'Camp'" describes as a "love of the unnatural: of artifice and exaggeration"), which though not reducible to one another have frequently been conflated in both popular entertainments and in criticism.[8] Critics such as Moe Meyer have claimed that "Camp, as specifically queer parody, becomes [. . .] the only process by which the queer is able to enter representation and to produce social visibility".[9] In contrast, Sontag's argument, which poses a "peculiar relation" between "camp taste" and homosexuality without designating them as self-same, usefully points to how codes of camp and gay might operate in relation to each other without entailing a necessary equivalence.[10] The wedding celebration in the film works similarly, deploying, but not conflating, codes of gay and camp, where one admits the possibility of the other, in order to create a kind of jubilant queer excess which, in the mass of the sailors, works also to create a community based on relationships outside the heteroerotic bonds proposed by the dynastic marriage of Miranda and Ferdinand.

The slippage in my discussion thus far between gay, homosexual, camp, queer, hetero- and homoerotic also identifies tensions concerning relationships between acts, identities and terminology in academic and popular discourses. These are tensions that recur in my discussion here as I negotiate the language used in the documents and by the individuals I consider in relation to acts, identities, cultures and community/ies. In particular, proponents of lesbian and gay rights in the 1970s and 1980s were invested in producing lesbian and gay visibility, often in the service of specific political and social goals, especially in relation to civil rights. But, in Michael Warner's words,

> [t]hough it has had importance in organizational efforts (where in circular fashion it receives concretization), the notion of a community has remained problematic if only because nearly every lesbian or gay remembers being such before entering a collectively identified space, because much of lesbian and gay history has to do with noncommunity, and because dispersal rather than localization continues to be definitive of queer self-understanding.[11]

For Warner, the notion of "community" is inadequate to describe the multiplicity of queer experiences and histories, even as it has enabled organisational efforts. To deploy "community" in the service of particular identities and political goals, even as this necessarily entails elisions and conflations can, though, be seen in Judith Butler's terms as "laying claim" to particular identities. For Butler, the act of laying claim works to "refute homophobic deployments of the terms in law, public policy, on the street, in 'private' life."[12] She argues "that the temporary totalization performed by identity categories is a necessary error" in that a category is "necessary as a term of affiliation, but it will not fully describe those it purports to represent. As a result, it will be necessary to affirm the contingency of the term", as I have done here.[13] In working through these terminological problems, I am indebted to queer reading practices, such as Butler's. These are practices that consider how sexualities might be understood as performative, constituted through citation and repetition, which entails the possibility of subjection, difference and intervention, and that bear the force of historical and cultural specificity. Here I have sought to respect the terminological choices of the individuals and groups I consider while calling into question the kinds of assumptions and tensions that inhere within these terms.

In the terms of the argument of this book, Jarman's *Tempest* can be seen as a response to the trauma of homophobia, offering a counter-narrative to histories of oppression, through its manipulation of the cinematic gaze and its deployment of codes of gay and camp. The production of homoerotic counter-narratives is a pattern that is repeated in Jarman's other "Renaissance" films. *The Angelic Conversation* sets a selection of Shakespeare's sonnets read by Judi Dench—primarily those addressed to the young man—to a series of grainy, textured images, produced by shooting on Super 8 film, which was then transferred successively from lowband video to high-band video to 35mm film. The images consist mostly of two young men swimming, wrestling, embracing, kissing, sleeping and walking.[14] By "reclaiming" what Jarman describes in his notebook for *The Angelic Conversation* as "small gestures", the film works to locate homoeroticism in historical and literary records as well as in the present of the film's production.[15] In particular, as the film was produced and released during the initial peak of the HIV/AIDS crisis in the United Kingdom, a period which brought anxieties about (male) same-sex sexual practices and identities into sharp relief, its images of homoeroticism offer—and continue to offer—a set of celebratory counter-images to prevailing discourses which associated homoerotic desire with disease and death. It is, however, in *Edward II* (1991) that Jarman addresses the violence of homophobia most trenchantly.[16] Indeed, Jarman prefaces his film script *Queer Edward II* with the assertion that:

> It is difficult enough to be queer, but to be a queer in the cinema is almost impossible. Heterosexuals have fucked up the screen so completely that there's hardly room for us to kiss there. Marlowe outs the past—why don't we out the present? That's really the only message this play has. Fuck poetry [. . .]

> *This book is dedicated to:*
> *the repeal of all anti-gay laws, particularly*
> *Section 28.*[17]

The film script also includes a series of slogans which pithily identify homophobia and the operations of heterosoc and offer pro-queer alternatives, such as "Land of hate and bigotry/ lesbian and gay rights *now*", "You Say Don't Fuck We Say FUCK YOU", "*its* [sic] *cool to be queer*", "never mind, we can't all be queer" and "HETEROPHOBIA *liberates*, HOMO-SEXISM *empowers*".[18] Just as the film script turns repeatedly to the trauma of homophobia and offers a response to its operation, so too does the film. In particular, it includes scenes that depict members of the self-described UK queer rights' group OutRage! who are rallied by Edward. The group carry placards protesting for gay rights and these images recall actions carried out by this group since its formation in May 1990, such as those in response to Section 28, to which I will return below.[19] The film also works to create alternative relationships to the structures of heterosoc by foregrounding the eroticism of Edward's relationship with Gaveston but also in its depiction of Edward's death as double vision, where the jailor/murderer Lightborn can also be read as Edward's lover. Finally, the silent tableau of OutRage! protesters over which the camera tracks at the end of the film stands as witness both to a history of homophobia and also to the possibilities for collective action in response to this history, especially with respect to a multitude of queer desires.

Tellingly, both *Edward II* and *This Island's Mine*, with their examination of anxieties surrounding sexuality, were produced some 10 years later than the jubilant excesses of the wedding scene in Jarman's *The Tempest* and a decade into Margaret Thatcher's Conservative Government which was first elected in 1979, returned for a second term in 1983 and for the final of three terms in 1987; John Major, who replaced Thatcher as leader of the Conservative Party from 1990, won a fourth term from 1992 until the landslide election of Tony Blair's Labour Government in 1997. The 1960s and 1970s saw some improvements in terms of civil liberties for those who engage in same-sex sexual practices, embodied in the decriminalisation of sexual acts between two consenting male adults in the 1967 Sexual Offences Act in the (delayed) wake of the recommendation of the 1957 Wolfenden Report, which recommended "[t]hat homosexual behaviour between consenting adults in private be no longer a criminal offence."[20] In contrast to the freedoms won by the revision to the law, in 1988 Thatcher's Government introduced Section 28, which offered a new legal instantiation of state-sponsored prejudice against homosexuality (and homosexuals). This legislation sought to limit the "promotion" of homosexuality by local authorities, and, as I will explore below, also made connections between homosexuality and disease. The 1980s also saw the emergence of the human immunodeficiency virus (HIV). Despite the fact that the virus does not discriminate on the basis of sexual identity, it was initially medicalised in early 1982 in such a way that gay men were identified as its subjects in the acronym, Gay Related Immune Deficiency Syndrome (GRIDS). As

Jonathan Dollimore trenchantly argues, in "homophobic representations of AIDS, homosexuality and death become inseparable; homoerotic desire is construed as death-driven, death-desiring and death-dealing".[21]

The film treatment for *28*, an unrealised project by Jarman and Keith Collins, offers a vision of the effects of prohibitive legislation such as Section 28 and homophobia in response to HIV/AIDS. The script centres on the character of a young actor who confuses himself with Edward II. The treatment sketches a desolate vision of Britain in the wake of HIV/AIDS and Section 28, described as "the first of many similar acts of legislation restricting human rights":

> The death penalty has been re-introduced. Homosexuality has been recriminalised with wide ranging penalties, the police have unlimited power of search and detention.
> The homophobia generated by the AIDS crisis has reached a new dimension, everyone caries identity cards (with HIV status), mass quarantining has been introduced, and holiday camps like Butlins have been requisitioned as detention centres.[22]

The Jarman archive thus encodes an instance of what I would describe as a proleptic traumatic response. As Shlomith Rimmon-Kenan notes, following Gérard Genette, in narratological theory a prolepsis "is a narration of a story-event at a point before later events have been told. The narration, as it were, takes an excursion into the future of the story".[23] This narratological device can be adapted for thinking about the "story time" of a performance text in relation to the "writing time" of a text. Thus the film script of *28* offers a traumatic flash forward in relation to the time of its writing, where trauma in the present is the ground upon which that which has not yet happened is imagined as having happened, articulated in the traumatic future-time envisaged by *28*. Furthermore, the opening "landscape" section finishes with the line "19XX is going to be a good year". The refusal to provide a date for the film's setting suggests that the future imagined by the treatment might become concrete with respect to any number of late twentieth-century possibilities. Osment's play, as I will explore below, has a different relationship to the temporality of Section 28: first drafted before the legislation came into effect, the passing of the Section into law, which occurred in May just after the play's first run from February to April, retrospectively informs an understanding of the "story time" and acts on the present-time of the production. In the remainder of this chapter I will focus on *This Island's Mine* to consider how this play and its performance, especially with respect to its engagement with *The Tempest*, and its material traces encode trauma produced in response to systemic oppression on the basis of lived and imagined sexual identifications and practices. In particular, I will consider the production's engagement with racist and homophobic discourses, the later of which bears witness to the HIV/AIDS crisis and the institution of Section 28. As with other case studies explored in this book, I also want to consider how trauma, perhaps perversely, provides the ground for the creation and affirmation of communities (and the ways in which these communities can, in turn, produce oppressions and exclusions of their own), which I explore here in relation to understandings of "gay community" in late twentieth-century Britain.

GAY SWEATSHOP

Gay Sweatshop emerged in the mid-1970s in the context of gay rights' movements, such as the Campaign for Homosexual Equality, the Gay Liberation Front and Gay Left, a gay socialist collective, and other consciousness-raising theatre groups such as the Women's Theatre Group (later Sphinx Theatre Company), Monstrous Regiment and Black Theatre Co-operative (later Nitro). The company produced a range of work, primarily focussed on plays but which also included readings, workshops, discussion groups, pantomimes, cabarets and performance clubs. A statement of intent from the mid-1970s held in the company's constitution and policy documents notes that it aimed "to discover and present all kinds of plays and entertainments which have gay themes, which are politically motivated, which explore the roots of gay oppression and which are designed to work some change in their audiences".[24] Here the company identifies its concerns with representation and effecting social change. In his history of Gay Sweatshop, Osment returns to and develops these points, noting that the plays were concerned with putting the "experiences of lesbians and gay men centre-stage" and the company aimed to provide "a context for gay people to work together and to allow their sexuality to inform their work in a positive way".[25] Osment's comment flags how theatre is conceived here (as it tends to be in other community-based theatre contexts) as offering a focus for creating a community (gay people can work together in an environment where same-sex sexual identifications are a positive contribution to the work of the company) and one that provides space (physical and cultural) for representing gay and lesbian experiences, exemplifying discourses on community which, as Miranda Joseph notes, tend to represent it as an "unequivocal good".[26] As I will explore below, the work of Gay Sweatshop certainly operated to produce a positive and productive sense of community and to create opportunities for representation both of itself and others; but the rhetoric and operation of community are also punctured by tensions, especially in relation to ethnicity. As Joseph notes, "[t]o invoke community is immediately to raise questions of belonging and of power", questions that I will consider here through an analysis first of the text and performance and then of the performance archive.[27]

TRAUMA, TEXT AND PERFORMANCE

This Island's Mine, which takes its title from Caliban's much-quoted resisting claim, was written on an Arts Council of Great Britain Bursary in 1986 for Gay Sweatshop. It was given its first public performance as a rehearsed reading as part of the Gay Sweatshop Times Twelve festival on 13 March 1987 and received its first full production at the Drill Hall Arts Centre in London on 24 February 1988. Subsequently the play was taken on tour in England in March and April 1988 and in Scotland in June 1988, variously supported by the Arts Council of Great Britain, Greater London Arts, North West, Southern Arts, the Scottish Arts Council and the Section 28 Arts Lobby. The play, which has been published in *Gay Sweatshop: Four Plays and a Company* and anthologised in Daniel Fischlin and Mark Fortier's *Adaptations of Shakespeare,* is for seven actors. Collectively, they perform 25 characters whose lives overlap in a series of Dickensian coincidences.[28] The characters include Luke, a gay teenager; Martin, Luke's gay uncle; Martin's wife Marianne, her lover Debbie and Debbie's child Dave; Selwyn, a gay black actor who plays Caliban; Mark, his white lover who is sacked from his job as a chef because of fears about HIV/AIDS (Osment based this part of the narrative on a news report of a similar incident in Barnstaple) and who becomes Luke's first lover; Miss Rosenblum, an elderly Jewish refugee and her wartime white American lover, Stephen, who is also Marianne's father and is implicated in the sale of contaminated blood to Third World countries. Threaded into the narrative are several rehearsal scenes for a production of *The Tempest*. Osment notes that he "didn't set off with the idea of it [*The Tempest*] being a central image for the play"; instead he

> began work on the play in 1985 at the height of the AIDS hysteria and it was unavoidable that this should inform the mood of the play. Indeed it was responsible for the theme of exile. I was beginning to feel that I no longer belonged in a Britain increasingly hostile to everything I believed in.[29]

While Osment positions *The Tempest* as secondary in relation to his concerns with exile, especially in relation to HIV/AIDS and contemporary British culture, the inclusion of traces of *The Tempest* focuses a series of traumatic responses. Here I am interested in examining the fragments of *The Tempest*, in conjunction with the body doubling, mode of performance and the politics of casting, with respect to the trauma of racism and homophobia, and also to the politics of community formation.

Following the opening six scenes, where the bulk of the play's characters are introduced, the action shifts, unannounced, to what transpires as a rehearsal for 1.2 of *The Tempest*, where one of the play's central characters,

Selwyn, a young, gay, black man, performs as Caliban. As Caliban/Selwyn speaks "There's wood enough within", the Director interrupts with:

> "No, no, no, no, no."
> In a draughty hall in Belsize Park
> Rehearsals are not going well:
> "Selwyn, darling,
> Caliban is a primitive,
> He tried to rape Miranda,
> So don't try and give us the noble savage,
> It just won't work,
> It's an oversimplification
> It will destroy the balance of the play.
> Prospero is the hero,
> Not Caliban."

The Director goes on:

> "He's raw physicality and sex.
> We'll dress you up in something skimpy
> Give the punters a treat."
> Under his breath:
> "God why have I got the only black actor
> Who doesn't know how to use his body?" (scene 7)

This rehearsal scene models a series of traumatic turns with respect to sexuality and ethnicity. On one level, the Director works to locate Caliban (and by association, Selwyn) as a stereotype of a black, sexually attractive and/or aggressive man. Here, the Director is depicted as a consumer of Western stereotypes concerning black men and sexuality, such as those articulated by Frantz Fanon in *Black Skin, White Masks* (1967) and Kobena Mercer in *Welcome to the Jungle* (1994), for example. In the context of a discussion of Michel Cournot's *Martinique* (1948), Fanon talks of how the black male body is metonymically reduced to the penis: "one is no longer aware of the Negro but only of a penis; the Negro is eclipsed. He is turned into a penis. He *is* a penis".[30] In the Director's foregrounding of Caliban's status as a rapist, his designation of him as "raw physicality and sex", and his desire to dress Selwyn in "something skimpy" so as to "[g]ive the punters a treat", he situates Caliban/Selwyn as a simultaneously attractive and repulsive figure of desire available for commercial consumption. The Director's "skimpy" costuming decision, coupled with his language—which includes "darling" and "punters", which resonates with stereotypical (and sometimes homophobic) images of gay men in theatrical contexts—admits a further layer of potential meaning.[31] That is, these images suggest that Selwyn might also be consumed visually as gay black exotica, hinting at the kinds of images that circulate in novels such as Alan Hollinghurst's *The Swimming Pool Library* (1988) and in Robert Mapplethorpe's photographs, notwithstanding the way in which these images might also be cited as affirmative rather than exploitative. Furthermore, the Director's question, "why have I got the only black actor who doesn't know how to use his body?" also reiterates stereotypes about blackness, physicality and desire. As Mercer argues, black men

> are implicated into the same landscape of stereotypes which is dominated and organized around the needs, demands and desires of white males. Blacks "fit" into this terrain by being confined to a narrow repertoire of "types"—the supersexual stud and the sexual "savage" on the one hand, or the delicate, fragile and exotic "oriental" on the other.[32]

In *Welcome to the Jungle*—a series of 10 essays, most of which were written between 1985 and 1990 in London, a period broadly synchronous with the production of *This Island's Mine*—Mercer works to interrogate stereotypes such as these and the politics of (self-)representation through a consideration of music, dancing, filmmaking, (hair)style, photography and politics.

As well as returning to the trauma of racism and the way this is tied to sexual objectification and oppression, *This Island's Mine* also works to critique the operation of racism, partially through the creation of counter-narratives. Following Selwyn's performance of Caliban's "You taught me language" speech (1.2.366–68), the Director asks him where his West Indian accent is, saying "I thought we agreed you were going to do it with a strong accent!" In this rehearsal sequence, Selwyn's refusal to use the accent required by the director, coupled with his "failure" to use his body in the prescribed way, marks an opposition to the Director's objectification of blackness and attendant racism. This is reinforced by Trevor Ferguson's performance of Selwyn, the grainy record of which survives in the Gay Sweatshop Archive, where he looks at the Director and then turns away from him.[33] This refusal also occurs in relation to Caliban's identification of the potential of language for cursing his master, even as he operates within this language. As Homi K. Bhabha notes, colonial efforts to produce docile mimetic subjects fail to be totalising as the difference admitted into the operation of mimicry also admits the potential for parody, which slips into mockery.[34] Selwyn's refusal to use language in the way he has been instructed thus creates an opening in the narrative for an opposition to the Director's discourse of racial commodification.

As the play draws to a close, Selwyn delivers Caliban's "This island's mine" speech (scene 33). In the recording of the performance Ferguson was positioned centre stage, arms by his side, as he addressed the audience directly, defiantly. If one strand of contemporary British racism operates, as Paul Gilroy suggests, by asserting "not that blacks are inferior but that we are different, so different that our distinctive mode of being is at odds with residence in this country" such that blackness and Britishness are rendered as "mutually exclusive social and cultural categories", Selwyn's speech works to make a claim for being at home in Britain not only as a black British man but also as a gay black British man.[35] As with many of *The Tempest*'s postcolonial counterparts, Caliban is used to make a claim for ownership and, by association, citizenship, which here crosses ethnic, national and sexual territories. In this vein Kate Chedgzoy suggests that *This Island's Mine*

> appropriates Shakespeare to insist that the history and culture of this island, which Caliban shares with the play's audience as much as with its other characters, are not merely monolithic and exclusive, but are also composed of, and belong to, the diverse voices of the exiled, marginal, dispossessed and oppositional individuals who populate it.[36]

This sense of diversity and ownership over these territories is not won unequivocally as the play suggests that the constituent parts of Selwyn's identity are fractured. Although his first lover, a gay black dance teacher, casts this fracturing in positive and enabling terms, encouraging Selwyn to "[b]reak the mould" (scene 17), by the end of the play, Selwyn announces his intention to return to his family in Hackney (scene 29), a family which feels he has been living "in another country" (scene 14). This works to mark his alienation from both white gay and black British cultures, which in the terms of the text are, for the most part, rendered as mutually exclusive. As Mary F. Brewer observes "[j]ust as his sexual 'otherness' means that Selwyn cannot fit comfortably in a Black social location, in the same way his racial 'otherness' means that he cannot feel at home in White society, either the straight mainstream or a White-dominated gay subculture".[37] Here Selwyn's inclusion in various subcultural communities is purchased through his exclusion from others, identifying tensions that inhere within community formation, to which I will return below. The performance, though, works to smooth over these tensions in its closing stages. The recording shows how Selwyn's former lover Mark embraces him as Luke makes his final speech in which he hopefully imagines his future as a young, gay man. The gesture of the embrace works to associate these characters harmoniously with one another, working to mitigate the tensions that have punctuated the narrative, especially with respect to ethnicity. As Luke's speech reaches its conclusion, Mark releases Selwyn from the embrace and all the characters stand separated from one another, gazing at the audience, as if making a silent demand on the spectators to acknowledge the collective diversity of the group and their various claims for ownership and citizenship.

The play's style of performance, with an emphasis on storytelling and the inclusion of moments, such as Luke's speech, which involves actors narrating their actions, was influenced by Osment's work with Shared Experience, a UK-based theatre company formed in 1975 that works to combine physical and text-based performances.[38] The play's mode of performance, where the characters partly speak their narrative in the third person and partly act it out in dialogue with other characters, offers, like the narrative, a return to the traumatic spectre of racism but this return also embeds a critique of racism. For example, the Director's racist aside which is narrated with the direction, "under his breath", works to denaturalise the racist content even as it reiterates it, instead positing it as an object of critique. The Director's language, which works to objectify Selwyn/Caliban's body in turn invites the spectator to consume the actor Trevor Ferguson's body in similar terms: in short, to imagine Ferguson in something skimpy. In the staging of the play, Ferguson was not presented in such a costume, but dressed instead in his "Selwyn" costume of skivvy, or turtleneck, and trousers (Figure 3.1). Due to the costuming decisions in *This Island's Mine*, the objectification of Ferguson's body was, to some extent, checked, making an opening in the performance for a consideration of the visual consumption processes at work on the stage and in culture more generally. The deployment of *The Tempest* and the Director's vision for the performance of Caliban thus folds the trauma of racist discourse, and how this intersects with sexuality, into the narrative of *This Island's Mine*, whilst simultaneously creating the potential

Figure 3.1 Trevor Ferguson (left) as Selwyn and Richard Sandells (right) as Mark in Philip Osment's 1988 production *This Island's Mine* for Gay Sweatshop Theatre. Photograph © Sunil Gupta, reproduced with his permission.

for a critique of this discourse. The traumatic folds of *The Tempest* are further multiplied, sometimes violently, through a consideration of the narrative, actor doubling, and casting practices, especially with respect to Selwyn.

The play thus tracks its Caliban figure, Selwyn, through a series of oppressions in relation to ethnicity, sexuality and their intersection. Barely a third of the way into the play, Selwyn is victimised on the street by three policemen, who stop him on suspicion of burglary. One taunts him with "He's a poof./ You a black pansy then?" and another adds "I thought you only got pink ones" (scene 13). The policemen threaten Selwyn with rape, inverting the earlier association between Selwyn/Caliban and rape such that he becomes victim rather than perpetrator; and they tell him to watch his lip "Unless you want a truncheon up your arse", before they assault him (scene 13). The violence of Prospero's threat to Caliban that he will "rack thee with old cramps,/ Fill all thy bones with aches" (1.2.372–73), which is repeated in scene 26, is here pre-empted as a violent physical assault.[39] The violence meted out by the policemen also manifests from within Selwyn's family, as his brother threatens to beat him up because he is gay (scene 17). Selwyn's relationship with his boyfriend Mark is implicated in a further layer of oppression as the actor who played Mark also played the Director, as well as doubling as one of the policemen. Osment says that he did not consciously choose the double of Mark and the Director in order to produce a particular effect but concedes that "it had a sort of potency".[40] This is a potency that I would suggest is caught between trauma and pleasure, as Mark's erotic interactions with Selwyn, where he figures sex as "The rush of excitement at the breaking of taboos/ Long-held by his race" (scene 14), is implicated within a dynamic of colonial specularisation of blackness reinforced by the Director's objectification of Selwyn. In performance, these dynamics of desire are replayed, with a difference, in a series of attractions between Martin and black men, all played by Ferguson: the man Martin cruises at the airport while waiting for Marianne is played by Ferguson, as is the man who fails to return Martin's smiles at the disco, and Martin also shares a lingering look with Selwyn when he visits to say thank you for looking after him following the assault. In each case the black character is performed by Ferguson in such a way that he is shown to have some measure of agency in the field of desire, either through reciprocating the gaze of the white other or choosing to ignore it, as is the case in the club sequence. In contrast to these flashes of agency, actor doubling is also used to suggest an additional traumatic experience on the basis of sexuality: the actor who played Selwyn/Caliban also played Dave, the 10-year-old son of Debbie, who is beaten up and called a "nancy boy" (scene 15) by his schoolmates because he lives with his mother and her girlfriend.

As the narrative tracks Selwyn/Caliban/Dave through a series of oppressions (and resistances), the play's performance mode again resists presenting this as mimetic traumatic playback. My interest is not in proposing that acts of alienation have a necessary social political and/or affective force on spectators, or that the realistic staging of violence is incapable of producing similar effects. Rather my concern with the alienation of verbal and physical violence is its *potential* to identify violent actions as objects of critique. This refusal of mimetic violence is most apparent in the assault on Selwyn, which as the video record of the performance shows, was not physically enacted. Rather "Punch", "Kick" and "They leave him in a heap" are verbalised by the performers (scene 13); on the utterance of "Punch", Ferguson clutches his face and on "Kick" he doubles over, offering a physical response to the verbal imperatives. He does not collapse into a "heap" until Luke and Miss Rosenblum discover him; they then take care of Selwyn following the assault. This sequence thus cites traumatic events ("real" gay bashings) but reworks them belatedly in modified form. The insertion of elements of narration and the decision not to enact the violence but rather to physicalise its effects refuses a cycle of mimetic violent repetition while identifying its operation and aftermath. When Luke and Miss Rosenblum—marginalised by their homosexuality and Jewishness, respectively—discover Selwyn they see in his injuries police brutality during the miners' strike and the disappearance of Jewish intellectuals. Here the narrative also works to attach homophobic violence to events perpetrated in other times and places, thus widening the traumatic frame. For Susan Bennett, the violated body becomes here a site of memory. She suggests that "in the pain of the remembered past, the continuity of experience of violence offers some pleasure at least in its recognition".[41] Although Bennett's guarded assertion of "pleasure" seems almost perverse given the various histories of violence and oppression that the play tracks, her identification of the recognition of violence, coded in terms of corporeal visibility, locates how the play works to make such histories visible, and in visibility there lies the potential for collective action, social change and resistance to oppression.

In the connections between Miss Rosenblum, Luke and Selwyn, the presentation of alternative family and community structures, the space of the gay disco and the gay pride march, the play depicts a series of communities. Indeed, Osment writes that "the play was to explore the idea of families and how we create alternative families for ourselves based not on blood ties but on a community of interest and ideas—pretended families if you like", directly alluding to the language of Section 28 and its opposition to the "promotion" of the "acceptability of homosexuality as a pretended family relationship", to which I will return below (95–96).[42] His suggestion that the play offers a series of "pretended families" thus identifies how the play, belatedly (given the temporal gap between Osment's introduction to *Gay Sweatshop* and his writing of the play), is offered as a challenge to the terms of Section 28. The play thus works to create alternative communities in response to traumatic histories and events. In so doing it also registers tensions in and between these communities or alternative families, as I suggested earlier in relation to Selwyn and his relationships with his family and his boyfriend Mark.

The tensions that surround the creation of gay communities in the narrative of the play recur in modified form in relation to the creative concerns of Gay Sweatshop and the politics of characterisation and casting. Osment notes that "the play came out of my involvement with Gay Sweatshop [. . . .] it's very much about what was current [. . .] the attempt to reach out to other communities [. . . .] get black people in the company with limited success".[43] He also notes that the company was interested in engaging "with debates around ethnicity" as this "was very much what all the funding bodies were wanting you to do [. . .] and we wanted to take it on".[44] Here Osment situates Gay Sweatshop in a programme of widening participation, which is driven both inside the community and in response to external forces. Nevertheless, Osment notes that the company had "limited success" in engaging black communities. This point is reiterated by Lois Weaver, joint artistic director, with James Neale-Kennerley, of Gay Sweatshop from 1992 until the Company closed in 1997, in her comments that the company tended "not to attract people of colour" which she attributes to Gay Sweatshop not "doing work that people of colour wanted to do", particularly with respect to form and the issues it engaged with.[45] This situation is also addressed in minutes of the company's meetings from 1985 and 1987, commensurate with the early development of *This Island's Mine*; the minutes record the relative absence of black performers and writers in Gay Sweatshop and suggest that more attention should be given to diversifying performance forms, such as including poetry, in order to attract black performers.[46] The efforts to involve black performers echo earlier work by the company in the mid- to late 1970s to interest women, regardless of ethnicity, to participate; this resulted in women joining the company in 1976 and the formation of a men's company and a women's company in 1977.[47]

Whereas the company had a measure of success in attracting primarily white women, in the mid-1980s it concentrated on attracting black women, especially through feminist networks, such as those that coalesced around the magazine *Spare Rib*; by contrast black men attract little attention in the records of these meetings. Osment talks further of the difficulty of finding "out" gay black actors, such as someone who was "right for the part" of Selwyn, observing that "it was easier to find [black] women who were out and willing" to be involved and that it was "less easy to find men".[48] The relative lack of involvement of black people in Gay Sweatshop productions is also mirrored by audience composition, insofar as this is possible to establish. An audience survey conducted by the company in 1989 reveals that 1% of the 329 people surveyed identified as black ("Afro/Caribbean", "African" or "Other" in the terms of the survey), 88% identified as "White European" and of the 11% who identified as "Other" 31% identified themselves as white.[49] It is not possible to extrapolate from these statistics to all Gay Sweatshop productions, or even to ascertain the veracity of these statistics in relation to the production in question. However, the survey results suggest that the company tended to attract a primarily white spectatorship. These comments and statistics identify how communities form in relation to exclusions from both within and outside themselves. The creation and performance of *This Island's Mine* thus bears witness to these social pressures surrounding ethnicity: these pressures are explored in the narrative and performance style, but also recur in the management discussions recorded in the company's archive. An examination of the production's archive in the next section will enable further consideration of the traumatic force of *This Island's Mine* and its relation to community formation and the tensions that inhere within these formations.

SECTION 28

As I noted earlier, the performance of *This Island's Mine* took place in the context of the passing into law of Section 28 of the Local Government Act. Section 28 (variously known as Clause 27, 28, and 29) was first put forward in 1986 as a Private Members Bill in the House of Lords, sponsored by John Giffard, Earl of Halsbury, with the intention "to restrain local authorities from promoting homosexuality".[50] The Bill was not passed, but following the 1987 general election, which returned Thatcher's Conservative Government to power for a third term, partly on the promise of promoting "family values", a new Bill was introduced by MP David Wilshire, based on the Halsbury format.[51] This Bill was passed into law as Section 28 of the Local Government Act, and came into force on 24 May 1988; it was subsequently repealed on 21 June 2000 in Scotland and on 18 November 2003 in the rest of the United Kingdom. Section 28 states that:

(1) A local authority shall not–
    (a)   intentionally promote homosexuality or publish material with the intention of promoting homosexuality;
    (b)   promote the teaching in any maintained [government funded] school of the acceptability of homosexuality as a pretended family relationship.
(2) Nothing in subsection (1) above shall be taken to prohibit the doing of anything for the purpose of treating or preventing the spread of disease.
(3) In any proceedings in connection with the application of this section a court shall draw such inferences as to the intention of the local authority as may reasonably be drawn from the evidence before it.[52]

As several commentators have noted, the language of Section 28 is vague, with the words "promote", "pretended", "homosexuality" and "intentionally" open to a variety of interpretations.[53] That said, in subsection (3) it is as if the constitution of the Section anticipates objections as to its lack of precision and the responsibility of determining "intention" is passed to the court. The legal power of Section 28 was, however, relatively limited, leading Philip Thomas and Ruth Costigan to assert that in "*strict legal terms*, Section 28 is of little effect" and this is measured by the lack of prosecutions.[54] Furthermore, Jackie Stacey notes that "one of the chief targets of the section, education, was covered by the Education Bill, rather than the Local Government Bill, thus rendering the section legally redundant".[55] Despite its lack of legal effectiveness, Section 28 was (and its effects linger still) a powerful piece of legislation for three main reasons. First, even though the Earl of Caithness asserted during debate in the House of Lords that the Section "in no way imposes some form of discrimination against homosexuals", it offered a legal basis for homophobia in local authority contexts.[56] Second, although the legislation had limited legal force, it did have the power to produce self-censorship. In this way it had the potential to minimise or censor gay and lesbian visibility as constituted by various groups, particularly in the arts where "fringe" theatre groups are often dependent on local authority funding.[57] Third, the Section, in its assertion that "nothing in subsection (1) above shall be taken to prohibit the doing of anything for the purpose of treating or preventing the spread of disease" links homosexuality with the spread of disease and works to reinforce negative perceptions of homosexuality, especially in relation to gay men, compounded by the HIV/AIDS crisis.

In contrast to the restrictions of Section 28, civil liberties related to sexual orientation (defined legally in the 2006 Equality Act as "orientation towards—(a) persons of the same sex as him or her, (b) persons of the opposite sex, or (c) both") have improved for those of us living in the United Kingdom with same-sex "orientations", in particular, since the turn of the millennium.[58] This is in part due to the work of direct action groups such as OutRage! and the lobby group, Stonewall, which was formed in 1989 by individuals who were active in protests against Section 28. In particular, the age of consent for hetero- and homo- sexual acts was equalised to 16 in the 2000 Sexual Offences (Amendment) Act; Section 28 was repealed in 2003; the Civil Partnership Act 2004, offers legal protections to same-sex couples akin to those afforded by marriage (but it is only available to same-sex couples, ensuring that discrimination remains embedded in the legal system); the Employment Equality (Sexual Orientation) Regulations, 2003 offers work-place protections in relation to discrimination and harassment on the grounds of sexual orientation; and the Equality Act 2006 makes it illegal to discriminate with respect to the supply of goods, facilities and services on the grounds of sexual orientation.[59] These legal decisions thus operate as an index of how homophobia is variously enshrined and opposed in law; the freedoms won since the turn of the millennium bring into sharp relief the oppressions operating at the time of Section 28 to which *This Island's Mine* was subject.

ARCHIVES OF TRAUMA: DOCUMENTING COMMUNITY

A press release for the revival in June 1988 notes that *This Island's Mine* was "[w]ritten before the notorious Section 28 was even a Clause" and in an interview Osment notes that "it wasn't written as a response to Section 28 at all".[60] The kinds of anxieties identified by the Section, especially surrounding relationships between sexuality and disease and how families might be constituted, recur in the narrative as I have suggested above, and, as I will now explore, in the production history and reception. Indeed Osment remarks in the programmes for both the first production and the revival that the Section 28 debates gave "the play a topicality which I had not foreseen at that time".[61] This topicality can be considered in terms of the temporal relations between the institution of Section 28, the "story time" of Osment's script and the elements that make up the play's "production time" (especially "writing time" and "performance time") and their operation in relation to trauma. In so doing it is useful to return to the narratological devices of prolepsis, which I considered earlier in relation to Jarman's treatment for *28*, and analepsis. As Rimmon-Kenan notes, analepsis is "a narration of a story-event at a point in the text after later events have been told. The narration returns, as it were, to a past point in the story".[62] Analepsis thus both identifies a lacuna in the narrative (that which was not previously known to the reader/spectator) and works to fill it (with the "out-of-time" narration). I suggested in the introduction that trauma operates belatedly where the event is not able to be known or accounted for at the time of its occurrence. Trauma might, then, be thought of as inherently analeptic, repeatedly returning "out-of-time" to that which cannot be seamlessly incorporated into a linear narrative at the time of its occurrence. What is interesting about the unforeseen topicality of Section 28 in relation to the content of *This Island's Mine* is that the play at once seems to mark an analepsis (returning to an event) and a prolepsis (flashing forward to an event). That is, the play's concerns with non-nuclear families and relationships between homosexuality and HIV/AIDS at once offer a traumatic anticipation of Section 28 (the "writing time" of the play occurred before the Section came into force and yet the "story time" offers an uncanny foreshadowing of its chief propositions) and simultaneously seems to offer a response to Section 28 (the buildup of the passing into law of the Section during the "performance time" enables the "story time" to be read, retrospectively, as a response to the present of the "performance time", even though there is no necessary causal relationship). Thus, the traumatic force of the Section, which was not foreseen during the "writing time", belatedly informs an understanding of the "story time" and, crucially for what follows, affects the present of the "performance time", to which the production's archive bears witness.

I have suggested that there is no necessary causal relationship between the "writing time", "story time" and "production time". However, an analysis of several drafts of the script held in the Archives at Royal Holloway, University of London, suggests that the language of the Section may have infiltrated later drafts of the work, thus showing how "production time" might affect "writing time" and "story time". In what appears to be an earlier draft, the character Luke sees a newspaper headline that reads "GAY PLAGUE HITS THE CITY" and in later versions, including the published version, Luke sees two headlines that read: "DON'T TEACH OUR CHILDREN TO BE GAY!" and "GOVERNORS TAKE ACTION TO PROTECT HEALTH AND MORALS" (scene 1). Here it would seem that the language of the Section, specifically relating to education and sexuality, permeates the language of the script identifying how the force of the Section comes to bear on the writing time and story time of the play.[63]

The performance's archive both records homophobia and its material effects but also works to locate the production as a site of oppositional politics that seek to oppose and disable the operation of homophobia. In the next part of this discussion I will examine how the work of the production and the company around the Section and other instances of homophobia enables the creation and affirmation of gay identities, relationships and communities drawing, on occasion, on the cultural authority of Shakespeare. The work of Gay Sweatshop might, here, be seen as part of a process of gay community formation and consolidation in response to negative external pressures; as the UK lobby group Stonewall note: "as well as stigmatising gay people it [Section 28] also galvanised the gay community", a point that resonates with Stacey's assertion that "[a]s well as greater visibility in the media there was a consolidation, rather than the intended disintegration, of lesbian and gay communities and identities".[64] The archive thus stands as monument to the traumatic effects of homophobia but also encodes how trauma can be used to mobilise resistance and create communities, even as these communities entail exclusions and homogenisation. To explore these issues I will turn now to an analysis of elements of Gay Sweatshop's archive.[65]

An excavation of the archive, stratified by a series of pre- email, web and mobile telephone communications and publicity circa 1987–1988, reveals the company's efforts, through phone logs and letters, to seek venues for the production. An analysis of these documents identifies how Section 28 is brought to bear on the performances both before and after the Section passed into law. Letters written by Gay Sweatshop to secure venues identify anxieties about the effects that the Section might have on funding applications. In a letter seeking support from the Southampton City Council Arts Department for a subsidy to tour the production to the South of England, Gay Sweatshop's administrator writes: "I realise the wider implications of Clause 27 of the Local Government Bill currently under Parliamentary debate may well make applications for subsidy of this kind impossible in the future" to which the following reply was received: "[w]e are still unsure about the full implications of Clause 27. I am confident that, assuming it is passed, the venues we fund could still promote gay work, but I think that we would not be able *directly* to support that work financially. This is still not clear".[66] In this exchange, anxieties about how Section 28 might affect future funding opportunities emerge. The reply, like the analyses of the law I referred to earlier, marks the difficulty in establishing clearly the force of Section 28. Here the letter writer acknowledges that it might not be possible to fund the work under the auspices of one organisation. His suggestion that it might still be possible to do so under the auspices of another organisation does, however, create the possibility for the work still to be shown in venues funded by local authorities after the Section has passed into law. The optimism of this exchange is shadowed by letters which hint at the potential difficulty of programming the work in the aftermath of the Section, such as a letter from the Pegasus Theatre to Gay Sweatshop which notes that plans for an Autumn tour "will need to be strategized carefully in the light of the new dark ages".[67]

The possible difficulties in securing tour venues are also highlighted by the mass of news media clippings—previews, listings, interviews and reviews—included in the archive.[68] These clippings from a variety of sources including the broadsheets and the gay press chart how Section 28 was cited as a threat to the work of the company as this series of examples illustrates: "Gay Sweatshop's appearances [on the local authority Arts Centre circuit] are threatened by the notorious Clause 29", "For all the show's elegiac appeal, I trust current legislation will not render this the Sweatshop's farewell tour" and "many of the venues at which they hope to perform will be local council run. Each, therefore, is under threat from Clause 29".[69] While the legal efficacy of the Section was, as I have suggested, limited, the extent to which its discursive framework might be said to legitimise certain homophobic actions emerges sharply in relation to two Gay Sweatshop tour dates, even before the Section became law. A note in the programme states that in Exeter "the County Council cut £10 000 from the Local Arts Centre's grant as a punishment for booking the company which it declared 'a health risk to young people'" following Gay Sweatshop's *Compromised Immunity* tour in 1987.[70] Although the cut was not made within the remit of the yet-to-be-established law, the language of the proposed law which associates homosexuality with disease traces this decision. The ways that local authorities might intervene in arts programming with respect to sexuality also emerged in relation to the possibility of touring the performance in Swansea; an article in *Gay Times* reported that "Conservative councillor Richard Lewis has pledged to do all he can to stop Gay Sweatshop including the city in the company's tour of their latest production *This Island's Mine*".[71] Furthermore, while the Secretary General of the Arts Council notes that "at no stage has the issue of not funding the Company because of Section 28 even been mentioned, let alone given any consideration", when the company faced serious financial difficulties in 1990, the force of the Section recurred again in a letter written by a supporter of the company to the Secretary General of the Arts Council as a marker of the "threat" facing lesbians and gay men.[72] Again, the Section is identified as contributing to homophobia, even as its actual legal powers were limited, with the national Arts Council falling outside local government jurisdiction.

Alongside the institutionalised homophobia that gravitates around the Section, the archive also records other instances of homophobia. The tour reports note the display of an "anti-gay 'joke' poster in the toilet" in one of the accommodation venues and "a disturbance in the auditorium [. . .] when someone voiced disapproval of the play towards the end".[73] Most strikingly, after a performance in Croydon, a tour report states: "for future reference: Croydon is the H.Q. of the National Front. Holding hands at the railway station—esp. late on Saturday nights might not be advisable. Look out for skinheads first!!"[74] This incident is also recorded in Gay Sweatshop's report for the Arts Council of Great Britain where it noted a "violent and unprovoked incident of 'queer-bashing' when two of the Company, making their way to the station following a performance in Croydon, were attacked by a group of youths".[75] A similar violent incident also occurred during the company's earlier tour of *The Dear Love of Comrades* in Birmingham in April 1979; the logbook for the production notes that "We got beaten up near the Grosvenor Hotel on the first night. We held a meeting at the Gay Community Centre and they leafletted [*sic*] pubs about recent harassment of Gays. Contact Gay Centre when we have bookings in B'ham".[76] The archive for *This Island's Mine* (and that of *The Dear Love of Comrades*) stands as a testament to the material effects of homophobia, which are graphically illustrated in the assault of two of the company's members, echoing an element of the narrative of *This Island's Mine*. This incident also raises issues related to the temporality of the archive in relation to trauma and performance. That is, this traumatic event, which was unforeseen at the time of the play's development and early performances (notwithstanding the way in which queer bashing shadows queer cultures and the earlier Gay Sweatshop tour), is, through the process of archiving, retrospectively incorporated into the field of a performance's documentation. The performance thus returns to a history of traumatic events and, at a further remove, the archive belatedly records a specific, localised instance of trauma.[77]

The archive certainly encodes the material effects of homophobia. In contrast, in the last part of this chapter, I would like to suggest that the trauma produced by the Section and other forms of homophobia, perhaps paradoxically, enables the creation and affirmation of affective and effective community relationships, such as the mobilisation of the gay community group in Birmingham who leafleted pubs in response to acts of homophobia. Thus, Section 28 was mobilised by the company to provide a mechanism by which to generate interest in the performance and also as a platform for producing a collective response to the legislation. For example, a letter from Gay Sweatshop seeking tour support notes that *This Island's Mine* "now has added significance at this time with the far-reaching effects of the proposed Local Government Bill".[78] Here the Section is used to increase the play's topicality and value as a theatrical commodity. Another letter notes that "Sweatshop is acting as co-ordinator for a 'Stop Clause 27 Campaign' from an arts angle" and the archive also documents the support received from the Section 28 Arts Lobby which helped to fund the revival of the production after the Section had passed into law.[79]

Drawing on Jackie Stacey's arguments in "Promoting Normality", Chedgzoy notes that the Arts Lobby sought to oppose the Section on the grounds that it would, potentially, restrict "public access to great works of gay art and literature—Marlowe's *Edward II* and Shakespeare's *Sonnets* were frequently cited as being in danger, along with the works of Oscar Wilde and David Hockney, among others".[80] Stacey notes that the strategy was effective "[s]ince many of these 'masters' were a fundamental component of British cultural education, their exclusion from publicly funded bodies such as schools, museums and art galleries became increasingly unrealistic as more and more of them were associated with homosexuality".[81] Stacey also identifies how the work of the Lobby worked to affirm "dominant notions of the universality and excellence of British high culture, a model which feminists and other radical critics have previously attempted to challenge".[82] Exemplifying this engagement with "high culture", the Section 28 Arts Lobby, which was led by Richard Sandells of Gay Sweatshop, co-opted the help and support of famous (Shakespearean) actors such as Judi Dench, John Gielgud, Ian McKellen, Vanessa Redgrave, Antony Sher, Imelda Staunton, Patrick Stewart and Juliet Stevenson.[83] Many of these performers participated in a gala benefit performance, *Before the Act*, at the Piccadilly Theatre on 5 June 1988 to protest against Section 28. The gala focussed on the performance of work by lesbian and gay artists, including Michael Tippett's compositions of songs from Shakespeare's plays.[84] In the activist work of these high-profile performers, the cultural authority of Shakespeare was tacitly mobilised in the service of anti-homophobic protest, even as Shakespeare was not specifically identified as a "gay author" in the "anthology of love poetry" section of the evening, which included work by Sappho, Carol Ann Duffy, A. E. Housman, Tennessee Williams, Christopher Marlowe and Oscar Wilde, among others.[85] The positioning of Gay Sweatshop and *This Island's Mine* in the context of the arguments of the Arts Lobby worked to imbue the project with the cultural authority of the "gay masters" and, given the play's title and central narrative, the authority of Shakespeare in particular; the work of the Arts Lobby also points to how groups formed in response to the perceived negative effects of the legislation, with Gay Sweatshop pivotal to this work, as I will now explore more fully.

In addition to performances of the play, Gay Sweatshop offered pre-show discussions, which can be read as an alternative mode of performance. In an interview in the *Pink Paper*, Margaret Robinson, who played Miss Rosenblum in the production, says that "[p]art of Gay Sweatshop is an understanding that you are prepared to take part in workshops, talks, chats, particularly on tour with young people who are uncertain about being gay, more than talking about the play".[86] Thus the work of the company is once again situated as part of a broader project, which works to create a sense of community, a project that in Robinson's formulation, seems to supersede the importance of the play. Similarly, a letter from the Pegasus Theatre in Oxford points to how Gay Sweatshop's tour of the play was identified as a platform from which to address issues relating to Section 28, especially in the perceived absence of other forms of protest; as the letter writer notes:

> with the evil Clause 28 (27) throwing people's lives and well-being in jeopardy, it feels appropriate to invite the company to hold a discussion with local interested people in the Pegasus [. . .] before the second performance. It seems also appropriate because the show is about people claiming their rights to exist in this country so there's a good tie-in. When we considered this last week it was because there had not been an organized Oxford response to Clause 28 (27) locally that we knew of [. . . .] We're glad now to report that GLO (Gay Lesbian Oxford Rights Campaign) exists and will go to this week's meeting [. . . .] I would imagine that we will quite explicitly relate the discussion (if you agree to it) to Clause 28 (27).[87]

Here the content of the play is cited as a useful adjunct to the Pegasus Theatre's main concern, which is opposition to Section 28; in effect it is Gay Sweatshop's function as makers of "gay theatre" that is used as a platform for the discussion, rather than the specific content or form of the play itself. At the end of the performance of *This Island's Mine* captured on film, there is a strategic deployment of the play's narrative in relation to gay community formation. As the applause died down at the end of the curtain call, Richard Sandells, who played Mark, among several other characters, stepped forward and spoke directly to the audience:

> There are people who would say that what you've just watched promotes homosexuality. Well if it does then I think we can all be rather proud of that. But as you're probably aware some people feels so threatened and frightened by that prospect that recently they passed a law against it and Section 28 of the Local Government Act is now a threat not only to the future work of this company but to the happiness and dignity of every lesbian and gay man in the country. But this island's ours too and we're going to make sure that it's repealed, this wicked legislation.[88]

Sandells goes on to invite spectators to make a donation to the Arts Lobby to assist in efforts to "make sure that it [the Section] is thrown out".

Sandells explicitly identifies the play's narrative in terms of its potential to "promote" homosexuality and in so doing uses the play as an example of the kind of work that might be threatened by Section 28. He also works to challenge the negative force of the legislation by co-opting the language of pride. In effect the performance is cast as performative, working to bring a certain conception of homosexuality into being, the act of which is yoked to the production of a sense of collective pride. Strikingly, he also appropriates the language of the play's title in his assertion that "this island's ours". Here Caliban's claim, which is repeatedly attached to calls for sovereignty in the face of colonisation, and which in the play has been reworked in the context of black gay British identities, is here used to stake a claim for lesbians and gay men in the United Kingdom more generally. In Sandells's use of collective forms of address—we, our—he works to produce the spectators and the performers as a unified group who can be mobilised against the Section. This production of the collective does, however, work to elide other differences, exemplified by the assignment of Caliban/Selwyn's claim as part of a collective gay resistance, shorn of engagements with ethnicity. Sandells's use of the categories "lesbian and gay" also works to homogenise difference in terms of sexual identities and practices. In the talks and post-show addresses, the force of the Section, unknown at the time of the play's creation, thus returns to work on the present of the play's "production time". In the deployment of these modes of address it is also clear that the threat of the Section becomes a trigger for community creation and mobilisation.

This relationship between trauma and the creation of community recurs strikingly in a letter from a spectator who attended the performance and the discussion at the Pegasus Theatre, which is worth quoting at length:

> I am gay, and came out about two and a half years ago, but have not met any other gay people during that time, so it was amazing for me to be surrounded by other gay people—the atmosphere amongst you all made me very proud of being gay, and reassured me that it is a good and positive thing to be. I also went to the Clause 28 discussion before the performance, and was angered and depressed to learn what the clause will mean to gay people.
>
> I am moving to London [. . . and] I would very much like to get involved with fighting against the clause and helping other gay people generally.[89]

This letter identifies how the trauma produced by Section 28 (the spectator feels "angered and depressed"), coupled with the sense of community produced by the production and the discussion, provided the grounds for an affirmative sense of individual subjectivity (the spectator is "proud of being gay") and the basis for a collective community identity (the spectator wants to fight against the Clause and help "other gay people"). Similarly, Gay Sweatshop's report to the Arts Council of Great Britain notes that

> Letters of thanks, support and congratulations from isolated lesbians
> & gay men re-emphasised the importance of the Sweatshop tours to
> many homosexuals who have never or rarely seen a true representation
> of their own lifestyles on stage; equally such letters were received from
> newfound heterosexual supporters of the Company.[90]

Here the work of the company is positioned as making connections between
"isolated" individuals and a larger community via "a true representation
of their own lifestyle"; while the representations are couched in terms of
veracity and authenticity, the representations offered by Gay Sweatshop
might again be seen as operating performatively, working to bring a certain
(but not exclusive) understanding of what it might mean to identify as gay
or lesbian.

The tour reports, similarly, identify the creation of affirmative communities and include a series of observations about spectators such as: "very
warm: particularly impressed with age ranges—some older straight couples
and sixth formers [. . .] less vocal but they were definitely 'with' us", "*very*
warm and attentive throughout. Mainly students", "Very enthusiastic both
nights", "first night *very* quiet—but attentive. Very warm applause. Second
night quite the opposite—plenty of laughs. Wonderful silence at end before
applause" and "Very warm—very gay—a great boost for all of us!"[91] It is
unclear what the criteria are for determining audience demographics with
respect to sexuality (or indeed other factors such as "middle class").[92] It is
also unclear what the criteria are for determining "warmth" but it is striking how often this adjective is used in the repeated figuration of the applause
as "warm". In my viewing of the performance video I too find myself compelled to use this adjective. Even as I know I cannot know how individual
spectators felt and that an adjective like "warmth" appears abstract and
vague, working to mystify the event of live performance, this term, which
is unquantifiable in relation to performance, repeatedly institutes itself in
both the reports and my sense of the performance. I would suggest that
these assertions of "warmth" (recorded with respect to six of the eight
tour venues), coupled with claims that the audience was "with us", work
to record and produce a supportive community of spectators and performers. That is, the spectators are identified, through certain behavioural cues
(applause, laughter) as complicit with the work of the performance—coded
in terms of warmth—and are called into a relation of community with one
another through these communal behaviours, notwithstanding the acts of
resistant spectators. As I mentioned earlier, these reports also record acts
of homophobia such as the assault on two of the company's members in
Croydon (after a "warm and enthusiastic" reception to the performance)
and a negative interjection by a member of the audience, as well as identifying cases where the production played to "bemused" spectators or small
houses.[93] However, the dominant strain to emerge from these reports is
the way in which the production participates in what is perceived by the

company to be the creation of an affirmative, gay-positive environment. As with Jarman's projects, Shakespeare's text has been neatly co-opted as part of this cultural work.

Whereas the letter, the tour reports and the Arts Council report identify how a sense of community might be produced by the actions of Gay Sweatshop, another letter expresses anxieties about the efficacy of the creation of gay and lesbian (theatre) communities:

> I am left, though with a feeling of sorrow that the production will not be seen by a wider audience. Because of your company's name, you are bound to attract a mainly gay or lesbian audience.
>
> I happen not to be gay [. . . .] It was only my indignation at the implication of Clause 28 (now 29 I believe) which persuaded me to come along [. . . .]
>
> I understand the importance of being able to openly represent your sexuality on stage, but by restricting your audience to gays and lesbians you will fail to reach the very audiences who need to be emotionally stirred by your plays and the whole exercise ends up by being self-indulgent.[94]

Here the writer exhibits concerns about the efficacy of gay and lesbian theatre to attract audiences outside its own constituency. The writer thus identifies a tension in the operation of communities with respect to relationships between those "inside" and "outside" a given community. Whereas the community created by Gay Sweatshop is seen in efficacious terms by the letter writer cited earlier who wants to help gay people, for the writer of the second letter, it is cast in terms of failure. That said, it is interesting to note that although the second letter writer notes that s/he is "not gay", and in the terms of the letter, outside the target community, s/he, along with others indicated by the Arts Council Report and letters to the company, has still participated in this theatre event. This suggests that the community boundaries that the letter writer presents as sharply defined are more porous and thus entail the possibility of efficacious traffic between communities. The flyer used to advertise the production (Figure 3.2) also bears analysis in terms of this idea of community, visually playing out this tension between inclusion and exclusion. Here the multitude of faces is united under the sign of the Union Jack, suggesting the possibility for a collective that is marked by difference (or, indeed, by similarities, which may, or may not be legible visually). But the form of the image—produced such that some of the individuals appear fragmented and disjointed in relation to one another—might be read as undermining the possibility of an idea of a collective community, even as the flag operates, perhaps ironically, as the signifier which unites this group.

In the context of these debates about community formation, it is useful to think of the work of Weaver and Neale-Kennerley. They were appointed

Figure 3.2   Flyer for Gay Sweatshop's 1988 production, *This Island's Mine*. Reproduced with the permission of the Archives, Royal Holloway, University of London (GS/3/20/1 RHUL Archives).

co-artistic directors of Gay Sweatshop following the award of Arts Council revenue funding in 1991 and worked to produce a more porous understanding of both the community the company might engage and create, and the kinds of performance work it might produce. While the Arts Council provided its funding on the basis of mid-scale touring of plays, Weaver and Neale-Kennerley also worked to develop the work of individual artists, through events such as the *Queer School* professional development summer workshops, where Weaver notes that anyone who chose to lay claim to "queer" could participate. They also produced *One Night Stands*, which sought to "bring together established and blossoming lesbian and gay performers and writers to create evenings of one-off performances drawn from the worlds of theatre, dance, music and live art".[95] As Weaver explains:

> we were trying to introduce new ways of working that got away from the traditional writer, director, actor, theatre company model and also asking people to experiment with form and encouraging more radical solo/independent performance based work. It was more of a performance platform with a party atmosphere inspired by my work at WOW and other downtown New York performance venues in the 80s and 90s [. . .] rather than gay cabaret.

As Gay Sweatshop approached closure in 1997, the company created *Club Deviance*, a performance club night that mixed various media including dance, live art and photography, described in a press release as a "visceral mix of traditional settings, theatrical skills, subcultural aesthetics and queer politics".[96] Projects such as these worked to diversify both the work that the company was producing and its constituency, shifting its focus away from touring "product" toward participation and experimental projects. The work of Weaver and Neale-Kennerley also marked a shift from what Weaver describes as the more "assimilationist" politics of "gay" toward a "queer" politics that refuses assimilation and works to articulate difference. Weaver also notes tensions between the work she and Neale-Kennerley were producing and the work the company's board and the Arts Council wanted to be made (i.e., mid-scale touring "gay" plays, of the kind *This Island's Mine* typifies). Talking of the same period, Osment suggests that it was no longer clear what Gay Sweatshop was "meant to be doing" at the end of the 1990s and how it should define itself, especially in relation to "postmodern definitions" of "queer", which Osment suggests did not "sit well with the company's original philosophy".[97] Osment and Weaver also note that gay theatre work of the kind Gay Sweatshop had primarily produced, was also being taken up by other companies in both metropolitan and regional centres, perhaps reducing the need for a dedicated touring company such as Gay Sweatshop.[98] Here, then, the "community" of Gay Sweatshop is again subject to internal and external pressures in response to changing performance and identity politics, which threatened its capacity to sustain itself. It was not, however, a debate about identity and performance politics that finally led to the winding up of the company in 1997 but, rather, the loss of Arts Council funding which had rescued the company from financial collapse in 1991, pointing to "the inevitable implication of community in [financial] capital", as Joseph has trenchantly argued.[99]

In this chapter I have attempted to show how the text, performance and archive of *This Island's Mine* encode and respond to various traumas which weave themselves into what Ann Cvetkovich describes as the "textures of everyday experience", especially with respect to sexuality and its intersection with discourses of racism and homophobia.[100] In so doing the performance works to remember and witness the trauma produced through homophobia and racism, archiving it in the moment of performance, primarily through operation of the play's *Tempest* narrative, and in the performance's material traces. I have also considered how performances and their associated archival records generate possibilities for understanding how traumatic events and histories might also be used as the basis for the development of alternative communities and identities. Although it occupies a relatively peripheral position to the work of Gay Sweatshop more generally, the cultural authority of Shakespeare was, on occasion, mobilised in the service of these projects, even as this authority can also work to elide difference and uphold dominant power relations and conceptions of art. The performance and archival records thus stake a powerful claim for the possibilities for countering homophobia through community performance actions but simultaneously identify tensions, marginalisation and exclusions that inhere within community formations. I will turn now to the final chapter where I will consider relationships between performance and the traumatic event of war through an analysis of Nicholas Hytner's production of *Henry V* (2003) for the National Theatre in London.

4 Theatres of War
Nicholas Hytner's *Henry V*

"The wasteland and anarchy of Iraq in the aftermath of our illegal 2003 invasion is reflected in so many of Shakespeare's plays that one can move effortlessly between the tragedies and the histories to read of present-day civil war Baghdad", wrote Robert Fisk, Middle East correspondent for the UK-based newspaper *The Independent*, in a 2007 article for the paper.[1] In support of his argument, Fisk proceeded to catalogue a series of parallels between Shakespeare and war: Henry's pre-Agincourt speech is likened to "Saddam's prelude to the 'Mother of All Battles' where Prospero-like purity [which isn't clarified] is espoused for the Arab 'side'"; General Norman Schwarzkopf's report of American and Iraqi deaths during the first Gulf War (1990–91) is taken as an echo of Henry's announcement of the asymmetrical battle casualties sustained at Agincourt; and a US Marine's 2003 confrontation with an Iraqi soldier-demonstrator in which he tells him to "[s]hut the fuck up" before asking his translator "[w]hat the fuck's he saying?" is taken as an analogue for Pistol's treatment of a French prisoner (4.4), to name but three such comparisons from *Henry V*. Similar observations are made elsewhere in the article in relation to *Julius Caesar*, *The Tempest*, *Othello* and *King Lear*.

Fisk reads Shakespeare's plays and historical events as analogous in a mutually supporting self-sustaining loop, which I would suggest is premised on an understanding of universal human nature that elides cultural and historical difference. Fisk's argument is symptomatic of repeated associations made between the action and characterisation of Shakespeare's plays and historical and contemporary events, such as those I have examined at other points in this book. With respect to relationships between Shakespeare's plays and war, one such striking (but by no means isolated) example is Michael Bogdanov and Michael Pennington's *War of the Roses* cycle of both tetralogies (1986–89) for the English Shakespeare Company. This cycle drew on Britain's war with Argentina over the Falkland Islands (April–June 1982), crystallised in the inclusion of a placard held by the Chorus that reproduced a daily tabloid newspaper's headline "Gotcha" in response to the British attack on the Argentine ship, the *General Belgrano*. Looking further back in the twentieth century, Richard Loncraine's film

Richard III (1995) locates the action of the play in the context of 1930s Britain and invites spectators to make comparisons between Richard's reign and both Nazi Germany and a nightmare fantasy of Britain under an Oswald Mosley-style fascist rule. More recently, Nicholas Hytner's *Henry V* (2003) for the National Theatre in London, which is the subject of this chapter, gave the play a resolutely contemporary setting in the context of British and American military action in Afghanistan following the attack on the World Trade Center on 11 September 2001. As the production entered its rehearsal phase it also engaged with military action in Iraq, which was launched on 20 March 2003, three days after the rehearsal period began. Indeed, Hytner reiterates the self-supporting "loop of relevance" between the play and contemporary events in his claim that "the play was illuminated by current events and, I hope that for the audiences who saw the play, current events were illuminated by the play".[2]

In their consideration of art produced in response to terrorism, Graham Coulter-Smith and Maurice Owen argue that "[a]llegory is most certainly one of the most powerful weapons at an artist's disposal when confronted with the need to visualize that which is so traumatic that a direct treatment appears obscene".[3] While they use the term "allegory", where a subject is considered "under the guise of some other subject of aptly suggestive resemblance" (*OED* 1), their claim might apply equally well to analogy, or the "[e]quivalency or likeness of relations" (*OED* 3). For Coulter-Smith and Owen, direct engagement with a traumatic event is rendered obscene, or grossly offensive, such that an indirect relation to the event provides an artist with a more effective means of visualising trauma. I am less convinced by Coulter-Smith and Owen's argument that a direct relation to the event appears obscene, as they seem to privilege some forms of representation over others in terms of an ethics of taste. But their point does identify how an indirect relation to the subject under discussion might provide a mechanism (or the allure of a mechanism) through which to engage with the traumatic force of that event.

Through a consideration of Hytner's "indirect" treatment of events in Afghanistan and Iraq via the performance of one of Shakespeare's plays, I want to analyse the production's relationship to contemporary acts of warfare, especially with respect to the production and framing of traumatic images of war. This is not with a view to showing that such analogies either "work" or break down at the level of content or narrative; relationships denoted by analogy, as I have indicated elsewhere in this book, necessarily entail a breakdown as the structural similarity (or sameness) an analogy denotes rests on difference (or a refusal of sameness) between phenomena. Rather, I am interested in taking the proposed connection between one of Shakespeare's narratives and contemporary war seriously so as to consider what's at stake in this connection, especially with respect to the representation of violence and its effects and the political and ethical implications of this work. To borrow from Judith Butler, what are the "frames of war"

through which spectators are invited to look?[4] What ideological imperatives do they embed?

In its treatment of war, I suggest that Hytner's production was not so
much interested in sustaining an analogy between two phenomena such
that their difference is apparent, but in collapsing the distinction between
the production and the real events that it invoked, such that the theatre
might stand as an instantiation of the "reality" of war. In so doing I argue
that the production identified the failure of representational theatre to
articulate the horror of war and the messy affectiveness of the trauma that
it generates, and that it worked to occlude this failure under the signs of
"truth" and "realism". It also functioned, especially in its closing sequences,
to resolve, to some extent, the trauma of war by using the play's narrative
to consign violence to the past through the rhetoric of victory (even as the
play and production look forward to further cycles of violence in the *Henry
VI* plays), which was also repeated in discourse surrounding the production. In contrast, a consideration of the production's documentary traces—
held in the National Theatre's archive and online as part of Stagework,
the National's website of production resources—offers a more complicated
set of temporal relationships between violent events, performance and its
documentary traces.[5] The following reading of the archive and other documentary traces, which pays particular attention to the claims that photographs make upon viewers, considers how the inclusion of photographic
documentation in the archive and programmes embeds the ongoing traumatic effects of war.

IN TIME: NATION(AL) BUILDING

Hytner officially commenced his role as the new Director of the National,
following Trevor Nunn's tenure, on 1 April 2003. His decision to direct
Henry V in his opening season of plays was, as I will explore below, in part
made in response to contemporary events and in part because, as Hytner
explains, "[i]t has never been done at the National, perhaps because the
great wartime film made by the National's first Director, Laurence Olivier,
casts such a long shadow. But it's time we did it".[6] The programme, which
depicts images from the play's performance history from Charles Kean's
1859 production to Kenneth Branagh's 1989 film, implicitly positions Hytner's production as the latest in a lineage of famous productions of Shakespeare's play—Kean, Calvert, Olivier, Quayle, Barton, Hands, Branagh.[7]
The images, coupled with Hytner's comment, work to locate his production
as heir to these forebears and in conjunction with his Travelex-sponsored
initiative—designed to make tickets more affordable to a wider audience
demographic by selling two thirds of the Olivier tickets for £10—to cement
his position as the Director of the National and, by extension, the inheritor of Olivier's legacy. In his "Welcome to the National Theatre" in the

programme to the 2003 season of plays, Hytner positions the work of the National thus:

> It's a great time to be a national theatre and to rise to the challenge of living up to our name. We want to chart the way the nation is changing, and to tell the stories that pull our audiences into new ways of understanding what's happening around them. We want to bring frontline reports from new communities and generations, and to see the present redefined in the context of the past.
>
> Above all, while we're doing all this, we want to give as many people as possible a really good time [. . .]
>
> [. . . .] *Henry V* is the indispensable play about the British at war.

Hytner's note immediately signals the National Theatre's role in the project of nation building through the engagement with communities, generations and histories, incorporated under the sign of a *national* theatre. Adrian Lester, the production's Henry, cites *Henry V* as a vision of national unity, in his assertion that "Shakespeare was creating a Great Britain before there was a Great Britain". He extrapolates this assessment of the play to the work of the production, arguing that the play depicts people from different cultures—Welsh, Irish, Scottish—standing together to fight for an English King and "on this stage you've got a mix of cultures all doing that very same thing".[8] The production is here presented as bringing people of different backgrounds together for a common (English) cause. The selectively "colour blind" casting of the play, where black British actors were cast as Henry, Westmorland and Pistol, is cited by Faz Singhateh, who played Westmorland, as offering audiences "an updated version of what it is on the streets of London, in their own towns, there are black people everywhere [. . . .] I think as young kids that's quite an important thing that they see the world as it is on stage".[9] Just as authenticity is claimed for the production in terms of its representation of war, as I will explore further below, it is also claimed here for its engagement with ethnicity. In Hytner's, Lester's and Singhateh's comments, the work of the National—and *Henry V* in particular—is offered as a positive model of national unity, smoothing over traumatic histories of racism in Britain, of the kind I engaged with in Chapter 3, and historical inequalities in the British theatre industry in relation to ethnicity and national identity. The emergence of the first productions by the National Theatre of Scotland in 2006 and the National Theatre Wales in 2010 perhaps speaks, in part, however, to the limited capacity of the National Theatre—based in London and partially funded by Arts Council England—to speak adequately to "Britain" and its constituent nations, as well as indexing the operation of devolution in the United Kingdom, where political power was redistributed to a restored Scottish parliament and assemblies were established in Wales and Northern Ireland under Tony Blair's Labour Government.[10]

Importantly, for Hytner, the project of staging the nation is compatible with giving people "a really good time". The theatre is positioned as cutting edge, at the front line of the project of narrativising and theatricalising the nation as part of an entertainment and leisure economy premised on the production of pleasure. *Henry V*—"the indispensable play about the British at war"—is located as a key part of this project, specifically with respect to defining the nation at war. In Hytner's production, the general designation of the "British at war" was localised in relation to the invasions of Afghanistan and Iraq. The production thus shrewdly capitalised on contemporary events as part of the National's entertainment economy such that war became packaged as entertainment. This is an economy that is dependent on programming a mixture of existing and new work. In his description of factors involved in the selection of "old" plays, Hytner says, "what you're always looking for is a play that might connect specifically to today".[11] As with other productions that I have discussed in this book, the temporality of the production of *Henry V* in relation to both past and contemporary events sustains exploration in relation to histories of violence and their traumatic after-effects. Indeed, Hytner's comment in the programme that the National aims "to see the present redefined in the context of the past" offers a gloss on traumatic temporality where that which is past does not remain in the past but instead returns to inform the present. In what follows I aim to tease out some of the implications of Hytner's decision to programme *Henry V* in relation to contemporary war, both those known and those yet unknown at the time of programming. In so doing I want to consider how these wars inform the "present" (defined here in terms of "production time"), the "writing time" of this book and the future to which it speaks.

Reflecting on his decision in the summer of 2002 to direct *Henry V*, Hytner notes on the Stagework website that "we had just been at war in Afghanistan".[12] Here war in Afghanistan is consigned to the past, no doubt in part due to the "fall" of the Taliban in late 2001; Hytner's claim that this war is an event of the past is mocked by the grim irony that some nine years later in the summer of 2010, US, British and coalition forces are still operational in Afghanistan, as are the Taliban, and civilian and military casualties and injuries continue to be sustained. Whereas Hytner consigned war in Afghanistan to the past, his decision to programme *Henry V* offered an anticipatory relationship to future military action: "the reason we did the play was because it felt like it would connect very strongly to what *might* be going on. I had no idea that we would be rehearsing it as we invaded Iraq [. . . .] It wasn't an enormous surprise".[13] Similarly, in a post-show Platform discussion at the National Hytner notes:

> when I started to think about the play we had not long ago been at war in Afghanistan. It seemed *likely* that in the wake of the terrorist attacks in New York we would be gathering ourselves or we would be

marshalled by our leaders to go to war again and it obviously felt like
[. . .] a play that would speak very directly now.[14]

In these comments, the production is positioned in relation to the "past"
war in Afghanistan and, in the use of the words "might" and "likely", anticipates a future war with an as-yet-to-be-determined referent, even as UK, US
and UN responses to the work of the UN weapons' inspectors in Iraq during 2002 and 2003 suggested that it would be the *likely* target of military
action. The production was thus set up to register a response to a war of
the past (Afghanistan), which in its ongoing effects refuses to be consigned
to the past, and offers an anticipatory engagement with a potential war-to-
come (Iraq). Motivated by a desire for the production to speak to "now",
Hytner's decision to present the play "uncomplicatedly in modern dress"[15]
works to deploy the trauma of contemporary warfare in the service of what
the programme promises to be a "really good time". As I will explore below,
the modern dress is far from uncomplicated, enmeshing the production in
the difficult business of representing contemporary warfare, and the "really
good time" that is claimed for the production and the work of the National
more generally invites consideration in terms of how the presentation of the
trauma of war as entertainment positions spectators.

In a temporal coincidence, Hytner's anticipation of an as yet unnamed
but predictable war—marked by his claim that "[i]t wasn't an enormous
surprise"—was literalised on 17 March 2003, the first day of the six-week
rehearsal period. Specifically, George W. Bush demanded that Saddam
Hussein leave Iraq in 48 hours or face war; the US-led invasion, supported
by the British and other coalition forces, commenced on 20 March 2003. In
Hytner's comment that he "had no idea that we would be rehearsing [. . .
the play] as we invaded Iraq", the work of the theatre is placed in relation
to the work of the state, such that the activities of both entities are synchronised with each other. This works to reiterate the absolute in-timeness or
relevance of the production to contemporary events.

The temporal coincidence between the action of the play and current events
recurred at several points throughout the rehearsal process, as documented in
the rehearsal diary, written by Peter Reynolds and Lee White.[16] For example,
the first rehearsal of 1.2, where Henry seeks assurance from the Archbishop
of Canterbury that his invasion of France has a sound legal basis, took place
on 18 March, the same day that the UK Parliament debated the legitimacy of
invading Iraq.[17] This debate culminated in the House of Commons voting to
go to war, partly in order to uphold UN Security Council Resolution 1441;
the Resolution noted that Iraq was in "material breach" of earlier resolutions
regarding its weaponry and gave it "a final opportunity to comply with its
disarmament obligations under relevant resolutions of the Council".[18] 1.2,
which is often cut or truncated in performance (as it was here, in addition to
being conflated with 1.1) on account of its long and complicated discussion
of Salic law, was here staged as a cabinet room, complete with 17 dossiers

comprised of 300 pages, complete with fold-out maps.[19] Speaking in the post-show Platform discussion about the extent to which particular scenes were shaped in response to world events, Hytner responded by saying, "we are in the theatre entirely opportunistic". For Hytner the dossier "is the Iraq dossier", a reference to the Blair Government's somewhat slimmer 50-page dossier, "Iraq's Weapons of Mass Destruction"—published by the Government and discussed in Parliament on 24 September 2002—which detailed Saddam Hussein's alleged holdings of weapons of mass destruction and violations of UN Security Council resolutions.[20] Furthermore, the rehearsal diary notes that "[o]n Friday 21 March, the day after the invasion of Iraq began, the company undertook their first rehearsal of the English retreat from Harfleur. The irony of 'playing' with guns on such a day was not lost on the company".[21] It is also noted in the diary that the images of the actors dressed in military clothing and holding guns in this exercise were "startlingly familiar from the television news of the night before, or the images dominating the front pages of the newspapers. Once again, the fictional world of the play was linked to the real military events unfolding in a foreign land".[22] The action of the play and contemporary events are repeatedly folded together and a condition of realism is claimed for the production as the images of the rehearsing "soldiers" are read as versions or ciphers of the images depicted in the media coverage. The rehearsal diary also notes "a particular irony in discussing the legitimacy of Saddam's execution on the same day as the actors were preparing to rehearse Act 3 scene 6, in which Pistol's pleas for the life of Bardolph are rebuked and the King [. . .] executes him with a shot to the head".[23] The designation of the rehearsals in terms of their ironic relation to contemporary events works to suggest that that which is unexpected in relation to the rehearsals—the invasion of Iraq and so on—is, in fact, synchronous with the work of the production; the doubleness that irony denotes thus functions to unify the two phenomena. The parallels noted in the rehearsal diary, which was available for sale in the National's bookshop during the production's run, thus served to reinforce the production's efforts to market itself as absolutely "in time" or synchronous with contemporary events.

This synchronicity suggests that performance is capable of folding the trauma of war smoothly into its representational machinery, imbuing the production with an authority and authenticity of the real. Lester exemplifies this position in his claim that "[t]he play brought great focus to the conflict we were all watching on our TV screens. I think it was fascinating for audiences to see on stage what they had read about in the papers that morning".[24] The production was thus offered as a three-dimensional version of the events that are reported by the media. In this way the work of the production seems to map neatly onto contemporary events such that it became an instantiation of contemporary events. This convergence between the production and contemporary events was supported by Hytner's decision to use video clips at various points during the production and to include the figure of an embedded reporter, familiar from televised newscasts, when Henry goes to war in France.[25] The videos identify how events of war are carefully managed as mediatised images—Henry speaks to the English about the need for war (1.2.304–10) in the style of a prime-ministerial or presidential broadcast, for example.[26] This again worked to imbue the production with an authentic understanding of the operation of contemporary warfare and its documentation and reception. Indeed, Hytner notes that one of his ideas for the production was to explore "the way contemporary media spin is involved in the waging of war nowadays".[27]

This claim for a neat correlation between the production and contemporary events is reiterated and also complicated by Robert Blythe, the production's Llewellyn, in his comment that:

> when we looked at the 9 o'clock news it was like watching rehearsals in a way but with live bullets. It made it seem to me anyway [. . .] it's one's personal views of the war, I don't think it was necessary [. . .] I mean public opinion seemed to express that at the time as well as beforehand, so it was a painful experience doing it.[28]

Blythe denotes the production as being synchronous with contemporary events such that the rehearsal seems neatly to shadow contemporary events but for the (not significant) presence of live ammunition, thus working to locate the rehearsal (and production) as authentic instantiations of war. But the neatness of the comparison is punctured by Blythe's assertion that it was "painful" to perform in a play that dramatises a nation going to war in the context of a contemporary war that he does not agree with. Here Blythe registers the difficulty of engaging with contemporary traumatic experience in the service of theatrical representation, and hints at the ethical difficulties of engaging in a production that narrates "successful" military action, even as it attempts to capture aspects of the violent realities of contemporary warfare. In the next section—which explores the production's efforts to represent the reality of contemporary war—the performance identifies its failure to embody the horror of war. As ever, trauma resists representation as the thing itself, but the representational system used by the production worked to occlude this resistance.

STAGING WAR

As with Doran's production of *Titus Andronicus*, those involved in Hytner's *Henry V* were concerned to stage the "truth" of the external events to which the production referred. The production's engagement with contemporary events is even represented in the rehearsal diary as a kind of compulsion, born of a need to "work through" the mediatised images broadcast on the television news:

[n]ight after night television news contained the sounds and images of war, the pyrotechnics of exploding ordnance and cruse missiles over Baghdad and Basra, the miserable sight of often terribly wounded civilians, including many children [. . . .] On entering the rehearsal room in the morning it was as if everyone had seen the same compelling and troubling footage the previous night and now felt compelled to discuss it.[29]

Here the rehearsal room is coded as a space for sharing and discussing "troubling" images of war; these images, in turn, provided the basis for the production's engagement with the "truth" of warfare. This desire to stage the "truth" of war, is made explicit in Lester's reiteration of Hytner's advice that "[t]he best thing we could do is to watch the news and read the papers and bring every opinion on to the stage with us so that we find the truth of what it must be like for those guys over there doing this".[30] The aim of the production is defined as a search for the "truth" of the experience of warfare in Afghanistan and Iraq, predicated on an understanding of performance as capable of replicating this "truth". This figuration is reiterated in Lester's claim that:

[w]hen we were starting it [. . .] we decided the best thing we could possibly do would be to have someone who has been over to Afghanistan and Baghdad, who could sit down and watch the production and say: "Yeah, I got that." [. . .] then you've taken Shakespeare, you've taken theatre [. . .] and you've made it absolutely, realistically relevant to someone's experience today.[31]

Lester's comments suggest a desire to offer an accurate, realistic portrayal of contemporary warfare, such that it might be recognised as an authentic copy by someone who has experienced military action in Afghanistan and Iraq. The production is coded here in terms of realism, especially with respect to its capacity to capture and reproduce the experience of war. A number of activities were undertaken to imbue the production with realism but as I will suggest, these served primarily to identify the gap between the production and the traumatic experiences it sought to replicate.

In order to achieve a realistic representation of contemporary warfare, the actors underwent a series of training exercises with the production's Military Adviser (MA), Richard Smedley, who along with another former member of the military, was Hytner's "chief source" for what he describes as "the visceral impact of battle".[32] As noted in the rehearsal diary, "for the purpose of the training, the actors were to address the MA as 'sergeant' to establish a relationship akin to that in a real military training situation".[33] In addition to establishing relationships designed to simulate military-style discipline, hierarchies and "army behaviour",[34]

Figure 4.1   Rehearsal photograph of Nicholas Hytner's 2003 production of *Henry V* for the National Theatre. Photograph © Ivan Kyncl, reproduced with the permission of Alena Melichar.

the cast were trained in the use of replica firearms, based on the models of weapons being used by British troops in Iraq; Figure 4.1 depicts one of these training exercises and a selection of additional images are collated on the Stagework website.[35] Lester described how the cast "concentrated on the very real experience of battle; what it might be like to be out there facing death".[36] Here the drive was toward producing the physical and emotional realities of warfare, including, in the terms of PTSD, the traumatic experience of feeling that death is immanent or threatened. Lester's summary assumes that it is possible to acquire some kind of emotional verisimilitude in relation to the experiences of military conflict. The production sought to facilitate this work and in so doing points up both the ideological imperatives that inform the production's representation of military behaviour as well as identifying the failure of the representations to carry the weight of the "real" thing of the traumatic experience of war, as I will now consider.

The production's efforts to imbue the characterisations with the experience of emotional shock are evident in some of the tasks the actors were given in the production of the Stagework website. The website records two video interviews with actors, one with Robert Blythe who speaks in character as Llewellyn and one with Rupert Wickham, who speaks about the experiences of his character, Captain Gower. Speaking of Gower, Wickham comments:

I don't think he's totally equipped to deal with the horrors of this particular war [. . . .] In the course of the play he's confronted with some very difficult choices and some acts of inhumanity which he finds very difficult to deal with [. . . .] He encounters things which he's not able really to deal with in a war situation.[37]

Wickham here registers the traumatic effects of war on the character with respect to the difficulty of assimilating or accounting for this experience. Whereas Wickham describes Gower as if he was a real person suffering from PTSD-like symptoms, Blythe's interview collapses this distinction such that he is invited to speak *as* Llewellyn. Blythe/Llewellyn is framed in a headshot against a black background, reminiscent of the style of confessional television interviews. Dressed in his military uniform/costume, Blythe speaks about "his" experiences as Llewellyn, with particular reference to the sequence where Henry orders him to execute the French prisoners:

[w]ell, it's quite painful to talk about. It relates to the order that I was given directly by the King to execute prisoners of war. That wasn't an easy thing to do and I think that will have affected me, in the future. I don't think I'll be quite the soldier I was before.[38]

Blythe speaks in a manner that suggests the emotional difficulty of recounting this situation as he works through a traumatic aspect of warfare. Here the actor offers himself as a surrogate for the character, working to develop a psychological profile that registers the effects of warfare such that "he" seems to be diminished in his capacities as a solider by the effect of individually executing all the prisoners. This process of surrogation and the drive for realism recurs in Hytner's claim in the Platform discussion that "by the time this cast of actors had really started to inhabit the notion that they were the contemporary British Army it felt impossible to most of them to carry out that order" to kill the French prisoners. Talking further in the Platform discussion of the depiction of the soldiers Hytner says, "one of the things I hope this production is, is respectful of the common British soldier". In particular, he sees his representation of the soldiers as working against a performance tradition that "writes the English Army off as thugs". In justifying his representation of the soldiers, he collapses the distinction between the play and contemporary events with his comment that "it didn't seem to me that we were sending thugs into Iraq". He goes on to note that he "didn't particularly want to put on this stage something which was an insult to people who have more difficult jobs than we do, I would imagine". This again shows how the production in driven by a desire for veracity but also points to how veracity is ideologically inflected. Hytner's comment thus offers the actors as successful surrogations of the contemporary British Army and works to situate the army as offering compassionate and humane treatment of prisoners of war, both on and off stage.

These efforts to depict the humane treatment of prisoners, which are underpinned by a set of beliefs about how members of the contemporary British Army would behave in a combat situation, are, however, compromised both by the action of the play and contemporary news reports. Thus Hytner follows through with a modified version of Henry's instruction that "every soldier kill his prisoners" (4.6.37), a scene that was cut in both Olivier's (1944) and Branagh's (1989) films, among other productions, so as to present Henry in a sympathetic light. Indeed Branagh comments, "I think I rather flunked and avoided [. . .] I could have possibly been braver about the way we presented it and not, as I feared we would, lose the sympathy of the audience for the central character".[39] In Hytner's production, Llewellyn is instructed by Henry to "Give the word through" (4.6.38); with a call of "ready, aim, fire" he ordered his men to kill the prisoners but, after raising their guns in readiness, they refused the order, turning away, the word "shit" audible amid the prisoners' pleas for their lives. In staging the reluctance of the soldiers to carry out Henry's order such that Llewellyn carried out all the executions, the production offered an implicit critique of Henry's actions and worked to present the army as avoiding unnecessary violence, especially in relation to prisoners of war. In her reading of this sequence, Lois Potter suggests that this act invites consideration "as evidence of the ordinary soldiers' humanity compared with the commander's callous indifference", an indifference, which as the interview with Blythe/Llewellyn suggests was enacted with difficulty.[40] While this scene might suggest that the soldiers are "humane", this humanity is rendered ineffectual as the prisoners are still executed in a burst of machine gun fire, followed by a close-range execution of one prisoner who failed to die immediately and was shot as he attempted to crawl away.

Presented alongside the reluctant English soldiers, the images of the French prisoners, sitting on the stage, hooded, with their hands behind their heads, facing away from the audience were, as the Stagework website notes, "copied from news photographs of captured Iraqi prisoners".[41] The insertion of contemporary English dialogue into the scene, as the prisoners were instructed to sit down and cross their legs, further wrests the scene from an early modern to a contemporary context. Here the production co-opted and exploited the experiences of faceless (literally) others—others who are denied the capacity to speak for themselves—in order to invest the production with authentic images of contemporary warfare. Whereas Hytner carefully considered the representation of the "common British soldier" in terms of a "respectful" representation, similar care was not, insofar as the documentary traces suggest, accorded the faceless others through whom the British soldiers are able to purchase their integrity and humanity. The image economy of war photography, which works to aestheticise war even as it seeks to document its horror, is here reused in the service of theatrical spectacle for consumption as part of the experience of play-going.

The reiteration of scenes from contemporary news reports as part of the presentation of Shakespeare's play invites a consideration in terms of the ethics of spectatorship. That is, what is at stake in watching "real" violence recycled in the service of theatrical entertainment, especially when the violence on stage ultimately goes unchallenged and is sanctioned by the King/state? To some extent spectators might be positioned as complicit in the staging of violence as they enter (presumably) willingly into the space of the theatre to watch the action. And yet spectators might take an ethical position to the action by *acknowledging* their complicity and participation within the theatrical economy and its representational machinery. This does not, of course, change the fact of prisoner abuses, either on stage or in Iraq, but it does create the space for a consideration of how violence is repackaged as part of both media and theatrical entertainments. The challenge that these phenomena pose to spectators is for "us" to take some responsibility for "our" participation in the circulation and reiteration of images and, potentially, to use this as a basis for ethical action in relation to others.

While the actors playing the prisoners worked to perform emotions of fear and terror as they begged for their lives, raising their arms in supplication toward their captors, these sequences worked to highlight, for me at least, the distance between the stage representation and the reality of the experiences of prisoners of war. As Anthony Kubiak writes in his account of the staging of terror,

> [i]n the final analysis, we are still faced with a theatre whose violence, no matter how "real," still exists primarily as a sign of itself, while the violence of the interrogation cell is precisely that which is unsignifyable. (It is also worth noting that the theatrical ordeal, no matter how intense, is undergone voluntarily, while the very terror of torture rests in part on the victim's absolute lack of control).[42]

Kubiak points to how mimetic theatre operates as a signification system; its representations function as representations, rather than instantiating the trauma—or "terror", in the context of Kubiak's formulation—of the thing itself. He also identifies how theatre refigures the distribution of power in situations of conflict such that inequalities of conflict are rendered benign in performance. The actor enters willingly into the system of theatrical representation and the environment is monitored for risk and safety. Indeed, the rehearsal notes for 4.7 include a request for "6 sandbags to go over their [the actors'] heads that are loosely woven for them to see through & also to be able to breath [*sic*] through".[43] In this carefully monitored and controlled environment, the situation is divested of much, if not all, of the affect of terror or trauma that comes from the helplessness of the "real" situation of a prisoner of war, which the production seeks to represent, with particular recourse to the experiences of Iraqi prisoners. In contrast, the absolute lack of control and subjugation that marks the experiences of prisoners of war emerges more clearly, although, of course, not fully, not on stage but in the photographs circulated by the British media contemporaneous with the opening of the production on 13 May 2003, detailing alleged abuses of Iraqi prisoners by British troops. These images offer a disturbing and violent counter-narrative of unethical behaviour to the one of integrity and humanity that the production worked to develop.[44]

The drive toward realism through weapons training and character creation exercises was augmented by the use of replica military uniform and kit, the results of which are shown in Figure 4.2; Lester's Henry stands wearing combat uniform, a pistol in one hand, surrounded by four soldiers who are similarly dressed, two with rifles raised as if they are about to fire out of the frame of the photograph. Despite this attention to detail, the production, by virtue of its status as a theatrical representation, cannot but identify its failure to instantiate the real thing. Instead the production works to highlight the carefully produced theatricality of the scenes, as Ivan Kyncl's elegantly composed photographs of the production and its rehearsal phase, two of which are reproduced in this book, illustrate. In the rehearsal photograph (Figure 4.1), for example, some of the actors wear elbow and knee pads so as to aid them in the choreography of the battle sequences in the space of the rehearsal room. Given the demands of working on the large Olivier stage, both in terms of the number of actors on stage and the

Figure 4.2 Adrian Lester (centre) as Henry V in Nicholas Hytner's 2003 production of *Henry V* for the National Theatre. Photograph © Ivan Kyncl, reproduced with the permission of Alena Melichar.

technical demands of staging battle sequences, these spectacles were, as noted in the rehearsal diary, subject to "meticulous planning and military style logistics".[45] This led to conflict between efforts to stage the "reality" of battle and the technical and theatrical demands of the sequences. This is most clearly revealed in the rehearsal diary, which records Smedley's concerns that:

> the action had also become too slick and had none of the "mess" of real conflict [. . . .] The shooting of two of the soldiers leads the army to take cover but too many of the actors were anticipating the shootings and reacting too early. But when Richard fixed this, the spontaneous reaction to the shootings created so much hurried movement on stage that Hytner became worried that it would distract the audience from reading the actual shootings. He conceded that they would have to "cheat the image" by making the deaths bigger and delaying the outbreak of panic.[46]

Here Smedley's desire to reproduce something of the "'mess' of real conflict" is subordinated to Hytner's concerns with staging spectacle within a carefully controlled theatrical environment. The rehearsal notes, which identify, for example, where the shell explosions in 3.2 should fall, the use of makeup in order that the soldiers in 3.3 be shown with "charred looking faces and look a real mess", the complexity of the technical rehearsal and video footage of the production reveal the careful choreography of the battle sequences.[47]

Rather than showing the reality of contemporary warfare, the rehearsal notes and footage instead draw attention to the theatricality of staged warfare and the failure of the spectacle of men moving across the stage in military kit with replica weapons and "charred" faces to embody the mess of "real" conflict. To return to Kubiak's arguments, "[t]heatre always seems to leave real violence behind because this is precisely theatre's function—to conceal violence even when (or especially when) it is seemingly exposing it in the violent spectacle".[48] Rather than showing "real" violence, which Kubiak argues, may in part be due to the prosaic fact that "real violence in performance [. . .] is not as efficient as its mimetic representation" (repertory theatre relies, after all, on the capacity to "reuse" the actor from performance to performance), theatre works instead to conceal its operation.[49] But, given that spectators (presumably) know that they are not watching the "real thing" of warfare and its traumatic after-effects, what does it matter that the production fails, as it must, to instantiate it? Here I would argue that the issue is not the failure of representation to instantiate the real thing (this is, after all, the condition of realism), but rather the way that the production worked to occlude this failure. That is, the production was presented as if it had special access to the physical and emotional reality of contemporary warfare, capitalising on events just prior to and concurrent with the production to authenticate (and sell) the production. Here the "real" trauma of warfare is co-opted in the service of the production of a theatrical commodity designed to participate in Hytner's project of nation(al) building.

OUT OF TIME 1: MEMORIALISING THE PAST

In contrast to the moments of coincidence between the rehearsal process, the play's opening and contemporary events, in a letter to *The Stage* on 27 March 2003 Gary Tewson suggested that the play will look out of date when it opens: "[w]ith Saddam toppled and the Iraqi people dancing in the streets, Mr Hytner's conceptual tomfoolery will be out of date as well as out of its depth".[50] Tewson's comment here looks forward to the future of the production's opening in May in order to identify it as being out of time, or asynchronous with contemporary events, which are depicted here in terms of a fantasy of liberation for the Iraqi people. Tewson's comment also participates in the rhetoric of victory with respect to war in Iraq, which is reiterated by those involved in the production. Whereas earlier parts of the rehearsal diary had noted a synchronous relation between the war and the action of the play—"[a]s the campaign for the Olivier stage was being mapped out, the fighting in Iraq continued"—as the production entered its final week of preparation it is noted that "[t]he war in Iraq had ended, but the battle to successfully stage this play was far from won".[51] Here victory is implicitly claimed for the coalition military action in Iraq; the language of battle is also co-opted for the work of theatre, such that the production might, too, be positioned as a victor of sorts, echoing the language of the "campaign" for the Olivier.

Whereas Hytner claimed an anticipatory relation between the production and contemporary events for the preparation phrase of the project, in the post-show Platform discussion at the National he switched to the past tense in order to explain some of the production choices. He says "there were certain things which ultimately happened which I think wouldn't have happened if the war hadn't finished [. . . .] As an example [. . .] the celebratory victory video [shown near the end of the production]; I don't think I would have gone there if the war had been long and bloody and when we opened there were still British soldiers being killed". Hytner here locates the war against Iraq as an event of the past, which creates the space for him to consider Henry's victory as celebratory propaganda, exemplified by the "victory video", to which I will return below (125–26). Reading these comments at a remove of some seven years does, however, expose the failure of this temporal consignment of the war to the past as the United Kingdom and the United States didn't announce their intention to end their military operations in Iraq until 18 December 2008 and 31 August 2010, respectively; in the speeches announcing their decisions, Gordon Brown and Barack Obama downplayed some (but not all) of the rhetoric of victory, speaking in some measure to the significant loss of civilian and military lives during the campaign.[52]

Hytner could not, of course have predicted with absolute certainty the sustained military action in Iraq, which works, belatedly, as I have suggested, to undermine the rhetoric of victory that circulated in the wake of the initial assault on Iraq and the deposition of Saddam Hussein in March 2003, and which informed some of the production decisions. But reading the production retrospectively, or belatedly, the rhetoric of victory in the face of continued military action identifies the hollowness of that rhetoric and points to the ongoing and traumatic experiences of warfare, both for those who perpetrate it and those who are its victims. This is exemplified in the news reports of allegations of prisoner abuses that emerged concurrently with the production's opening to which I referred earlier, showing how the trauma of war refuses to be contained by rhetorical closure, working its way into the contemporary consciousness through the conduit of the media. In this section I want to consider how the production works, although not exclusively, to consign war (both the action narrated by the play and contemporary warfare) to the past. In so doing I want to consider how the production attempted to memorialise military action under the sign of a specifically British victory, even as it created space for a critique of the rhetoric of victory, and the implications this has for spectatorship.

The "celebratory" video Hytner mentioned that was shown near the end of the production, which can be viewed on the Stagework website under the not so subtle title "Propaganda Video", was shot in the style of a news broadcast trailer.[53] With its synthpop soundtrack it offers an upbeat, over-determined representation of Henry's victory. The video opens with the Union Jack fluttering across the screen, followed by the superimposition of the title credits "The Battle of Agincourt". The video then depicts images of Henry dressed in combat gear, sometimes with the Union Jack behind him, rousing his troops, who are presented as a unified mass. Across the bottom of the screen scroll the death statistics from Agincourt—10 000 French and 29 English deaths. The video finishes with the Union Jack once again rippling across the screen, this time with the word "Victory" superimposed upon it. This film thus offers a neatly mediatised version of events as they are recounted in the play's narrative and also identifies how "news" is packaged as "entertainment". In the depiction of Henry as a heroic military leader, steering his troops to victory in the name of the nation, "news" is shown to be far from ideologically neutral. Given the production's insistent engagement with contemporary conflict, which, in addition to the comments made by Hytner and the actors, was identified repeatedly in reviews of the production—"Henry Goes to Baghdad", "Henry Gets a Few Tips from Blair", "Iraq and a Hard Place", "Agincourt, near Basra", for example—spectators were invited to read the celebration of the victory at Agincourt as an analogue for British and American action in Iraq.[54] By the production's end, one of its publicity taglines—"The risks are huge; the cause debatable; and bloodshed certain"—comes to be resolved in Henry's successful and mostly casualty-free (for the English) campaign, enacted in the saccharine news broadcast under the sign of the Union Jack.[55] The use of the Union Jack is, of course, ahistorical in relation to both the historical time of the play's narrative (early 1400s) and original conditions of production (1599) of *Henry V*; the first union flag, which joined the English and Scottish crosses, wasn't produced until 1606 following James I's accession to the throne. The modern Union Jack, which dates from 1801 is, though, contemporary with the early twenty-first Britain of the production's setting.[56] The production's deployment of this sign in the onstage business of the post-Agincourt sequences (it is carried on and off stage by the victorious soldiers) and as a significant part of the "victory" video, works to relocate Henry's medieval victory under the sign of contemporary Britain. The production here consigns war to the past and it is memorialised in victorious terms, with minimal loss of life.

While the production maintained a relatively ambiguous position on Henry's decision to go to war—it is neither resolutely pro- or anti-war, in keeping with what Hytner describes in the Platform discussion as his "ambiguous response" to the war—the final sequences, in the wake of the defeat of the French, work to foreclose on this ambiguity, such that the production celebrates "victory", with the soldiers' celebratory dance to pumping heavy metal music, the reading aloud of the war casualties to Henry's and the soldiers' evident communal delight and relief, and the screening of the victory video. Here the production seemed to invite complicity from the spectators in relation to acts of war—Henry's and, if the production's analogy is taken seriously, Bush and Blair's. It did, though, create the space for such complicity to be refused. The overdetermined video, for example, could have been read, ironically, as a critique of the rhetoric of victory and the propaganda surrounding war. Furthermore, the awkward "comedy" that surrounds Catherine's enforced surrender to Henry (5.2) could have been considered in the context of the ongoing and pernicious effects of warfare, especially with respect to the treatment of women. Finally, the narrative closure of the play, in which the Chorus takes a proleptic excursion into the future to describe Henry VI's reign, where his "state so many had the managing/ That they lost France and made his England bleed" (Epilogue, 11–12), identifies the hollowness of the triumphal rhetoric at the close of *Henry V*'s fifth act and the production's performance of it. Given that *1 Henry VI*, *2 Henry VI* and *3 Henry VI* had already been written and staged by the time Shakespeare wrote *Henry V*, the play might also be read as an analepsis, marking a return to the past after future (and destructive) events have been told and, in this case, performed.[57] The play's excursions into the future of the narrative and the past of the production history are thus both marked by the failure of Henry VI to maintain Henry V's victory over France and control over England.

In this context, it is worth noting that in 2005 Hytner directed *1 Henry IV* and *2 Henry IV* at the National; rather than playing out the failure of Henry V's dynasty through the *Henry VI* plays, Hytner returned to an earlier stage in the historical narrative to depict the development of Prince Hal from playboy to the authoritative Henry V. Unlike the modern dress used for *Henry V*, the *Henry IV* plays were subject, for the most part, to a medieval dress aesthetic and setting. Despite this, the hoods that were used for the rebels at the end of *I Henry IV* resonated, for me at least, with images from the contemporary media and Hytner's *Henry V*, identifying how images of contemporary trauma can work their way insistently into contemporary representations of the past.[58] Devoid of the overt associations with Afghanistan and Iraq that marked *Henry V*, Hytner's productions of *1* and *2 Henry IV*, which took place as conflict in Afghanistan and Iraq was far from over, seemed to defer the invitation that his earlier production of *Henry V* offered in its conclusion to consider the failure of invasion, be it of France or, by analogy, Afghanistan and Iraq. Confronted with depictions of the "contemporary" as in *Henry V* or "the past" as in the *Henry IV* plays, the challenge for the spectator, then, is to resist letting theatre disappear under the rubric of a "really good time" and to hold it accountable for its representational politics, perhaps especially in cases where those politics work to elide marginal subject positions and foreclose on the trauma to which it lays claim. While the discourse surrounding *Henry V* worked to consign the war in Iraq to the past, a consideration of the photographs collated in the programme and the production's research materials shows how the trauma, or ongoing effects, of war continue to be felt. This material makes claims on the present of the "production time" and the future to come, marked here by the "writing time" of this critical project and the future to which it speaks. As Sontag notes in *On Photography* (1977), and the following section will consider, "[t]he force of a photograph is that it keeps open to scrutiny instants which the normal flow of time immediately replaces".[59]

OUT OF TIME 2: PHOTOGRAPHING FOR THE FUTURE

The programme for *Henry V* pays homage to a pictorial history of representations of war in its inclusion of images from ancient, medieval and early modern cultures. It also includes photographs of German stormtroopers "going over the top" in the First World War; the allied invasion of Sicily in 1943, with a stream of soldiers wading ashore under the weight of full military kit; and a photograph of British troops posed on a tank in Iraq in 1992, with one soldier positioned at the apex of the gun, flying a Union Jack embossed with the royal insignia. This drive to represent past conflicts is also present in the inclusion of images on the Stagework website of the Royal Artillery Memorial (1925), which commemorates members of the

Royal Regiment of Artillery who died during the First World War.[60] The programme and the Stagework website thus collectively archive a history of warfare, including the historical event that *Henry V* depicts in the inclusion of an image of the Battle of Agincourt from a fifteenth-century miniature. The use of images of war, like the military exercises and replica uniforms and kit, work to imbue the production with the aura of the "real" experience of warfare, situating the production in relation to a longer history than the contemporary conflicts to which the production most obviously points.

The programme, with its captioned pictures, also functions to delimit and bound the potential meanings of a given photograph (for example, the caption of the soldiers in Iraq in 1992 prevents me from reading this image as a representation of more recent conflict in Afghanistan and Iraq, with which it shares many visual codes). As Roland Barthes notes in his essay "The Photographic Message" (1961), photographic captions constitute "a parasitic message designed to connote the image, to 'quicken' it with one or more second-order signified. In other words [. . .] it is now the words which, structurally, are parasitic on the image".[61] Although it's worth qualifying Barthes's claim with Sontag's observation that "no caption can permanently restrict or secure a picture's meaning", the precisely dated captions in the programme work alongside the lengthy timescale that the images cover, to position these events as categorically of the past.[62] It is notable that the most recent photograph, taken in 1992 of British troops in Iraq, finishes the historical sequence of warfare, which has shown aspects of war to be inhospitable and violent, with an image of group solidarity as the soldiers smile directly at the camera and wave their arms in the air. The programme, with its compendium of images of war, placed alongside heroic images of Henry from the play's performance history—Laurence Olivier in medieval armour mounted on a horse with the St George's cross in the background (1944)—operates as a kind of sanitised souvenir *memento mori* of battles and productions of the past. It denotes shifts in documentary technologies, which, like aspects of the production, work to memorialise the dead; it collects images of others within its pages but the specificity of their claims and experiences goes largely unheard, neatly repackaged in the context of character assessments of Henry V, character and play, which dominate the programme.

Given Hytner's interest in having the play speak to "current events", what is striking about the collection of images in the programme is that it does not contain any images of contemporary military action in Afghanistan and Iraq. In contrast to the volume of information it contains and the images of historical conflicts it depicts, the programme only draws attention to contemporary conflicts verbally and comparatively fleetingly. For instance, it includes a fragment of an article in the tabloid *The Sun* that likened Lt Col Tim Collins's speech to the 1st Battalion of the Royal Irish Regiment outside Basra in 2003 to Henry's speech to his army before Agincourt; it also prints a comment from former Foreign Secretary Douglas

Hurd that Henry's "claim to France is more complicated even than Security Council resolution 1441 on Iraq". Images of these very recent and ongoing conflicts are, however, elided from the visual field of the programme. The programme thus registers a tension, where the production's central traumatic event is visually absent, even as it is called into being through the programme's text, which once again confers legitimacy upon the production decisions. This visual lacuna may, of course, speak to pragmatic concerns relating to the timescale of the programme preparation in relation to obtaining permission to reproduce images. But the elision of documentary photographic representation of action in Afghanistan and Iraq removes a point of comparison between the production and the "real" thing to which it refers. This has the effect of positioning the action of the performance as the primary visual signifier of contemporary warfare for its spectators, if only for the duration of the performance. Indeed, the only contemporary images in the programme consist of rehearsal photographs of the cast, several of which depict their military exercises. The elision thus works alongside the acting exercises, costumes and props, to imbue the production with the aura of the "real", the authentic inheritor of the performances and histories to which the programme refers. Whereas images of Iraq and Afghanistan are missing from the programme they are, as I mentioned earlier in relation to the image of the Iraqi prisoners, present in the research materials that the cast used as part of the rehearsal process.

Held in the National Theatre Archive in clear plastic sleeves, which give them the quality of specimens, collected for posterity, are newspaper clippings glued onto sheets of white A4 paper, included in a folder alongside production notes, costume fabric swatches and photographs of the actors.[63] Although mostly undated, the captions suggest that the images relate to the preparation and invasion of Iraq in March 2003: troops carry out exercises in north Kuwait; troops fit armour to a reconnaissance vehicle in the Kuwaiti desert; eight pairs of siblings pose for a photograph as they wait in the Kuwaiti desert; Royal Marines patrol in Kuwait, guns at the ready, their faces shielded by gas masks; two army engineers rest in Kuwait after clearing their camp out; two US marines trudge through mud outside Nasiriyah; troops shelter in a muddy dugout in the same area; a soldier stands guard as an oilfield burns in Rumaila; an Iraqi man cradles his son, slumped on the ground behind barbed wire in a prisoner of war camp in Najaf; a Royal Marine holds down a Fedayeen prisoner in Umm Qasr—the prisoner's face is pixellated, the marine looks directly at the camera; a Gurkha soldier guards Iraqi prisoners of war, who stand as a faceless out-of-focus mass in the background, the Gurkha soldier sharply etched in the foreground, his gun clearly visible. It seems likely from the comments in the rehearsal diary that images from contemporary news reports, if not these ones in particular, were referred to in the rehearsal process, alongside images from the Gulf War in the early 1990s that also lined the rehearsal room.[64] This kind of material, alongside images from the television news, provided grist for the production's image making with respect to the "reality" of battle and the treatment of prisoners, highlighting Sontag's assertion that "[t]he understanding of war among people who have not experienced war is now chiefly a product of the impact of these images".[65] War, in Sontag's terms, is known through images; the images stand in for experience to the extent that they become the experience of war. Hytner's theatre, at a further remove, attempts to offers itself as a three-dimensional image of the experience of war, for actors and spectators.

To read the images in the archive is, in one respect, to highlight how both photography and performance fail to capture the traumatic event of war, registering only its traces in after-images. The photographs reproduced in the clippings work to show something of the oppressiveness of day-to-day warfare, especially the atrocious weather conditions that are likened in one caption to the Somme battlefields of the First World War. They also depict the horrifyingly unequal relations of power that war produces. This is exemplified in the image of the prisoner whose head is held to the ground and his face pixellated, such that he becomes, literally, a faceless other, like the out-of-focus prisoners that the Gurkha soldier guards and the Iraqi man holding his son, his head covered by what looks to be a hood, familiar from other images of prisoners that circulated concurrently with the production. The horror of these images points up the hollowness of the image making on stage, such as I considered earlier in relation to the depiction of the French prisoners; the stage images, carefully managed and controlled, cannot help but identify their failure to capture the traumatic experience of warfare.

I do not, though, want to reify the photographs as offering access to the "real thing" of the experience of war. Here, then, it is worth remembering Sontag's claim that "the photographic image, even to the extent that it is a trace [. . .], cannot be simply a transparency of something that happened. It is always the image that someone chose; to photograph is to frame, and to frame is to exclude".[66] The photograph is not a one-to-one correspondence of the event but produced by the photographer and mediated and mediatised by the news media such that the photograph does not give access to the event itself. Instead it gives access to a version or representation of the event and this is always necessarily partial by virtue of the framing of the image. Like the operation of trauma, the photograph is belated, both in the action of the shutter and the production of the image for consumption. It registers, then, an effect, a trace of the event, which remains unknowable. In so doing it offers its own version of the event through the photograph's visual codes and "parasitic" captions (war is heroic, oppressive, violent, and so on). Writing of the difficulty that attends what might be described as the "photography of trauma", Barthes argues:

> trauma is a suspension of language, a blocking of meaning. Certainly situations which are normally traumatic can be seized in a process of photographic signification but then precisely they are indicated via a

rhetorical code which distances, sublimates and pacifies them. Truly traumatic photographs are rare, for in photography the trauma is wholly dependent on the certainty that the scene "really" happened [. . . .] the traumatic photograph [. . .] is the photograph about which there is nothing to say; the shock photo is by structure insignificant: no value, no knowledge, at the limit no verbal categorization can have a hold on the process of instituting the signification.[67]

Barthes here suggests that to photograph trauma is, by virtue of the photograph's participation in rhetorical codes, to distance, sublimate and pacify it; it thus becomes other than the thing it purports to be. He keeps open the possibility that a traumatic photograph might exist; this is a photograph that refuses categorisation and evades signification. But given the way that photographs of traumatic events are framed for consumption such that the horror of the image, at least in mainstream news media, very rarely stands alone, without comment, without interpretation, an image that resists signification seems phantasmic, flickering at the edges of discourse.

Although I would suggest that the photographic images, like the production, fail in their representation of the traumatic thing itself, they also, like the images in the programme, make claims upon the viewer to acknowledge the violence of war. I would argue that to engage with the images in the archive—to bring them into circulation as part of the production's discourse through the act of criticism—is to acknowledge, however inadequately, some of the experiences of war to which the production claims to speak. Whereas the production and the discourse around it work to consign the "event" of war to the past—"we had just been at war", "if the war hadn't finished"—the photographs in the archive, by keeping sometimes violent moments open to scrutiny, refuse such easy consignment to the past, especially when read belatedly in relation to ongoing UK and US military action in Afghanistan and Iraq. The photographs, by virtue of their temporality, are capable of making a claim on the spectator such that the ongoing force of war continues to be felt now and in the future.

In her consideration of photographs of prisoner abuses and torture by US military personnel at Abu Ghraib Prison in Iraq, which began to emerge in 2004, Judith Butler suggests that:

the efficacy of the camera works along a temporal trajectory other than the chronology it secures. The visual archive circulates. The date function on the camera may specify precisely when the event happened, but the indefinite circulability of the image allows the event to continue to happen and, indeed, thanks to these images the event has not stopped happening.[68]

That is, while the camera documents an event that takes place at a certain time the circulation and repetition of the image works to reiterate the image such that it continues to be announced, as if it were happening again and again. These images, which both document the past and announce it, repeatedly, for the future time in which the photographs will be viewed, invite spectators to be haunted by the horror of the images now and in the future. Butler goes on to argue that:

> the photograph acts on us in part through outliving the life it documents; it establishes in advance the time in which that loss will be acknowledged as a loss. So the photograph is linked through its "tense" to the grievability of a life, anticipating and performing that grievability. In this way, we can be haunted in advance by the suffering or deaths of others. Or we can be haunted afterwards, when the check against grief becomes undone.[69]

In response to Sontag's call for "the atrocious images to haunt us", Butler here mounts an argument about the photograph's power to act on its spectators.[70] Butler suggests that the photograph makes an argument "for the grievability of a life" in that "[i]f we can be haunted, then we can acknowledge that there has been a loss and hence that there has been a life".[71] The photograph seeks this acknowledgement through its tense. Butler thus makes a case for how the frozen moment of the photograph makes a claim on its viewers by anticipating the past (i.e., photographs document that which will have been). In so doing the photograph asks the spectator to acknowledge that life and to grieve for the life that will have been. I would suggest that it is here that the efficacy of war photography is clearest. Its power is not so much in its capacity to "capture" trauma, which as I have suggested via Sontag and Barthes borders on the impossible. Rather it is photography's capacity to make demands on spectators to acknowledge the lives that the images depict as grievable and hence to accord them value.

The images in the archive from contemporary war reports were not made available in the programme or circulated as part of the production's official discourse (programmes, posters, and so on). This is in sharp contrast to the 64-page A5 booklet for Deborah Warner's production of *Julius Caesar* for the Barbican.[72] Produced in April 2005, almost exactly two years after Hytner's production of *Henry V*—with British military action in Afghanistan and Iraq clearly not yet over—Warner's production used a visual economy, like Hytner's, to create resonances between contemporary events and the action of Shakespeare's play. This is especially clear in the use of military kit and clothing; the staging of the hundred-strong crowd of extras who forced their way past police barricades which, in their capacity to be incited to violence, offered a horrifying antithesis to the anti-war marches of February 2003; and, most particularly, the programme. Printed on high gloss paper the programme contains reproductions of eight images which are visually coded in such a way that they seem to depict contemporary warfare in Iraq. It also included two photographs by Philip-Lorca diCorcia of city street scenes and a host of ubiquitous rehearsal images. Inspection of the sparsely detailed credits list reveals that at least one of the eight "war" images refers to fighting in Afghanistan in the 1990s and for six of these images, the credits list withholds information about the photographs' subjects, detailing only the photographers and their agents. The high production values of the programme, which literally made the images available for consumption as part of the theatrical experience, as with the programme for *Henry V*, function, as Sontag suggests in relation to photography more generally, "to convert the world into a department store or museum-without-walls in which every subject is depreciated into an article of consumption, promoted into an item for aesthetic appreciation".[73] As with Hytner's production of *Henry V*, Warner's production seemed to echo some of the images. Strikingly, one of the images, of a soldier wrapped in a sleeping bag in a bombed-out building, binoculars fixed to his eyes, guns ready at his feet, was enacted in the image that opened the production's second half.

The images of war, printed without captions, sit in the programme for *Julius Caesar* unmoored and reliant on individual spectators' familiarity with images circulating in the contemporary media to provide them with referents. The lack of captions frees the images from a parasitic "quickening", calling upon the spectator to acknowledge scenes of trauma, such as Hayne Palmour IV's image of an unnamed man who sits, blindfolded, hands bound behind his back, armed troops and a burning landscape discernible in the out-of-focus background; a search of the website of Polaris Images, the photographer's agency, notes that the image was taken on 8 April 2003 in Iraq. It is described in the following way: "[a] terrified Iraqi enemy prisoner sings to himself while blindfolded as Marines run run [*sic*] into an industrial complex that they just set on fire by shooting at fuel tanks with machine guns".[74] The parasitic caption animates the image, drenching it with the sonic accompaniment of the man's terrified singing, naming his actions and emotions with assuredness, as if his experience was knowable, while still designating him as an absolute "other": the "enemy". To reproduce the image, with or without the caption, reiterates, once again, the man's powerlessness and, despite the caption's efforts to name it otherwise, the absolute unknowability of his experience. In stripping the images of their referents and providing them with a new frame of reference—*Julius Caesar*—the programme works to package the images of others, as with the images of prisoners in *Henry V*, as part of the theatrical spectacle, pacified and domesticated as part a commentary on the action of the play. Faced with the images of war in the programme and their imitations on the stage I would argue that it is here that the "loop of relevance" fails most spectacularly; the narrative of *Julius Caesar* or *Henry V*, or any of Shakespeare's plays for that matter, seems entirely inadequate to "illuminate" anything of the lived traumatic experiences of war. Instead the images of contemporary war in Warner's programme, especially that of the blindfolded and bound prisoner, demand acknowledgement from the spectator with respect to the specificity of the traumatic experiences that they mark, a specificity that the programme and production work to deny. And yet the horror of the image still calls out to the spectator to acknowledge the life of the prisoner, in Butler's terms, as grievable.

To give weight to the images collected in the archives as I have done in relation to *Henry V* or to find a caption for a faceless and unnamed other as I have done in relation to *Julius Caesar*, however inadequate it may be, is to attempt a critical project that seeks to acknowledge, if only in a necessarily partial way, some of the individuals and circumstances that these productions stripped of their referents in the course of their theatrical reproduction. In so doing I have tried to keep open to scrutiny the ongoing trauma of war that photographs enable, by virtue of their "tense" and relation to future spectators. In this work I am all too acutely aware, as I have been throughout this book in my attempts to excavate the ongoing traumatic effects of violent events and histories, of the limitations not only of performance, but also of criticism, in acknowledging (and writing) the trauma of others. Indeed, my consideration of how performance works to memorialise, remember and witness violent events and histories, indexing their traumatic after-effects in performance and in the field of documentation, also acknowledges the failure of representation to call the traumatic thing itself into being. Efforts to represent and know trauma are never ideologically neutral and always serve particular cultural and political agendas, as the foregoing chapters have demonstrated. In attempting to account for—but not to rationalise—the ongoing effects of violence as it manifests in performance and its documentary traces, this book has sought to identify how performances of Shakespeare variously enfold the traumatic legacies of these events. In so doing I have sought to consider the political and ethical implications of performance's engagements with trauma, especially with respect to performing, spectatorship and community formation.

Performance can thus be used to uphold essentialist narratives about Shakespeare's relevance and universalism that can work to occlude difference and, on occasions, to perform further violence on individuals and groups. But it also enables, as I have suggested, the formation of productive and effective responses to violence that strive to acknowledge difference and counter oppression. Here it is worth noting that *This Island's Mine* and *The Maori Merchant of Venice*, produced on the fringes of mainstream metropolitan productions of Shakespeare—marked by organisations such as the National Theatre and the Royal Shakespeare Company—seem to afford more scope to counter and redress the traumatic effects of violence than *Titus Andronicus* and *Henry V*, co-produced and produced by the National, respectively. While the marginal might seem more efficacious in this respect, it is worth remembering that even in cases where a production might reproduce or produce forms of violence, spectators and writers can still choose to acknowledge, critique and oppose such representations, as I have tried to do at various points in this book.

The invitation that *Shakespeare, Trauma and Contemporary Performance* offers is to find ways of making performances of Shakespeare's plays and writing about them that keep open to scrutiny the ongoing trauma of violent events and histories to which productions variously lay claim, without producing further violence. Importantly, this is not a call for censorship but rather a call to consider how violence might be staged so as to foreground and critique the ways in which it is offered for consumption and the possibilities that performance might offer to counter violence. Such work invites theatre makers, writers, spectators and readers to stand as witness to trauma such that they might feel the weight of responsibility toward others and work to acknowledge and oppose inequalities born of violence.

Notes

Unless otherwise indicated all websites were operational as of 1 October 2010; it is not possible to guarantee the stability of these websites or that the content will remain appropriate. All references to Shakespeare's plays are to *The Norton Shakespeare*, ed. Stephen Greenblatt *et al*. (New York: Norton, 1997).

NOTES TO THE INTRODUCTION

1. *Titus*, DVD, directed by Julie Taymor (Los Angeles: Twentieth Century Fox Home Entertainment, 2000).
2. Ann Cvetkovich, *An Archive of Feelings: Trauma, Sexuality, and Lesbian Public Cultures* (Durham: Duke University Press, 2003), 11.
3. Cvetkovich, *An Archive of Feelings*, 10.
4. Miranda Joseph, *Against the Romance of Community* (Minneapolis: University of Minnesota Press, 2002), vii.
5. Julie Taymor, *Playing with Fire: Theater, Opera, Film*, co-authored with Eileen Blumenthal and Antonio Mondo, 3rd ed. (New York: Abrams, 1999), 219.
6. For a discussion of connections between Taymor's film and the Holocaust, see Richard Burt, "Shakespeare and the Holocaust: Julie Taymor's *Titus* Is Beautiful, or Shakesploi Meets (the) Camp," *Colby Quarterly* 37.1 (2001): 78–106.
7. Julie Taymor, *Titus: The Illustrated Screenplay, Adapted from the Play by William Shakespeare* (New York: Newmarket Press, 2000), 182.
8. Bill Moyers, interview with Julie Taymor, "America Responds: Tuesday, September 11, 2001," PBS, broadcast 20 September 2001, http://www.pbs.org/americaresponds/moyers920.html.
9. Taymor, interview with Moyers.
10. Courtney Lehmann, Bryan Reynolds and Lisa Starks, "'For such a sight will blind a father's eye': The Spectacle of Suffering in Taymor's *Titus*," in *Performing Transversally: Reimagining Shakespeare and the Critical Future*, by Bryan Reynolds (New York: Palgrave, 2003), 226, Lehmann *et al*.'s emphasis.
11. Tim Etchells, *Certain Fragments: Contemporary Performance and Forced Entertainment* (London: Routledge, 1999), 17.
12. Helena Grehan, *Performance, Ethics and Spectatorship in a Global Age* (Basingstoke: Palgrave, 2009), 21. For Emmanuel Levinas's elucidation of his philosophy of the "other", see, for example: *Totality and Infinity: An Essay*

on Exteriority, trans. Alphonso Lingis (Pittsburgh: Duquesne University Press, 1969), especially 187–219.

13. Kim Solga, *Violence Against Women in Early Modern Performance: Invisible Acts* (Basingstoke: Palgrave, 2009); see especially the introduction (1–28) and afterword (176–79).

14. Taymor, *Playing with Fire*, 242.

15. Taymor, *Titus: The Illustrated Screenplay*, 166.

16. Mark Thornton Burnett, "Remembrance, Holocaust, Globalization," in *Filming Shakespeare in the Global Marketplace* (Basingstoke: Palgrave, 2007), 87–106.

17. Jason Burt, "Chelsea Players Hold Inquest after Trauma of Spurs Defeat," *Independent*, 29 February 2008, http://www.independent.co.uk/sport/football/fa-league-cups/chelsea-players-hold-inquest-after-trauma-of-spurs-defeat-789249.html; Graeme Wearden, "Stockmarkets Spooked by Fresh Credit Crunch Fears," *Guardian*, 8 July 2008, http://www.guardian.co.uk/business/2008/jul/08/marketturmoil.creditcrunch.

18. Roger Luckhurst, *The Trauma Question* (London: Routledge, 2008), 34; see Luckhurst for a nuanced analysis of the development of psycho/physical accounts of trauma, especially 34–49.

19. Sigmund Freud, *Beyond the Pleasure Principle*, vol. 18, in *The Standard Edition of the Complete Psychological Works of Sigmund Freud*, trans. James Strachey (London: Hogarth Press, 1955), 12. My reading of Freud has benefitted from Cathy Caruth's work in *Unclaimed Experience: Trauma, Narrative and History* (Baltimore: Johns Hopkins University Press, 1996), 10–24 and 57–72, and Cvetkovich's work in *An Archive of Feelings*, 52–56.

20. Freud, *Beyond the Pleasure Principle*, 29.

21. Sigmund Freud, "Moses, His People and Monotheist Religion," in *Moses and Monotheism*, vol. 23, in *The Standard Edition of the Complete Psychological Works of Sigmund Freud*, trans. James Strachey (London: Hogarth Press, 1964), 54–137.

22. See Caruth, *Unclaimed Experience*, 10–24, especially 16–18.

23. Freud, "Moses, His People and Monotheist Religion," 67.

24. Freud, "Moses, His People and Monotheist Religion," 75–76.

25. Freud, *Beyond the Pleasure Principle*, 32.

26. Freud, *Beyond the Pleasure Principle*, 32.

27. Freud, "Moses, His People and Monotheist Religion," 77.

28. Cvetkovich, *An Archive of Feelings*, 52.

29. See Jacques Derrida, "Plato's Pharmacy," in *Dissemination*, trans. Barbara Johnson (London: Athlone, 1981), 61–171, especially 95–117.

30. Cvetkovich, *An Archive of Feelings*, 30.

31. See American Psychiatric Association, "Post-traumatic Stress Disorder," in *Diagnostic and Statistical Manual of Mental Disorders: DSM-III*, 3rd ed. (Washington, D.C.: American Psychiatric Association, 1980), 236–39; American Psychiatric Association, "Post-traumatic Stress Disorder," in *Diagnostic and Statistical Manual of Mental Disorders: DSM-III-R*, 3rd rev. ed. (Washington, D.C.: American Psychiatric Association, 1987), 247–51; American Psychiatric Association, "Posttraumatic Stress Disorder," in *Diagnostic and Statistical Manual of Mental Disorders: DSM-IV*, 4th ed. (Washington, D.C.: American Psychiatric Association, 1994), 424–29; American Psychiatric Association, "Posttraumatic Stress Disorder," in *Diagnostic and Statistical Manual of Mental Disorders: DSM-IV-TR*, 4th rev. ed. (Washington, D.C.: American Psychiatric Association,

2000), 463–68. *DSM-IV-TR* lists identical diagnostic criteria for Posttraumatic Stress Disorder to *DSM-IV* and contains some minor revisions to the remainder of the entry in relation to associated descriptive features, prevalence, course and familial pattern.

32. American Psychiatric Association, "Posttraumatic Stress Disorder," *DSM-IV-TR*, 467.
33. American Psychiatric Association, "Posttraumatic Stress Disorder," *DSM-IV-TR*, 464.
34. American Psychiatric Association, "Posttraumatic Stress Disorder," *DSM-IV-TR*, 468.
35. See American Psychiatric Association, "Post-traumatic Stress Disorder," *DSM-III*, 236; American Psychiatric Association, "Post-traumatic Stress Disorder," *DSM-III-R*, 247; the wording in *DSM-III-R* was revised in the following way: the "stressor producing this syndrome would be markedly distressing to almost anyone" (247).
36. Laura S. Brown, "Not Outside the Range: One Feminist Perspective on Psychic Trauma," in *Trauma: Explorations in Memory*, ed. Cathy Caruth (Baltimore: Johns Hopkins University Press, 1995), 107.
37. Caruth, *Unclaimed Experience*, 11; see also 91.
38. Caruth, *Unclaimed Experience*, 91–92.
39. Caruth, *Unclaimed Experience*, 25–56.
40. Caruth, *Unclaimed Experience*, 34, 27, Caruth's emphasis.
41. Caruth, *Unclaimed Experience*, 4.
42. Caruth, *Unclaimed Experience*, 11, Caruth's emphasis.
43. Caruth, "Introduction," in Caruth, *Trauma*, 11.
44. *The Trauma Industry*, Panorama, presented by Allan Little, produced by Kevin Toolis, BBC 1, 27 July 2009.
45. Kirby Farrell, *Post-traumatic Culture: Injury and Interpretation in the Nineties* (Baltimore: Johns Hopkins University Press, 1998), x.
46. Roger Luckhurst, *The Trauma Question* (London: Routledge, 2008).
47. Ruth Leys, *Trauma: A Genealogy* (Chicago: University of Chicago Press, 2000), 15–16, Leys's emphasis.
48. Cvetkovich, *An Archive of Feelings*, 10.
49. Cvetkovich, *An Archive of Feelings*, 3.
50. Cvetkovich, *An Archive of Feelings*, 3–4.
51. Cvetkovich, *An Archive of Feelings*, 10.
52. Cvetkovich, *An Archive of Feelings*, 10.
53. Farrell, *Post-traumatic Culture*, 12.
54. Farrell, *Post-traumatic Culture*, 2.
55. Dominick LaCapra, *Writing History, Writing Trauma* (Baltimore: Johns Hopkins University Press, 2001), 21.
56. Leys, *Trauma: A Genealogy*, 285.
57. Peggy Phelan, *Mourning Sex: Performing Public Memories* (London: Routledge, 1997), 3.
58. Phelan, *Mourning Sex*, 12.
59. Phelan, *Mourning Sex*, 17.
60. Cvetkovich, *An Archive of Feelings*, 3–4.
61. Jacques Derrida, *Archive Fever: A Freudian Impression*, trans. Eric Prenowitz (Chicago: University of Chicago Press, 1996), 17, Derrida's emphasis.
62. Derrida, *Archive Fever*, 13–20.
63. Cvetkovich, *An Archive of Feelings*, 8.
64. Michael D. Bristol, *Shakespeare's America, America's Shakespeare* (London: Routledge, 1990), 62–90.

65. Thomas P. Anderson, *Performing Early Modern Trauma from Shakespeare to Milton* (Aldershot: Ashgate, 2006), 3; Patricia A. Cahill, *Unto the Breach: Martial Formations, Historical Trauma, and the Early Modern Stage* (Oxford: Oxford University Press, 2008), 3; Heather Hirschfeld, "Hamlet's 'first corse': Repetition, Trauma, and the Displacement of Redemptive Typology," *Shakespeare Quarterly* 54.2 (2003): 424–48; Deborah Willis, "'The gnawing vulture': Revenge, Trauma Theory, and *Titus Andronicus*," *Shakespeare Quarterly* 53.1 (2002): 25.
66. Willis, "'The gnawing vulture'," 32.
67. Willis, "'The gnawing vulture'," 51.
68. Willis, "'The gnawing vulture'," 51.
69. Willis, "'The gnawing vulture'," 51, 52.
70. David McCandless, "A Tale of Two *Tituses*: Julie Taymor's Vision on Stage and Screen," *Shakespeare Quarterly* 53.4 (2002): 490, 489.
71. Timothy Murray, *Drama Trauma: Specters of Race and Sexuality in Performance, Video and Art* (London: Routledge, 1997), 4.
72. Murray, *Drama Trauma*, 4. For Murray's discussion of Luhrmann's and Moshinsky and Miller's films see 1–4 and 194–98, respectively.
73. Murray, *Drama Trauma*, 21.
74. Murray, *Drama Trauma*, 33.
75. Willis, "'The gnawing vulture'," 29.
76. Murray Cox, ed., *Shakespeare Comes to Broadmoor: "The Actors Are Come Hither"; The Performance of Tragedy in a Secure Psychiatric Hospital* (London: Kingsley, 1992); Amy Scott-Douglass, *Shakespeare Inside: The Bard Behind Bars* (London: Continuum, 2007).

NOTES TO CHAPTER 1

1. *Shakespeare in Love*, DVD, directed by John Madden (Culver City, C.A.: Columbia TriStar Home Video, 1999).
2. Marc Norman and Tom Stoppard, *Shakespeare in Love* (London: Faber, 1999), 53; all subsequent references will be given in parentheses in the text.
3. For a discussion of the authorship debate and a case for the play's co-authorship with George Peele, see Brian Vickers, *Shakespeare, Co-Author: A Historical Study of Five Collaborative Plays* (Oxford: Oxford University Press, 2002), 148–243.
4. Richard Burt, "Shakespeare and the Holocaust: Julie Taymor's *Titus* Is Beautiful, or Shakesploi Meets (the) Camp," *Colby Quarterly* 37.1 (2001): 89.
5. This chapter is a revised and expanded version of my article, "'Honour the real thing': Shakespeare, Trauma and *Titus Andronicus* in South Africa," *Shakespeare Survey* 62 (2009): 46–57.
6. The 23rd session of the United Nations' General Assembly adopted Resolution 2396 (XXIII) of the Committee on the Policies of Apartheid of the Government of South Africa (A/7348, par. 12, 20) on 2 December 1968; this document is accessible via http://www.un.org/documents/ga/res/23/ares23.htm (italics in original).
7. The 46th session of the United Nations' General Assembly adopted Resolution A/RES/46/79[A] of the Committee on the Policies of Apartheid of the Government of South Africa (A/7348, par. 9) at its 72nd plenary meeting on 13 December 1991; this document is accessible via http://www.un.org/documents/ga/res/46/a46r079.htm.

8. Programme, *Titus Andronicus*, directed by Gregory Doran, Market Theatre/ National Theatre, Cottesloe, London, 1995, National Theatre Archive, RNT/ PP/1/4/175; all references to the programme in this chapter are to this document.

9. Percy Mtwa, Mbongeni Ngema and Barney Simon, *Woza Albert!* (London: Methuen, 1983), n.p.

10. I am grateful to Lusanda Zokufa at the Market Theatre for providing me with details about the history of Shakespeare productions at the Market.

11. See Martin Orkin, *Shakespeare Against Apartheid* (Craighall: Donker, 1987); David Johnson, *Shakespeare and South Africa* (Oxford: Clarendon Press, 1996).

12. Natasha Distiller, *South Africa, Shakespeare and Post-colonial Culture* (Lewiston, N.Y.: Edwin Mellen Press, 2005), 203; Distiller offers a trenchant critique of both Orkin's and Johnson's critical projects (*South Africa*, 199–209).

13. Statistics South Africa, *Quantitative Research Findings on Rape in South Africa* (Pretoria: Statistics South Africa, 2000), http://www.statssa.gov. za/publications/Rape/Rape.pdf; South Africa Law Commission, *Research Paper on Domestic Violence* (Pretoria: South Africa Law Commission, 1999), 7, http://www.justice.gov.za/salrc/rpapers/violence.pdf.

14. Gregory Doran, *Woza Shakespeare! "Titus Andronicus" in South Africa* (London: Methuen, 1997), 179. *Woza Shakespeare!* is divided into sections variously written by Sher and Doran; all subsequent references will be given in parentheses in the text.

15. Natasha Distiller, "Tony's Will: *Titus Andronicus* in South Africa 1995," in *The Shakespearean International Yearbook 9*, ed. Laurence Wright (Farnham: Ashgate, 2009), 156.

16. Distiller, "Tony's Will," 156.

17. Distiller, "Tony's Will," 160.

18. Digby Ricci, "Titus Topples into the 'Relevant' Pit," review of *Titus Andronicus*, Market Theatre, *Weekly Mail & Guardian*, 31 March 1995; Michael Coveney, "A Magical Mastery Tour," review of *Titus Andronicus*, Courtyard, *Observer*, 16 July 1995; Charles Spencer, review of *Titus Andronicus*, Courtyard, *Daily Telegraph*, 14 July 1995.

19. Ricci, "Titus Topples into the 'Relevant' Pit,"; Mark Gevisser, "What's Wrong with Relevance?" review of *Titus Andronicus*, Market Theatre, *Weekly Mail & Guardian*, 7 April 1995; Robert Greig, "Schlock-horror, Elizabethan-style," review of *Titus Andronicus*, Market Theatre, [South Africa] *The Sunday Times*, 2 April 1995; Nick Curtis, "Classic Colonised in Clumsy Fashion," review of *Titus Andronicus*, Cottesloe, *Evening Standard*, 19 July 1995; Benedict Nightingale, "Tyranny Lives in Every Century," review of *Titus Andronicus*, Courtyard, *The Times*, 14 July 1995.

20. Gregory Doran, interview with Robert Lloyd Parry, "*Titus* in South Africa," *Plays International* August 1995: 11 (10–11).

21. Christopher Thurman, "Sher and Doran's *Titus Andronicus* (1995): Importing Shakespeare, Exporting South Africa," *Shakespeare in Southern Africa* 18 (2006): 31.

22. Platform, *Titus Andronicus*, National Theatre, 21 July 1995, National Theatre Archive, audio recording, ref. no. RNT/PL/3/288; all references to the Platform discussion in this chapter are to this recording.

23. Richard Tomlinson, Robert A. Beauregard, Lindsay Bremner and Xolela Mangcu, "The Postapartheid Struggle for an Integrated Johannesburg," in *Emerging Johannesburg: Perspectives on the Postapartheid City*, ed. Richard Tomlinson *et al.* (New York: Routledge, 2003), 13.

24. Thurman, "Sher and Doran's *Titus Andronicus* (1995)," 32.
25. Thurman, "Sher and Doran's *Titus Andronicus* (1995)," 32.
26. Antony Sher, "Homecoming," *The Times*, 19 November 1994.
27. Peter Brook, *The Empty Space* (London: Penguin, 1990), 30.
28. Lauren Love, "Resisting the 'Organic': A Feminist Actor's Approach," in *Acting (Re)Considered: A Theoretical and Practical Guide*, ed. Phillip B. Zarrilli, 2nd ed. (London: Routledge, 2002), 278.
29. Doran, interview with Robert Lloyd Parry, 10.
30. Love, "Resisting the 'Organic': A Feminist Actor's Approach," 279.
31. Cathy Caruth, *Unclaimed Experience: Trauma, Narrative and History* (Baltimore: Johns Hopkins University Press, 1996), 5.
32. Cathy Caruth, "Introduction," in *Trauma: Explorations in Memory*, ed. Cathy Caruth (Baltimore: Johns Hopkins University Press, 1995), 8; Caruth, *Unclaimed Experience*, 4.
33. Trauma Clinic advertisement, *Star*, 8 May 1995.
34. For details of the Truth and Reconciliation Commission, including transcripts from individuals who gave testimony see http://www.doj.gov.za/trc/. For an analysis of the work of the Commission especially in relation to the treatment of black women, see Mark Sanders, "Ambiguities of Mourning: Law, Custom, and Testimony of Women before South Africa's Truth and Reconciliation Commission," in *Loss: The Politics of Mourning*, ed. David L. Eng and David Kazanjian (Berkeley: University of California Press, 2003), 77–98.
35. Ashley Dawson, "Documenting the Trauma of Apartheid: *Long Night's Journey into Day* and South Africa's Truth and Reconciliation Commission," *Screen* 46.4 (2005): 475.
36. Doug Moston, "Standards and Practices," in *Method Acting Reconsidered: Theory, Practice, Future*, ed. David Krasner (New York: St. Martin's, 2000), 141.
37. I am grateful to Natasha Distiller for helping me to formulate this point.
38. Antony Sher and Sello Maake ka Ncube, "We Were Told That Black People Would Murder Us in Our Beds," *Guardian*, 25 May 2004, http://www.guardian.co.uk/stage/2004/may/25/theatre2; all subsequent quotations in this paragraph are to this article.
39. For a discussion of the tendency to parallel Elizabethan England and Africa and the ideological implications of this comparison, see Natasha Distiller, "'Through Shakespeare's Africa': 'terror and murder?'" in *Shakespeare's World/World Shakespeares: The Selected Proceedings of the International Shakespeare Association World Congress Brisbane, 2006*, ed. Richard Fotheringham, Christa Jansohn and R. S. White (Newark: University of Delaware Press, 2008), 382–93.
40. Jan Kott, *Shakespeare Our Contemporary*, trans. Boleslaw Taborski, 2nd ed. (London: Methuen, 1967), 5.
41. Alan Sinfield, "Introduction: Reproductions, Interventions," in *Political Shakespeare: Essays in Cultural Materialism*, ed. Jonathan Dollimore and Alan Sinfield, 2nd ed. (Manchester: Manchester University Press, 1994), 155.
42. Jonathan Holmes, "'A World Elsewhere': Shakespeare in South Africa," *Shakespeare Survey* 55 (2002): 278.
43. Gys de Villiers, "Not to Praise, But to Conquer," [UK] *The Sunday Times Magazine*, 12 March 1995.
44. *Titus Andronicus*, VHS, directed by Gregory Doran, South African Broadcasting Corporation, Market Theatre, 13 May 1995, Shakespeare Centre Library and Archive, accession no. 83390189.
45. Ronald J. Pelias, "Empathy and the Ethics of Entitlement," *Theatre Research International* 16.2 (1991): 142.

46. Pelias, "Empathy and the Ethics of Entitlement," 151.
47. Pelias, "Empathy and the Ethics of Entitlement," 151.
48. Pelias, "Empathy and the Ethics of Entitlement," 151.
49. Pascale Aebischer, *Shakespeare's Violated Bodies: Stage and Screen Performance* (Cambridge: Cambridge University Press, 2004), 36.
50. Aebischer, *Shakespeare's Violated Bodies*, 36.
51. Julia Kristeva, *Revolution in Poetic Language*, trans. Margaret Waller (New York: Columbia University Press, 1984), 60.
52. M. M. Bakhtin, *The Dialogic Imagination: Four Essays*, ed. Michael Holquist, trans. Caryl Emerson and Michael Holquist (Austin: University of Texas Press, 1981), 272.
53. Distiller, "Tony's Will," 160.
54. Gevisser, "What's Wrong with Relevance?"
55. Distiller, "Tony's Will," 165.
56. For positive reviews of the Market production see, for example, Greig, "Schlock-horror, Elizabethan-style," and Michael Kustow, "Exorcising Apartheid," review of *Titus Andronicus*, Market Theatre, [UK] *The Sunday Times*, 9 April 1995; for negative reviews see, for example, Ricci, "Titus Topples into the 'Relevant' Pit," and Diane de Beer, "Please Drop the Affectation," *Pretoria News*, 31 March 1995.
57. Sher quoted in Clare Bayley, "Lines of Least Resistance," *Independent*, 31 May 1995.
58. Michael Owen, "Sher, Shaken to the Roots," *Evening Standard*, 30 July 1995; Antony Sher, "A Violent Reaction to a New Culture," [UK] *The Sunday Times*, 18 June 1995; Antony Sher, "SA Theatre Is in Deep Trouble," *Star*, 26 April 1995.
59. Barry Ronge, "So Where Are All the Lovers of Good English?" *Star Tonight*, 21 April 1995; Sher, "SA Theatre is in Deep Trouble."
60. Unless otherwise noted all subsequent quotations or paraphrases in this paragraph are to Sher, "SA Theatre is in Deep Trouble."
61. Anonymous quoted in Antony Sher, "A Fond Farewell—For Now," *Star*, 12 May 1995, Sher's ellipsis.
62. André P. Czeglédy, "Villas of the Highveld: A Cultural Perspective on Johannesburg and Its 'Northern Suburbs'," in Tomlinson, *et al.*, *Emerging Johannesburg*, 27, 28.
63. Advertisement, *Titus Andronicus*, Market Theatre, *Star*, 16 March 1995.
64. Hilary Burns, "The Market Theatre of Johannesburg in the New South Africa," *New Theatre Quarterly* 18.4 (2002): 365.
65. See Editorial, "Centre-stage Debate," *Star*, 4 May 1995; Israel Motlhabane, "The Answer to Theatre Blues," *Star*, 4 May 1995; Ian Fraser, "The Truth Is, You Just Can't Eat Art," *Star*, 5 May 1995; Garalt MacLiam, "There's No Business in Slow Business," *Star*, 8 May 1995; Joyce Ozynski, "Signs Look Fine for Theatre," *Star*, 11 May 1995; Sher, "A Fond Farewell—For Now."
66. Joyce Ozynski, "Signs Look Fine for Theatre."
67. Anonymous quoted in Sher, "A Fond Farewell—For Now."
68. Motlhabane, "The Answer to Theatre Blues"; all subsequent quotations from Motlhabane in this paragraph are to this article.

NOTES TO CHAPTER 2

1. Mark Thornton Burnett, *Filming Shakespeare in the Global Marketplace* (Basingstoke: Palgrave, 2007), 105.
2. Burnett, *Filming Shakespeare*, 91.

3. See Arthur Horowitz, "Shylock after Auschwitz: The Merchant of Venice on the Post-Holocaust Stage—Subversion, Confrontation, and Provocation," *Journal for Cultural and Religious Theory* 8.3 (2007): 14.

4. Arnold Wesker, *Shylock*, in *The Journalists, The Wedding Feast, Shylock* (London: Penguin, 1990), 189; all subsequent references will be given in parentheses in the text.

5. See Sabine Schülting, "'I am not bound to please thee with my answers': *The Merchant of Venice* on the Post-war German Stage," in *World-Wide Shakespeares: Local Appropriations in Film and Performance*, ed. Sonia Massai (London: Routledge: 2005), 69.

6. "Shylock in Germany: The Reception of Shakespeare's 'The Merchant of Venice' after 1945," http://www.geisteswissenschaften.fu-berlin.de/en/v/shylock/index.html; the website provides an index, in German, of German-language productions since 1945: http://www.geisteswissenschaften.fu-berlin.de/v/shylock/Inszenierungen/index.html.

7. Gregory Doran quoted in Heather Neill, "Shylock's Pounded Flesh," *The Times*, 9 December 1997.

8. Michael Billington, review of *The Merchant of Venice*, directed by Loveday Ingram, The Pit, *Guardian*, 8 November 2001.

9. *The Maori Merchant of Venice* [*Te Tangata Whai Rawa O Weniti*], directed by Don C. Selwyn (Auckland: He Taonga Films, 2001). Following Judith Pryor, I primarily use the designation "Aotearoa New Zealand" in place of the more familiar "New Zealand" as it combines "Māori and Pākehā [New Zealanders of predominantly British and Irish origin] names, in order to juxtapose two contesting national narratives" (Pryor, *Constitutions: Writing Nations, Reading Difference* [Abingdon: Birkbeck Law Press, 2008], 117, n1).

10. See, for example, Alan Sinfield, "How to Read *The Merchant of Venice* without Being Heterosexist," in *Alternative Shakespeares Volume 2*, ed. Terence Hawkes (London: Routledge, 1996), 122–39.

11. This chapter is a revised and expanded version of my article, "Speaking Māori Shakespeare: *The Maori Merchant of Venice* and the Legacy of Colonisation," in *Screening Shakespeare in the Twenty-First Century*, ed. Mark Thornton Burnett and Ramona Wray (Edinburgh: Edinburgh University Press, 2006), 127–45.

12. Long vowel sounds in Māori are denoted either by a macron or a double vowel (the difference is largely dependent on tribal affiliation); Maori can thus be expressed as "Māori" or "Maaori". In this chapter I have used macrons, the denotation preferred by Te Puni Kōkiri (Ministry of Māori Development), except where they are absent from the texts I cite.

13. My analysis of New Zealand history is indebted to Michael King's *The Penguin History of New Zealand* (Auckland: Penguin, 2003). The Treaty/Tiriti is held in the National Archives in Wellington and copies of the text, in English and Māori, can be located via http://www.waitangi-tribunal.govt.nz/treaty/. For a detailed analysis of demographic trends relating to Māori and non-Māori New Zealanders see Statistics New Zealand, http://search.stats.govt.nz/nav/0. For details about developments in Māori language acquisition and an indication of the work still to be done in relation to linguistic development see publications produced by Te Puni Kōkiri (Ministry of Māori Development), http://www.tpk.govt.nz/en/in-print/our-publications/?s=a568a773–1f8c-433c-8669–288ae44d2c6c.

14. Homi K. Bhabha, *The Location of Culture* (London: Routledge, 1994); Daiva Stasiulis and Nira Yuval-Davis, "Introduction: Beyond Dichotomies—Gender, Race, Ethnicity and Class in Settler Societies," in *Unsettling Settler Societies: Articulations of Gender, Race, Ethnicity and Class,* ed.

Stasiulis and Yuval-Davis, Sage Series on Race and Ethnic Relations 11 (London: Sage, 1995), 5.

15. Rustom Bharucha, *Theatre and the World: Performance and the Politics of Culture* (London: Routledge, 1993), 4, 241. See Ania Loomba, "'Local-manufacture made-in-India Othello fellows': Issues of Race, Hybridity and Location in Post-colonial Shakespeares," in *Post-Colonial Shakespeares*, ed. Ania Loomba and Martin Orkin (London: Routledge, 1998), 143–63; Phillip B. Zarrilli, "For Whom Is the King a King? Issues of Intercultural Production, Perception, and Reception in a *Kathakali King Lear*," in *Critical Theory and Performance*, ed. Janelle G. Reinelt and Joseph R. Roach, 2nd ed. (Ann Arbor: University of Michigan Press, 2007), 108–33; W. B. Worthen, *Shakespeare and the Force of Modern Performance* (Cambridge: Cambridge University Press, 2003), 117–68.

16. A slideshow of images from the film can be seen at http://homepages.ihug.co.nz/~hetaonga/merchant/Slideshow/slideshow.html.

17. *The Maori Merchant of Venice* Media Kit, 3. The Media Kit can be downloaded from http://homepages.ihug.co.nz/~hetaonga/merchant/Media_Files/media_files.html; all subsequent references to this document will be given as "Media Kit".

18. Ruth Kaupua Panapa quoted in Caitlin Sykes, "Manukau Film-Maker at Forefront of Industry," *Manukau Courier*, 7 March 2002.

19. Emma Cox, "Te Reo Shakespeare: *Te Tangata Whai Rawa o Weneti/The Maori Merchant of Venice*," *Kunapipi* 28.1 (2006): 81–82.

20. Claire Murdoch, "Holy Sea-Cow," *Landfall* 206 (2003): 103.

21. Kaupua Panapa quoted in Sykes, "Manukau Film-Maker."

22. Valerie Wayne, review of *Te Tangata Whai Rawa O Weniti/The Māori Merchant of Venice*, *The Contemporary Pacific* 16.2 (2004): 428.

23. Media Kit, 3; Sam Edwards, review of *The Maori Merchant of Venice/Te Tangata Whai Rawa O Weniti*, *Waikato Times*, 18 February 2002; Mark Houlahan, "Hekepia? The *Mana* of the Maori *Merchant*," in Massai, *World-Wide Shakespeares*, 148.

24. The script of *Manawa Taua/Savage Hearts* is unpublished but a first draft by David Geary, Christian Penny and Anna Marbrook entitled *Savage Hearts* (1994) is held at Playmarket's archive in Wellington; this document was substantially reworked in performance.

25. See Catherine Silverstone, "*Othello*'s Travels in New Zealand: Shakespeare, Race and National Identity," in *Remaking Shakespeare: Performance Across Media, Genres and Cultures*, ed. Pascale Aebischer, Edward J. Esche and Nigel Wheale (Basingstoke: Palgrave, 2003), 84–89.

26. For a fuller discussion of this storyline see Silverstone, "*Othello*'s Travels in New Zealand," 78–84.

27. A. C. Bradley, *Shakespearean Tragedy: Lectures on "Hamlet", "Othello", "King Lear", "Macbeth"*, ed. Robert Shaughnessy, 4th ed. (Basingstoke: Palgrave, 2007). Bradley's book, first published in 1904, is now in its fourth edition. While Bradley's central claims about character have been challenged, especially in the wake of studies informed by poststructuralism, new historicism and cultural materialism, his analysis was enormously influential in the development of twentieth-century Shakespeare studies and English studies more broadly.

28. *God and Shakespeare*, digital video file, directed by Sándor Lau (Auckland: Paper Tiger Detective Agency, 2001). The film can be viewed online at http://www.nzshortfilm.com/film,261.sm.

29. Mau, *Tempest: Without a Body*, http://www.mau.co.nz/artists/tempest.php; this webpage contains a link to a short video of extracts from the production.

30. Media Release, *Tempest: Without a Body*, Sydney Festival, 2009, http://www.sydneyfestival.org.au/uploads/Tempest.pdf.
31. Mark Houlahan, "*Romeo and Tusi*: An Eclectically Musical Samoan/Māori *Romeo and Juliet* from Aotearoa/New Zealand," *Contemporary Theatre Review* 19.3 (2009): 280.
32. Pei Te Hurinui [Jones], trans., *Te Tangata Whai-Rawa O Weniti* [*The Merchant of Venice*], by William Shakespeare (Palmerston North, New Zealand: Young, 1946).
33. Pei Te Hurinui [Jones], trans., *Owhiro: Te Mua o Weniti* [*Othello: The Moor of Venice*], by William Shakespeare, unpublished typescript [1944], University of Waikato Library, Hamilton, New Zealand; Pei Te Hurinui [Jones], trans., *Huria Hiha* [*Julius Caesar*], by William Shakespeare, unpublished typescript, fMS-225, 1959, National Library of New Zealand/Te Puna Mātauranga o Aotearoa, Wellington. I am grateful to Mark Houlahan for drawing these texts to my attention.
34. Merimeri Penfold, trans., *Nga Waiata Aroha a Hekepia: Love Sonnets by Shakespeare; Nine Sonnets*, by William Shakespeare (Auckland: Holloway Press, University of Auckland, 2000).
35. *Te Po Uriuri (The Enveloping Night)*, digital video file, directed by Toby Mills (Auckland: Tawera Productions and Independent and General Productions, 2001). The film can be viewed online at http://www.nzonscreen.com/title/te-po-uriuri-2001.
36. For a discussion of historical records of cannibalism in Aotearoa New Zealand see Anne Salmond, *The Trial of the Cannibal Dog: Captain Cook in the South Seas* (London: Penguin, 2004), especially 136–37, 141–45, 222–26, 228–30. The sensitivities involved in this issue are highlighted in responses to New Zealand Prime Minister John Key's "joke," made during a tourism conference in Auckland in May 2010, when he said: "[t]he good news is that I was having dinner with Ngati Porou as opposed to their neighbouring iwi, which is Tuhoe, in which case I would have been dinner, which wouldn't have been quite so attractive"; Key quoted in Derek Cheng, "PM's joke inflames dispute with Tuhoe," *New Zealand Herald*, 14 May 2010, http://www.nzherald.co.nz/politics/news/article.cfm?c_id=280&objectid=10644826.
37. MacDonald Jackson offers a summary of the film's narrative elisions and rearrangements and an acute list of errors in the subtitles in "All Our Tribe," *Landfall* 204 (2002): 156–57.
38. Jacques Derrida, "What Is a 'Relevant' Translation?" trans. Lawrence Venuti, *Critical Inquiry* 27.2 (2001): 177, Derrida's emphasis.
39. Media Kit, 38.
40. Selwyn quoted in Veronica Schmidt, "Te Bard," *Listener*, 2 February 2002, 52.
41. Scott Morrison quoted in Media Kit, 17.
42. Morrison quoted in Media Kit, 17.
43. Morrison quoted in "Shakespeare Goes Maori," *BBC News*, 4 December 2001, http://news.bbc.co.uk/1/hi/entertainment/film/1691261.stm.
44. Media Kit, 8–9.
45. Walter Benjamin, "The Task of the Translator: An Introduction to the Translation of Baudelaire's *Tableaux parisiens*," in *Illuminations*, ed. Hannah Arendt, trans. Harry Zohn (London: Fontana, 1992), 75, 80.
46. Jacques Derrida, "Des Tours de Babel," trans. Joseph F. Graham, in *Difference in Translation*, ed. Joseph F. Graham (Ithaca: Cornell University Press, 1985), 191.
47. Waihoroi Shortland quoted in Margo White, "Shakespeare Korero," *Metro*, March 2002, 115; Selwyn quoted in "The Bard in Te Reo," *Waikato Times*, 9 February 2002.

48. Lawrence Venuti, *The Scandals of Translation: Towards an Ethics of Difference* (London: Routledge, 1998), 4.
49. Don Selwyn, interview, "The Bard of Aotearoa," *Onfilm*, February 2001, 15 (15–16).
50. See Jacques Derrida, *Of Grammatology*, trans. Gayatri Chakravorty Spivak, 2nd ed. (Baltimore: Johns Hopkins University Press, 1997), 141–64.
51. Jacques Derrida, *Acts of Literature*, ed. Derek Attridge (New York: Routledge, 1992), 188.
52. Samuel Lee, preface to Thomas Kendall, *A Grammar and Vocabulary of the Language of New Zealand* (London: Church Missionary Society, 1820), n.p.
53. Thomas Babington Macaulay, "Indian Education: Minute on the 2nd of February, 1835," in *Prose and Poetry*, ed. G. M. Young (London: Hart-Davis, 1952), 729. For a discussion of the ideology underpinning English studies in India see Gauri Viswanathan, *Masks of Conquest: Literary Study and British Rule in India* (London: Faber, 1990).
54. Selwyn quoted in Peter Calder, "Footy to Fairies—and Way Beyond," *New Zealand Herald*, 16 February 2002, http://www.nzherald.co.nz/lifestyle/news/article.cfm?c_id=6&objectid=939653.
55. Andy Sarich quoted in Media Kit, 28.
56. Te Puni Kōkiri (Ministry of Māori Development), *He Reo E Korerotia Ana—He Reo Ka Ora, A Shared Vision for the Future of Te Reo Māori*, March 2003, http://www.tpk.govt.nz/en/publications/docs/korerotia_english.pdf/, 6 (accessed: 22 September 2005); this document is no longer accessible. This vision of 2028 as the target date by which "the Māori language will be widely spoken by Māori" and appreciated by "[a]ll New Zealanders" is codified in *Te Rutaki Reo Māori—The Māori Language Strategy*, 2003, produced by Te Puni Kōkiri (Ministry of Māori Development) and accessible via http://www.tpk.govt.nz/en/in-print/our-publications/publications/the-maori-language-strategy/download/tpk-maorilangstrat-2003.pdf, 5.
57. Jacques Derrida, *Specters of Marx: The State of the Debt, the Work of Mourning, and the New International*, trans. Peggy Kamuf (New York: Routledge, 1994), xix, Derrida's emphasis.
58. Jacques Derrida, *Specters of Marx*, xix, Derrida's emphasis.
59. Selwyn quoted in Lindsey Birnie, "Film-maker Honoured," *Dominion*, 6 May 2002, ellipsis and round brackets in original.
60. Shortland quoted in Media Kit, 13.
61. Selwyn quoted in "The Bard in Te Reo."
62. Waitangi Tribunal, "Size of Claims," Chapter 12.3.3, *The Taranaki Report—Kaupapa Tuatahi*, 1996, http://www.waitangi-tribunal.govt.nz/reports/download pdf.asp?reportid=3FECC540-D049–4DE6-A7F0-C26BCCDAB345.
63. Tariana Turia quoted in "What Tariana Turia Said—In Full," *New Zealand Herald*, 31 August 2000, http://www.nzherald.co.nz/nz/news/article.cfm?c_id=1&objectid=149643.
64. Winston Peters and Roger Sowery quoted in Audrey Young, "Minister Hammers Colonial 'Holocaust'," *New Zealand Herald*, 30 August 2000, http://www.nzherald.co.nz/nz/news/article.cfm?c_id=1&objectid=149518.
65. "Audio and Transcript: Tariana Turia's Apology," *New Zealand Herald*, 6 September 2000, http://www.nzherald.co.nz/nz/news/article.cfm?c_id=1&objectid=150332.
66. Helen Clark quoted in Audrey Young, "Holocaust Apology Puts Minister in Hot Water," *New Zealand Herald*, 6 September 2000, http://www.nzherald.co.nz/nz/news/article.cfm?c_id=1&objectid=150333; square brackets in original.
67. Clark quoted in Young, "Holocaust Apology."

68. Wendy Ross quoted in Young, "Holocaust Apology."
69. Selwyn quoted in White, "Shakespeare Korero."
70. David E. Stannard, *American Holocaust: The Conquest of the New World* (New York: Oxford University Press, 1992).
71. See Miranda Joseph, *Against the Romance of Community* (Minneapolis: University of Minnesota Press, 2002).
72. *Te Tangata Whai Rawa O Wēniti*, resource kit, [written and compiled by the Ministry of Education] (Te Whanganui-a-Tara, Aotearoa [New Zealand]: Te Pou Taki Kōrero, 2004); Pei Te Hurinui Jones, trans., *Te Tangata Whai Rawa O Weneti* [*The Merchant of Venice*], by William Shakespeare, rev. ed. ([Wellington]: Ministry of Education/Te Tāhuhu o te Mātauranga, 2008).
73. Selwyn quoted in Calder, "Footy to Fairies—and Way Beyond."
74. Te Māngai Pāho/Māori Broadcasting Funding Agency, http://www.tmp. govt.nz/index.html.
75. Wairoa Maori Film Festival, http://www.manawairoa.com.
76. New Zealand Film Commission, Statistics, http://www.nzfilm.co.nz/ FilmCatalogue/Statistics.aspx; Te Māngai Pāho, http://www.tmp.govt.nz/ index.html.
77. Whenua Films, http://www.whenuafilms.co.nz/about.htm.
78. Nga Aho Whakaari, http://www.ngaahowhakaari.co.nz.
79. Selwyn quoted in Libby Middlebrook, "Language Test for Shakespeare Play," *New Zealand Herald*, 24 November 2000, http://www.nzherald. co.nz/nz/news/article.cfm?c_id=1&objectid=161717.
80. Houlahan, "Hekepia?"; Silverstone, "Speaking Māori Shakespeare"; Cox, "Te Reo Shakespeare." After the small cluster of articles published by Houlahan (2005), Silverstone (2006) and Cox (2006), *The Maori Merchant* has not, at the time of writing, received further sustained critical attention.
81. Judith McCann, quoted in "In Memoriam: Don Selwyn 1935–2007," *Onfilm*, June 2007, 18 (18–19).
82. Denise Irvine, "Taumarunui's Storyteller Ends Tale," *Waikato Times*, 18 April 2007.
83. Judith Tizard, "Acting Arts Minister Honours Don Selwyn," Radio New Zealand Newswire, 13 April 2007; Pita Sharples, "Poroporoaki: Don Selwyn," The Maori Party, Press Release, 16 April 2007.
84. Ian Mune quoted in Houlahan, "Hekepia?" 148.

NOTES TO CHAPTER 3

1. See, for example, Gordon McMullan, *Shakespeare and the Idea of Late Writing: Authorship in the Proximity of Death* (Cambridge: Cambridge University Press, 2007), especially 318–53. McMullan offers a trenchant critique of ideas of Shakespeare, authorship and lateness; this includes a consideration of *The Tempest* and how Prospero is deployed "as a figure both of the late Shakespeare and of the late career in general" (320); Paul Brown, "'This thing of darkness I acknowledge mine': *The Tempest* and the Discourse of Colonialism," in *Political Shakespeare: Essays in Cultural Materialism*, ed. Jonathan Dollimore and Alan Sinfield, 2nd ed. (Manchester: Manchester University Press, 1994), 48–71; Rob Nixon, "Caribbean and African Appropriations of *The Tempest*," *Critical Inquiry* 13.3 (1987): 557–78.
2. Dev Virahsawmy, *Toufann: A Mauritian Fantasy*, trans. Nisha Walling and Michael Walling (London: Border Crossings, 2003), 32; all subsequent references are to this edition and will be given in parentheses in the text. *Toufann* is also published in *African Theatre: Playwrights and Politics*, ed. Martin

Banham, James Gibbs and Femi Osofisan (Oxford: James Currey, 2001), 217–54.

3. Michael Walling, interview with Jane Wilkinson, "Staging Shakespeare across Borders, 12 December 1999," in Banham, Gibbs and Osofisan, *African Theatre*, 122.

4. Wilkinson, "Staging Shakespeare Across Borders," 122.

5. *The Tempest*, DVD, directed by Derek Jarman (London: Second Sight Films, 2004). See BFI Jarman Collection I, Box 5, Items 1–6, Box 6, Items 7–10 and Box 7, Item 11, for Jarman's design concepts, production notes and scripts for *The Tempest* from 1974 to 1979. Items from the Jarman collection are cited by permission of the Derek Jarman Estate and Peake Associates. For discussions of heterosoc see Jarman, *At Your Own Risk: A Saint's Testament*, ed. Michael Christie (London: Vintage, 1993).

6. Niall Richardson, *The Queer Cinema of Derek Jarman: Critical and Cultural Readings* (London: Tauris, 2009), 154.

7. Jarman, notebook, *The Angelic Conversation*, BFI Jarman Collection II, Box 5, n.p.

8. Susan Sontag, "Notes on 'Camp'," *Against Interpretation and Other Essays* (New York: Octagon, 1982), 275.

9. Moe Meyer, "Introduction: Reclaiming the Discourse of Camp," in *The Politics and Poetics of Camp*, ed. Moe Meyer (London: Routledge, 1994), 11; Meyer's anthology comprises a selection of essays on camp that are specifically concerned with camp and queer identities. For key texts in scholarship on camp, beginning with Christopher Isherwood and Susan Sontag, see also Fabio Cleto, ed., *Camp: Queer Aesthetics and the Performing Subject, A Reader* (Edinburgh: Edinburgh University Press, 1999).

10. Sontag, "Notes on 'Camp'," 290.

11. Michael Warner, "Introduction: Fear of a Queer Planet," *Social Text* 29 (1991): 15.

12. Judith Butler, *Bodies That Matter: On the Discursive Limits of "Sex"* (New York: Routledge, 1993), 230.

13. Butler, *Bodies That Matter*, 229.

14. *The Angelic Conversation*, DVD, directed by Derek Jarman (London: BFI, 2007).

15. Jarman, notebook, *The Angelic Conversation*, BFI Jarman Collection II, Box 5, n.p.

16. *Edward II*, DVD, directed by Derek Jarman (London: Second Sight Films, 2010).

17. Derek Jarman, *Queer Edward II* (London: BFI Publishing, 1991), n.p., Jarman's emphasis and layout.

18. Jarman, *Queer Edward II*, 110, 114, 74, 126, 168; I have attempted to preserve elements of the script's typography in the presentation of these quotations.

19. For further information about the history and actions of OutRage! see http://www.petertatchell.net/; Ian Lucas, *Outrage! An Oral History* (London: Cassell, 1998).

20. Sexual Offences Act 1967, http://www.opsi.gov.uk/RevisedStatutes/Acts/ukpga/1967/cukpga_19670060_en_1; John Wolfenden, Chairman, Committee on Homosexual Offences and Prostitution, *Report of the Committee on Homosexual Offences and Prostitution. Presented to Parliament by the Secretary of State for the Home Department and the Secretary of State for Scotland, etc.* (London, 1957), para. 355(i), 155.

21. Jonathan Dollimore, "Sex and Death," *Textual Practice* 9.1 (1995): 27.

22. Jarman and K[eith] C[ollins], *Treatment for a New Film "28"*, BFI Jarman Collection II, Box 43, Item 9. These elements of *28* recur in the script for

Jarman's unrealised project *Sod'Em* (1986), published in Derek Jarman, *Up in the Air: Collected Film Scripts* (London: Vintage, 1996), 183–225.

23. Shlomith Rimmon-Kenan, *Narrative Fiction: Contemporary Poetics*, 2nd ed. (London: Routledge, 2002), 46.

24. Gay Sweatshop, "A Statement of Intent," Constitution and Policies, n.d. GS/1/1/1/1 RHUL Archives. The archive for *This Island's Mine* comprises two box files—GS/3/20/1 and GS/3/20/2—and is held in the Archives, Royal Holloway, University of London (noted as RHUL Archives in all subsequent references).

25. Philip Osment, "Finding Room on the Agenda for Love: A History of Gay Sweatshop," in *Gay Sweatshop: Four Plays and a Company*, vii, ix. For examples of how members of Gay Sweatshop conceived of the work of the company see Nöel Greig, Philip Osment, Philip L. Timmins, Martin Panter, Drew Griffiths and Jill Posener, "Why I Joined Gay Sweatshop," in *Gay Left: A Gay Socialist Journal* 7 (1978/79): 25–28, http://www.gayleft1970s.org/issues/gay.left_issue.07.pdf; for a brief history of Gay Sweatshop in the context of feminist and gay theatre history and sexual politics, see Michelene Wandor, *Carry On, Understudies: Theatre and Sexual Politics*, 2nd ed. (London: Routledge, 1986), especially 53–57.

26. Miranda Joseph, *Against the Romance of Community* (Minneapolis: University of Minnesota Press, 2002), vii.

27. Joseph, *Against the Romance of Community*, xxiii.

28. *This Island's Mine* is published in *Gay Sweatshop: Four Plays and a Company*, ed. Philip Osment (London: Methuen, 1989), 83–120, and *Adaptations of Shakespeare: A Critical Anthology of Plays from the Seventeenth Century to the Present*, ed. Daniel Fischlin and Mark Fortier (London: Routledge, 2000), 258–84; all references to the play will be given as scene numbers in parentheses in the text.

29. Philip Osment, telephone interview with the author, 31 May 2001; Osment, "Finding Room," lxi.

30. Frantz Fanon, *Black Skin, White Masks*, trans. Charles Lam Markmann (London: Pluto, 1986), 170, Fanon's emphasis.

31. For a discussion of links between theatre and homosexuality in twentieth-century Anglo-American theatre see Alan Sinfield, *Out on Stage: Lesbian and Gay Theatre in the Twentieth Century* (New Haven: Yale University Press, 1999).

32. Kobena Mercer, *Welcome to the Jungle: New Positions in Black Cultural Studies* (New York: Routledge, 1994), 133.

33. *This Island's Mine*, DVD transferred from VHS, directed by Philip Osment, Gay Sweatshop, n.d., GS/7/2 RHUL Archives. Given Sandells's post-show speech (discussed on 102–03), it is likely that the DVD dates from the revival of the play in June 1988.

34. Homi K. Bhabha, "Of Mimicry and Man: The Ambivalence of Colonial Discourse," in *The Location of Culture* (London: Routledge, 1994), 85–92.

35. Paul Gilroy, *Small Acts: Thoughts on the Politics of Black Cultures* (London: Serpent's Tail, 1993), 91–92, 58.

36. Kate Chedgzoy, *Shakespeare's Queer Children: Sexual Politics and Contemporary Culture* (Manchester: Manchester University Press, 1995), 2.

37. Mary F. Brewer, *Staging Whiteness* (Middletown, C.T.: Wesleyan University Press, 2005), 181.

38. Osment, "Finding Room," lxii. For further information about Shared Experience see http://www.sharedexperience.org.uk.

39. The actor playing Prospero was doubled as Stephen, making a neat equivalence between Prospero's threat of violence toward the indigenous inhabitants of the island and Stephen's sale of contaminated blood to Third World countries.

40. Osment, telephone interview.
41. Susan Bennett, "Rehearsing *The Tempest*, Directing the Post-Colonial Body: Disjunctive Identity in Philip Osment's *This Island's Mine*," *Essays in Theatre* 15.1 (1996): 41.
42. Osment, "Finding Room," lxi.
43. Osment, telephone interview.
44. Osment, telephone interview.
45. Lois Weaver, telephone interview with the author, 17 August 2009. All subsequent quotations from Weaver are to this interview.
46. See GS/1/2/3 RHUL Archives and GS/1/2/4 RHUL Archives.
47. See GS/1/2/1/4 RHUL Archives.
48. Osment, telephone interview.
49. Audience Survey Results, GS/5/2 RHUL Archives. This box consists of 329 audience survey forms from 1989; the statistical analysis is my own.
50. John Giffard, Earl of Halsbury, Local Government Act 1986 (Amendment), 25 November 1986, vol. 482, col. 438, http://hansard.millbanksystems.com/lords/1986/nov/25/local-government-act-1986-amendment-bill.
51. For a discussion of the Thatcher era, sex, and "family values" see Martin Durham, *Sex and Politics: The Family and Morality in the Thatcher Years* (Basingstoke: Macmillan, 1991), and Jackie Stacey, "Promoting Normality: Section 28 and the Regulation of Sexuality," in *Off-Centre: Feminism and Cultural Studies*, ed. Sarah Franklin, Celia Lury and Jackie Stacey (London: Harper Collins Academic, 1991), especially 286–91.
52. Section 28 of the Local Government Act 1988, "Prohibition on promoting homosexuality by teaching or by publishing material," http://www.legislation.gov.uk/ukpga/1988/9/section/28/enacted.
53. For discussions of the language of Section 28 and attempts to clarify the Section's terminology see Philip Thomas and Ruth Costigan, *Promoting Homosexuality: Section 28 of the Local Government Act 1988* (Cardiff: Cardiff Law School, 1990), 10–14; Stonewall, *Section 28—Draft Briefing* (London: Stonewall, [1988]), 3–5; Madeleine Colvin with Jane Hawksley, *Section 28: A Practical Guide to the Law and Its Implications* (London: National Council for Civil Liberties, 1989), 11–14.
54. Thomas and Costigan, *Promoting Homosexuality*, 18, Thomas and Costigan's emphasis.
55. Stacey, "Promoting Normality," 286.
56. Earl of Caithness, *Hansard*, House of Lords, 1 February 1988, vol. 492, col. 889, http://hansard.millbanksystems.com/lords/1988/feb/01/local-government-bill.
57. See Stacey, "Promoting Normality," 286.
58. Equality Act 2006, http://www.opsi.gov.uk/acts/acts2006/pdf/ukpga_20060003_en.pdf.
59. Sexual Offences (Amendment) Act 2000, http://www.opsi.gov.uk/acts/acts2000/ukpga_20000044_en_1; Civil Partnership Act 2004, http://www.opsi.gov.uk/acts/acts2004/ukpga_20040033_en_1; Employment Equality (Sexual Orientation) Regulations 2003, http://www.opsi.gov.uk/si/si2003/20031661.htm; Equality Act 2006, http://www.opsi.gov.uk/acts/acts2006/pdf/ukpga_20060003_en.pdf.
60. *This Island's Mine*, press release, GS/3/20/2 RHUL Archives; Osment, telephone interview.
61. Philip Osment, author's note, programme, *This Island's Mine*, directed by Osment, Drill Hall Arts Centre, London, 1988, GS/3/20/1 RHUL Archives (unless otherwise noted, all subsequent references to the programme in this chapter are to this document); Osment, author's note, programme, *This Island's Mine* (Revival, June 1988), GS/3/20/1 RHUL Archives.
62. Rimmon-Kenan, *Narrative Fiction*, 46.

63. Four draft copies of the script are held in the Gay Sweatshop Archive at Royal Holloway. GS/3/20/1/1 RHUL Archives and GS/3/20/1/2 RHUL Archives are identical, save for the fact that /2 is photocopied at half-scale; these scripts appear to have been used for the first production in February 1988. GS/3/20/1/4 RHUL Archives contains an author's note referring to the first production and seems to be the script used for the revival in June 1988, especially as it notes a casting change that occurred during the revival. GS/3/20/1/3 RHUL Archives, however, looks like an earlier draft (one of the central character's names is different, no speech prefixes are included, and the headlines that Luke sees echo the language of Section 28 much less overtly than the subsequent drafts and published script); this script may, therefore, have been the basis of the rehearsed reading in March 1987.
64. Stonewall, "Brief Overview of Stonewall," http://www.stonewall.org.uk/about_us/2532.asp; Stacey, "Promoting Normality," 302.
65. See note 24 above in this chapter.
66. Letter from Gay Sweatshop to Civic Centre, Southampton, 18 December 1987, GS/3/20/1 RHUL Archives; Letter from Civic Centre, Southampton to Gay Sweatshop, 21 December 1987, GS/3/20/1 RHUL Archives (emphasis in original).
67. Letter from Pegasus Theatre to Gay Sweatshop, 25 January 1988, GS/3/20/1 RHUL Archives.
68. Previews, listings, reviews and interviews are collated as part of GS/3/20/1 RHUL Archives.
69. Educational Supplement, *The Times*, 11 March 1988; Jim Hiley, "Gay Hurrah," *Listener*, 10 March 1988; "Under Threat," *Gay Times*, April 1988, GS/3/20/1 RHUL Archives.
70. Osment discusses this issue in "Finding Room," lxiii.
71. "Tory Councillors Ready to Pounce on Local Gay Initiatives," *Gay Times*, February 1988, GS/3/20/1 RHUL Archives.
72. Letter from Secretary General of the Arts Council to Mark Fisher, Shadow Arts Minister, 12 December 1990, GS/1/3/2/5/18 RHUL Archives; Letter from Anonymous (by request of RHUL Archives), to Secretary General of the Arts Council, 4 December 1990, GS/1/3/2/5/20 RHUL Archives.
73. *This Island's Mine* Tour Reports: Harlow Playhouse, 15–16 March 1988; Green Room, Manchester, 22–23 March 1988, GS/3/20/1 RHUL Archives.
74. *This Island's Mine* Tour Reports: Croydon Warehouse, 19–24 April 1988, GS/3/20/1 RHUL Archives.
75. Gay Sweatshop, *This Island's Mine* Tour Report for the Arts Council of Great Britain, 29 June 1988, GS/3/20/2 RHUL Archives.
76. Logbook of *Dear Love of Comrades* Tour, 2–7 April 1979, n.p., GS/3/11/4/2 RHUL Archives.
77. I am grateful to Erika T. Lin for helping me to formulate my thinking on this issue.
78. Letter from Gay Sweatshop to Yorkshire Arts Board, 18 Dec. 1987, GS/3/20/2/3/3/1–3 RHUL Archives.
79. Letter from Gay Sweatshop to Civic Centre, Southampton, 18 December 1987, GS/3/20/1 RHUL Archives; Gay Sweatshop to Southern Arts, 19 May 1988, GS/3/20/2/3/1/1–6 RHUL Archives.
80. Chedgzoy, *Shakespeare's Queer Children*, 187.
81. Stacey, "Promoting Normality," 294.
82. Stacey, "Promoting Normality," 295.
83. Ian McKellen, Judi Dench and John Gielgud wrote to the Prime Minister expressing concern about the effect of Section 28 on the arts and

homosexuals, 12 February 1988, http://www.mckellen.com/activism/section 28.htm.

84. For a review of this event see http://www.mckellen.com/stage/00564.htm.

85. For the running order of *Before the Act* see http://www.mckellen.com/stage/00564b.htm.

86. Margaret Robinson, "From Shakespeare to Sweatshop with a Little Murder on the Side," interview by Fiona Cooper, *Pink Paper*, 30 June 1988, GS/3/20/1 RHUL Archives.

87. Letter from Pegasus Theatre, Oxford to Gay Sweatshop, 25 January 1988, GS/3/20/1 RHUL Archives.

88. Richard Sandells, post-show announcement, *This Island's Mine*, DVD.

89. Letter from Anonymous (by request of RHUL Archives) to Gay Sweatshop, 28 March 1988, Pegasus Theatre, GS/3/20/1 RHUL Archives.

90. *This Island's Mine* Tour Report submitted to the Arts Council, 29 June 1988, GS/3/20/2 RHUL Archives.

91. *This Island's Mine* Tour Reports: Harlow Playhouse, 15–16 March 1988; Leeds Polytechnic Studio, 17–18 March 1988; Green Room, Manchester, 22–23 March 1988; Pegasus Theatre, Oxford, 25–26 March 1988; Nottingham University Studio, 16 April 1988, GS/3/20/1 RHUL Archives (emphasis in original).

92. In the 1989 audience survey 70% of those surveyed identified as gay, lesbian or bisexual (GS/5/2 RHUL Archives).

93. *This Island's Mine* Tour Reports, Croydon Warehouse, 19–24 April 1988; Green Room, Manchester, 22–23 March 1988; Bellerby Theatre, Guilford, 5 April 1988; Hornpipe Portsmouth, 13–14 April 1988, GS/3/20/1 RHUL Archives.

94. Letter from Anonymous (by request of RHUL Archives) to Gay Sweatshop, 26 March 1988, Drill Hall, GS/3/20/1 RHUL Archives.

95. *One Night Stands*, Press Release, GS/3/40 RHUL Archives, 1993.

96. *Club Deviance*, Press Release, GS/3/44/6–8 RHUL Archives, 1997. RHUL holds documentation for *Queer School* 1992–1996, GS/3/42 RHUL Archives, *One Night Stands* 1993, GS/3/40 RHUL Archives and *Club Deviance* February–May 1997, GS/3/44 RHUL Archives.

97. Osment, telephone interview.

98. Osment, telephone interview.

99. Joseph, *Against the Romance of Community*, xxv. GS/1/3/2/5/1–21 RHUL Archives documents the threat of closure to the company in 1990 and the efforts to secure revenue rather than project funding for the company.

100. Ann Cvetkovich, *An Archive of Feelings: Trauma, Sexuality, and Lesbian Public Cultures* (Durham: Duke University Press, 2003), 3–4.

NOTES TO CHAPTER 4

1. Robert Fisk, "Shakespeare and War," *Independent*, 30 March 2007, http://www.independent.co.uk/opinion/commentators/fisk/robert-fisk-on-shakespeare-and-war-442400.html; all subsequent quotations from Fisk in this paragraph are to this article.

2. Nicholas Hytner, "Contemporary Context," video, Stagework, http://www.stagework.org.uk/webdav/harmonise@Page%252F@id=6012& Document%252F@id=2546.html.

3. Graham Coulter-Smith and Maurice Owen, "Introduction," in *Art in the Age of Terrorism*, ed. Graham Coulter-Smith and Maurice Owen (London: Paul Hoberton, 2005), 3.

4. Judith Butler, *Frames of War: When Is Life Grievable?* (London: Verso, 2009).
5. The Stagework website for *Henry V* can be accessed via the following link: http://www.stagework.org.uk/webdav/harmonise@Page%252F@id=6004& Section%252F@id=26.html.
6. Hytner, "Behold the Swelling Scene," *Times Literary Supplement*, 1 November 2002.
7. Programme, *Henry V*, directed by Nicholas Hytner, Olivier, National Theatre, London, 2003, National Theatre Archive, RNT/PP/1/3/249; all references to the programme in this chapter are to this document.
8. Adrian Lester, "Great Britain," video, Stagework, http://www.stagework. org.uk/webdav/harmonise@Page%252F@id=6012&Document%252F@ id=2508.html.
9. Faz Singhateh, "Appeal to Young Audiences," video, Stagework, http://www. stagework.org.uk/webdav/harmonise@Page%252F@id=6012&Document% 252F@id=2509.html.
10. For a discussion of the impact of the acts of devolution (1998) in relation to national identities and performance practices see Jen Harvie, *Staging the UK* (Manchester: Manchester University Press, 2005), especially 24–35.
11. Hytner, "Contemporary Context."
12. Hytner, "Contemporary Context."
13. Hytner, "Contemporary Context," my emphasis.
14. Nicholas Hytner, Platform, *Henry V*, National Theatre, 20 June 2003, National Theatre Archive, audio recording, ref. no. RNT/PL/3/775, my emphasis; all subsequent references to the Platform discussion in this chapter are to this recording.
15. Hytner, Platform, *Henry V*.
16. Peter Reynolds and Lee White, *A Rehearsal Diary: Henry V at the National*, ed. Lyn Haill (London: NT Publication, 2003); the diary is also included, with some modifications, on the Stagework website for *Henry V*, accessible via the following webpage http://www.stagework.org.uk/webdav/harmonise@ Page%252F@id=6016&Section%252F@id=29.html.
17. Reynolds and White, *A Rehearsal Diary*, 9; Hansard, "Iraq," 18 March 2003, col. 760–911, accessible via http://www.publications.parliament.uk/ pa/cm200203/cmhansrd/vo030318/debindx/30318-x.htm.
18. UN Security Council Resolution 1441; this document can be accessed via http://www.un.org/Docs/scres/2002/sc2002.htm.
19. Rehearsal Notes, 24 March 2003, *Henry V*, National Theatre, 2003, National Theatre Archive, RNT/SM/1/498; all subsequent references to the rehearsal notes are to this document. A set of the rehearsal notes is also collected in folder RNT/CO/1/476.
20. "Iraq's Weapons of Mass Destruction," http://webarchive.nationalarchives. gov.uk/+/http://www.number10.gov.uk/Page271.
21. Reynolds and White, *A Rehearsal Diary*, 13.
22. Reynolds and White, *A Rehearsal Diary*, 13.
23. Reynolds and White, *A Rehearsal Diary*, 27–28.
24. Lester, quoted in James Rampton, "And for His Next Trick . . ." *Independent*, 23 February 2004.
25. The videos can be viewed via the "Using Video" section of the Stagework website at http://www.stagework.org.uk/webdav/harmonise@Page%252F@ id=6007&Section%252F@id=372.html.
26. "Prime Ministerial Broadcast," video, Stagework, http://www.stagework. org.uk/webdav/harmonise@Page%252F@id=6012&Document%252F@ id=2561.html.

27. Hytner, "Contemporary Context."
28. Robert Blythe, "Contemporary Appeal," video, Stagework, http://www. stagework.org.uk/webdav/harmonise@Page%252F@id=6012&Document %252F@id=2433.html; I have used the spelling Llewellyn, rather than the more conventional Fluellen, as this is the spelling that was used in the programme and on the Stagework website.
29. Reynolds and White, *A Rehearsal Diary*, 27.
30. Lester, quoted in Jasper Rees, "A King for Our Times," *Daily Telegraph*, 29 April 2003.
31. Lester, quoted in Michael Wright, "If the Crown Fits . . ." *The Sunday Times*, 27 April 2003.
32. Hytner quoted in Heather Neill, *Times Educational Supplement*, 16 May 2003.
33. Reynolds and White, *A Rehearsal Diary*, 25.
34. Reynolds and White, *A Rehearsal Diary*, 25.
35. "Weapons Training," Stagework, http://www.stagework.org.uk/webdav/ harmonise@Page%252F@id=6012&Document%252F@id=2469.html.
36. Lester quoted in Claire Allfree, "A Serious Business," *Metro*, 29 April 2003.
37. "Rupert Wickham Captain Gower," Stagework, http://www.stagework. org.uk/webdav/harmonise@Page%252F@id=6012&Document%252F@ id=2452.html.
38. Robert Blythe, "Execute the Prisoners," Stagework, http://www.stagework. org.uk/webdav/harmonise@Page%252F@id=6012&Document%252F@ id=2450.html.
39. Kenneth Branagh, interview with Ramona Wray and Mark Thornton Burnett, "From the Horse's Mouth: Branagh on the Bard," in *Shakespeare, Film and Fin-de-Siècle*, ed. Mark Thornton Burnett and Ramona Wray (Basingstoke: Macmillan, 2000), 172.
40. Lois Potter, "English and American Richards, Edwards, and Henries," *Shakespeare Quarterly* 55.4 (2004): 454.
41. "Images of War," Stagework, http://www.stagework.org.uk/webdav/harmonise@ Page%252F@id=6007&Section%252F@id=375.html.
42. Anthony Kubiak, *Stages of Terror: Terrorism, Ideology and Coercion as Theatre History* (Bloomington: Indiana University Press, 1991), 158.
43. Rehearsal Notes, 4 April 2003.
44. See for example "Coalition 'tortured Iraqi POWs'," BBC, 16 May 2003, http://news.bbc.co.uk/1/hi/world/middle_east/3034031.stm; "PoW 'torture photos' Investigated," BBC, 30 May 2003, http://news.bbc.co.uk/1/hi/ england/2949282.stm.
45. Reynolds and White, *A Rehearsal Diary*, 24.
46. Reynolds and White, *A Rehearsal Diary*, 26.
47. Rehearsal Notes, 17 April 2003 and 11 April 2003; see Reynolds and White, *A Rehearsal Diary*, 34–38, for a discussion of the technical rehearsals; *Henry V*, VHS, directed by Hytner, Olivier, National Theatre, National Theatre Archive, 17 May 2003, RNT/SO/2/2/170.
48. Kubiak, *Stages of Terror*, 160.
49. Kubiak, *Stages of Terror*, 160.
50. Gary Tewson, "Hytner's Shakespeare Comparison Is Way Off Mark," *The Stage*, 27 March 2003.
51. Reynolds and White, *A Rehearsal Diary*, 27, 32.
52. Gordon Brown, Hansard, 18 December 2008, col. 1233, http://www. publications.parliament.uk/pa/cm200809/cmhansrd/cm081218/ debtext/81218–0004.htm#08121882000157; Barack Obama, "Remarks by the President in Address to the Nation on the End of Combat Operations in Iraq," 31

August 2010, http://www.whitehouse.gov/the-press-office/2010/08/31/remarks-president-address-nation-end-combat-operations-iraq.

53. "Propaganda Video," Stagework, http://www.stagework.org.uk/webdav/harmonise@Page%252F@id=6012&Document%252F@id=2564.html.

54. Mark Steyn, "Henry Goes to Baghdad," *New Criterion*, September 2003; Georgina Brown, "Henry Gets a Few Tips from Blair," *Mail on Sunday*, 18 May 2003; Dan Hancox, "Iraq and a Hard Place . . ." *South London Press*, 25 May 2003; Susannah Clapp, "Agincourt, near Basra," *Observer*, 18 May 2003.

55. *Henry V*, National Theatre, http://www.nationaltheatre.org.uk/3109/productions/henry-v.html.

56. Union Jack, The British Monarchy, http://www.royal.gov.uk/MonarchUK/Symbols/UnionJack.aspx.

57. I am grateful to Sarah Annes Brown for drawing my attention to the proleptic ending of *Henry V*.

58. *Henry IV Part 1*, VHS, directed by Hytner, Olivier, National Theatre, National Theatre Archive, 27 August 2005, RNT/SO/2/2/243.

59. Susan Sontag, *On Photography* (London: Penguin, 2002), 111.

60. "Royal Artillery Memorial," Stagework, http://www.stagework.org.uk/webdav/harmonise@Page%252F@id=6012&Document%252F@id=2655.html.

61. Roland Barthes, "The Photographic Message," in *Image, Music, Text*, ed. and trans. by Stephen Heath (London: Flamingo, 1984), 25.

62. Sontag, *On Photography*, 108.

63. *Henry V*, 2003, Olivier, National Theatre Archive, RNT/CO/1/476.

64. Reynolds and White, *A Rehearsal Diary*, 11.

65. Susan Sontag, *Regarding the Pain of Others* (London: Penguin, 2004), 19.

66. Sontag, *Regarding the Pain of Others*, 41.

67. Barthes, "The Photographic Message," 30–31.

68. Butler, *Frames of War*, 85–86.

69. Butler, *Frames of War*, 98.

70. Sontag, *Regarding the Pain of Others*, 102.

71. Butler, *Frames of War*, 98.

72. Programme, *Julius Caesar*, directed by Deborah Warner, BITE: 05, Barbican, London, 2005.

73. Sontag, *On Photography*, 110.

74. Hayne Palmour IV, Polaris Images, http://www.polarisimages.com/Portfolios/Photographers/Hayne_Palmour_IV/.

Bibliography

This bibliography does not include individual production materials (including audiovisual material), newspaper and magazine reviews, articles and interviews (print or online) or websites; these documents are referenced in the notes to individual chapters.

Aebischer, Pascale. *Shakespeare's Violated Bodies: Stage and Screen Performance.* Cambridge: Cambridge University Press, 2004.

American Psychiatric Association. "Post-traumatic Stress Disorder." In *Diagnostic and Statistical Manual of Mental Disorders: DSM-III,* 3rd ed., 236–39. Washington, D.C.: American Psychiatric Association, 1980.

———. "Post-traumatic Stress Disorder." In *Diagnostic and Statistical Manual of Mental Disorders: DSM-III-R,* 3rd rev. ed., 247–51. Washington, D.C.: American Psychiatric Association, 1987.

———. "Posttraumatic Stress Disorder." In *Diagnostic and Statistical Manual of Mental Disorders: DSM-IV,* 4th ed., 424–29. Washington, D.C.: American Psychiatric Association, 1994.

———. "Posttraumatic Stress Disorder." In *Diagnostic and Statistical Manual of Mental Disorders: DSM-IV-TR,* 4th rev. ed., 463–68. Washington, D.C.: American Psychiatric Association, 2000.

Anderson, Thomas P. *Performing Early Modern Trauma from Shakespeare to Milton.* Aldershot: Ashgate, 2006.

Angelic Conversation, The. DVD. Directed by Derek Jarman. London: BFI, 2007.

Bakhtin, M. M. *The Dialogic Imagination: Four Essays.* Edited by Michael Holquist. Translated by Caryl Emerson and Michael Holquist. Austin: University of Texas Press, 1981.

Banham, Martin, James Gibbs and Femi Osofisan, eds. *African Theatre: Playwrights and Politics.* Oxford: James Currey, 2001.

Barthes, Roland. "The Photographic Message." In *Image, Music, Text,* edited and translated by Stephen Heath, 15–31. London: Flamingo, 1984.

Benjamin, Walter. "The Task of the Translator: An Introduction to the Translation of Baudelaire's *Tableaux parisiens.*" In *Illuminations,* edited by Hannah Arendt and translated by Harry Zohn, 70–82. London: Fontana, 1992.

Bennett, Susan. "Rehearsing *The Tempest,* Directing the Post-Colonial Body: Disjunctive Identity in Philip Osment's *This Island's Mine.*" *Essays in Theatre* 15.1 (1996): 35–44.

Bhabha, Homi K. *The Location of Culture.* London: Routledge, 1994.

Bharucha, Rustom. *Theatre and the World: Performance and the Politics of Culture.* London: Routledge, 1993.

Bradley, A. C. *Shakespearean Tragedy: Lectures on "Hamlet", "Othello", "King Lear", "Macbeth".* Edited by Robert Shaughnessy. 4th ed. Basingstoke: Palgrave, 2007.

Brewer, Mary F. *Staging Whiteness.* Middletown, C.T. : Wesleyan University Press, 2005.

Bristol, Michael D. *Shakespeare's America, America's Shakespeare.* London: Routledge, 1990.

Brook, Peter. *The Empty Space.* London: Penguin, 1990.

Brown, Laura S. "Not Outside the Range: One Feminist Perspective on Psychic Trauma." In Caruth, *Trauma: Explorations in Memory*, 100–112.

Brown, Paul. "'This thing of darkness I acknowledge mine': *The Tempest* and the Discourse of Colonialism." In Dollimore and Sinfield, *Political Shakespeare*, 48–71.

Burnett, Mark Thornton. *Filming Shakespeare in the Global Marketplace.* Basingstoke: Palgrave, 2007.

Burns, Hilary. "The Market Theatre of Johannesburg in the New South Africa." *New Theatre Quarterly* 18.4 (2002): 359–74.

Burt, Richard. "Shakespeare and the Holocaust: Julie Taymor's *Titus* Is Beautiful, or Shakesploi Meets (the) Camp." *Colby Quarterly* 37.1 (2001): 78–106.

Butler, Judith. *Bodies That Matter: On the Discursive Limits of "Sex".* New York: Routledge, 1993.

———. *Frames of War: When Is Life Grievable?* London: Verso, 2009.

Cahill, Patricia A. *Unto the Breach: Martial Formations, Historical Trauma, and the Early Modern Stage.* Oxford: Oxford University Press, 2008.

Caruth, Cathy. "Introduction." In Caruth, *Trauma: Explorations in Memory*, 3–12.

———. *Unclaimed Experience: Trauma, Narrative and History.* Baltimore: Johns Hopkins University Press, 1996.

Caruth, Cathy, ed. *Trauma: Explorations in Memory.* Baltimore: Johns Hopkins University Press, 1995.

Chedgzoy, Kate. *Shakespeare's Queer Children: Sexual Politics and Contemporary Culture.* Manchester: Manchester University Press, 1995.

Cleto, Fabio, ed. *Camp: Queer Aesthetics and the Performing Subject, A Reader.* Edinburgh: Edinburgh University Press, 1999.

Colvin, Madeleine with Jane Hawksley. *Section 28: A Practical Guide to the Law and Its Implications.* London: National Council for Civil Liberties, 1989.

Coulter-Smith, Graham and Maurice Owen. "Introduction." In *Art in the Age of Terrorism*, edited by Graham Coulter-Smith and Maurice Owen, 1–9. London: Paul Hoberton, 2005.

Cox, Emma. "Te Reo Shakespeare: *Te Tangata Whai Rawa o Weneti/The Maori Merchant of Venice.*" *Kunapipi* 28.1 (2006): 79–95.

Cox, Murray, ed. *Shakespeare Comes to Broadmoor: "The Actors Are Come Hither"; The Performance of Tragedy in a Secure Psychiatric Hospital.* London: Kingsley, 1992.

Cvetkovich, Ann. *An Archive of Feelings: Trauma, Sexuality, and Lesbian Public Cultures.* Durham: Duke University Press, 2003.

Czeglédy, André P. "Villas of the Highveld: A Cultural Perspective on Johannesburg and Its 'Northern Suburbs'." In Tomlinson *et al.*, *Emerging Johannesburg*, 21–42.

Dawson, Ashley. "Documenting the Trauma of Apartheid: *Long Night's Journey into Day* and South Africa's Truth and Reconciliation Commission." *Screen* 46.4 (2005): 473–86.

Derek Jarman Collection I and II. British Film Institute, London.

Derrida, Jacques. *Acts of Literature.* Edited by Derek Attridge. New York: Routledge, 1992.

———. *Archive Fever: A Freudian Impression*. Translated by Eric Prenowitz. Chicago: University of Chicago Press, 1996.

———. "Des Tours de Babel." Translated by Joseph F. Graham. In *Difference in Translation*, edited by Joseph F. Graham, 165–207. Ithaca: Cornell University Press, 1985.

———. *Of Grammatology*. Translated by Gayatri Chakravorty Spivak. 2nd ed. Baltimore: Johns Hopkins University Press, 1997.

———. "Plato's Pharmacy." In *Dissemination*. Translated by Barbara Johnson, 61–171. London: Athlone, 1981.

———. *Specters of Marx: The State of the Debt, the Work of Mourning, and the New International*. Translated by Peggy Kamuf. New York: Routledge, 1994.

———. "What Is a 'Relevant' Translation?" Translated by Lawrence Venuti. *Critical Inquiry* 27.2 (2001): 174–200.

Distiller, Natasha. *South Africa, Shakespeare and Post-colonial Culture*. Lewiston, N.Y.: Edwin Mellen Press, 2005.

———. "'Through Shakespeare's Africa': 'terror and murder'?" In *Shakespeare's World/World Shakespeares: The Selected Proceedings of the International Shakespeare Association World Congress Brisbane, 2006*, edited by Richard Fotheringham, Christa Jansohn and R. S. White, 382–93. Newark: University of Delaware Press, 2008.

———. "Tony's Will: *Titus Andronicus* in South Africa 1995." In *The Shakespearean International Yearbook 9*, edited by Laurence Wright, 152–70. Farnham: Ashgate, 2009.

Dollimore, Jonathan. "Sex and Death." *Textual Practice* 9.1 (1995): 27–53.

Dollimore, Jonathan and Alan Sinfield, eds. *Political Shakespeare: Essays in Cultural Materialism*. 2nd ed. Manchester: Manchester University Press, 1994.

Durham, Martin. *Sex and Politics: The Family and Morality in the Thatcher Years*. Basingstoke: Macmillan, 1991.

Edward II. DVD. Directed by Derek Jarman. London: Second Sight Films, 2010.

Etchells, Tim. *Certain Fragments: Contemporary Performance and Forced Entertainment*. London: Routledge, 1999.

Fanon, Frantz. *Black Skin, White Masks*. Translated by Charles Lam Markmann. London: Pluto, 1986.

Farrell, Kirby. *Post-traumatic Culture: Injury and Interpretation in the Nineties*. Baltimore: Johns Hopkins University Press, 1998.

Freud, Sigmund. *Beyond the Pleasure Principle*. Vol. 18, in *The Standard Edition of the Complete Psychological Works of Sigmund Freud*, translated by James Strachey, 1–64. London: Hogarth Press, 1955.

———. "Moses, His People and Monotheist Religion." In *Moses and Monotheism: Three Essays*. Vol. 23, in *The Standard Edition of the Complete Psychological Works of Sigmund Freud*, translated by James Strachey, 54–137. London: Hogarth Press, 1964.

Gay Sweatshop. Archives, Royal Holloway, University of London.

Gilroy, Paul. *Small Acts: Thoughts on the Politics of Black Cultures*. London: Serpent's Tail, 1993.

God and Shakespeare. Digital video file. Directed by Sándor Lau. Auckland: Paper Tiger Detective Agency, 2001 http://www.nzshortfilm.com/film,261.sm (accessed 1 October 2010).

Grehan, Helena. *Performance, Ethics and Spectatorship in a Global Age*. Basingstoke: Palgrave, 2009.

Harvie, Jen. *Staging the UK*. Manchester: Manchester University Press, 2005.

Henry IV Parts 1 and II. Directed by Nicholas Hytner, 2005. National Theatre Archive, London.

Henry V. Directed by Nicholas Hytner, 2003. National Theatre Archive, London.

Hirschfeld, Heather. "Hamlet's 'first corse': Repetition, Trauma, and the Displacement of Redemptive Typology." *Shakespeare Quarterly* 54.2 (2003): 424–48.

Hodgdon, Barbara. *The Shakespeare Trade: Performances and Appropriations.* Philadelphia: University of Pennsylvania Press, 1998.

Holmes, Jonathan. "'A World Elsewhere': Shakespeare in South Africa." *Shakespeare Survey* 55 (2002): 271–84.

Horowitz, Arthur. "Shylock after Auschwitz: The Merchant of Venice on the Post-Holocaust Stage—Subversion, Confrontation, and Provocation." *Journal for Cultural and Religious Theory* 8.3 (2007): 7–19.

Houlahan, Mark. "Hekepia? The *Mana* of the Maori *Merchant.*" In Massai, *World-Wide Shakespeares,* 141–48.

———. "*Romeo and Tusi*: An Eclectically Musical Samoan/Māori *Romeo and Juliet* from Aotearoa/New Zealand." *Contemporary Theatre Review* 19.3 (2009): 279–88.

Jackson, MacDonald. "All Our Tribe." *Landfall* 204 (2002): 155–63.

Jarman, Derek. *At Your Own Risk: A Saint's Testament.* Edited by Michael Christie. London: Vintage, 1993.

———. *Queer Edward II.* London: BFI Publishing, 1991.

———. *Sod'Em.* In *Up in the Air: Collected Film Scripts,* 183–225. London: Vintage, 1996.

Johnson, David. *Shakespeare and South Africa.* Oxford: Clarendon Press, 1996.

[Jones], Pei Te Hurinui, translator. *Huria Hiha [Julius Caesar].* By William Shakespeare. Unpublished typescript, fMS-225, 1959. National Library of New Zealand/Te Puna Mātauranga o Aotearoa, Wellington, New Zealand.

———. *Owhiro: Te Mua o Weniti [Othello: The Moor of Venice].* By William Shakespeare. Unpublished typescript, [1944]. University of Waikato Library, Hamilton, New Zealand.

———. *Te Tangata Whai-Rawa O Weniti [The Merchant of Venice].* By William Shakespeare. Palmerston North, New Zealand: Young, 1946.

———. *Te Tangata Whai Rawa O Weneti [The Merchant of Venice].* By William Shakespeare. Revised edition. [Wellington]: Ministry of Education, 2008.

Joseph, Miranda. *Against the Romance of Community.* Minneapolis: University of Minnesota Press, 2002.

King, Michael. *The Penguin History of New Zealand.* Auckland: Penguin, 2003.

Kott, Jan. *Shakespeare Our Contemporary.* Translated by Boleslaw Taborski. 2nd ed. London: Methuen, 1967.

Kristeva, Julia. *Revolution in Poetic Language.* Translated by Margaret Waller. New York: Columbia University Press, 1984.

Kubiak, Anthony. *Stages of Terror: Terrorism, Ideology, and Coercion as Theatre History.* Bloomington: Indiana University Press, 1991.

LaCapra, Dominick. *Writing History, Writing Trauma.* Baltimore: Johns Hopkins University Press, 2001.

Lee, Samuel. Preface to Thomas Kendall, *A Grammar and Vocabulary of the Language of New Zealand,* n.p. London: Church Missionary Society, 1820.

Lehmann, Courtney, Bryan Reynolds and Lisa Starks. "'For such a sight will blind a father's eye': The Spectacle of Suffering in Taymor's *Titus.*" In *Performing Transversally: Reimagining Shakespeare and the Critical Future,* by Bryan Reynolds, 215–43. New York: Palgrave, 2003.

Levinas, Emmanuel. *Totality and Infinity: An Essay on Exteriority.* Translated by Alphonso Lingis. Pittsburgh: Duquesne University Press, 1969.

Leys, Ruth. *Trauma: A Genealogy.* Chicago: University of Chicago Press, 2000.

Loomba, Ania. "'Local-manufacture made-in-India Othello fellows': Issues of Race, Hybridity and Location in Post-colonial Shakespeares." In *Post-Colonial Shakespeares*, edited by Ania Loomba and Martin Orkin, 143–63. London: Routledge, 1998.

Love, Lauren. "Resisting the 'Organic': A Feminist Actor's Approach." In *Acting (Re)Considered: A Theoretical and Practical Guide*, edited by Phillip B. Zarrilli, 2nd ed., 277–90. London: Routledge, 2002.

Lucas, Ian. *Outrage! An Oral History*. London: Cassell, 1998.

Luckhurst, Roger. *The Trauma Question*. London: Routledge, 2008.

Macaulay, Thomas Babington. "Indian Education: Minute on the 2nd of February, 1835." In *Prose and Poetry*, edited by G. M. Young, 719–30. London: Hart-Davis, 1952.

Maori Merchant of Venice, The [*Te Tangata Whai Rawa O Weniti*]. Film. Directed by Don C. Selwyn. Auckland: He Taonga Films, 2001.

Massai, Sonia, ed. *World-Wide Shakespeares: Local Appropriations in Film and Performance*. London: Routledge: 2005.

McCandless, David. "A Tale of Two *Tituses*: Julie Taymor's Vision on Stage and Screen." *Shakespeare Quarterly* 53.4 (2002): 487–511.

McMullan, Gordon. *Shakespeare and the Idea of Late Writing: Authorship in the Proximity of Death*. Cambridge: Cambridge University Press, 2007.

Mercer, Kobena. *Welcome to the Jungle: New Positions in Black Cultural Studies*. New York: Routledge, 1994.

Meyer, Moe. "Introduction: Reclaiming the Discourse of Camp." In *The Politics and Poetics of Camp*, edited by Moe Meyer, 1–22. London: Routledge, 1994.

Moston, Doug. "Standards and Practices." In *Method Acting Reconsidered: Theory, Practice, Future*, edited by David Krasner, 135–46. New York: St. Martin's, 2000.

Mtwa, Percy, Mbongeni Ngema and Barney Simon. *Woza Albert!* London: Methuen, 1983.

Murdoch, Claire. "Holy Sea-Cow." *Landfall* 206 (2003): 97–105.

Murray, Timothy. *Drama Trauma: Specters of Race and Sexuality in Performance, Video and Art*. London: Routledge, 1997.

Nixon, Rob. "Caribbean and African Appropriations of *The Tempest*." *Critical Inquiry* 13.3 (1987): 557–78.

Norman, Marc and Tom Stoppard, *Shakespeare in Love*. London: Faber, 1999.

Orkin, Martin. *Shakespeare Against Apartheid*. Craighall: Donker, 1987.

Osment, Philip. "Finding Room on the Agenda for Love: A History of Gay Sweatshop." In Osment, *Gay Sweatshop*, vii–lxviii.

———. *This Island's Mine*. In *Adaptations of Shakespeare: A Critical Anthology of Plays from the Seventeenth Century to the Present*, edited by Daniel Fischlin and Mark Fortier, 258–84. London: Routledge, 2000.

———. *This Island's Mine*. In Osment, *Gay Sweatshop*, 83–120.

Osment, Philip, ed. *Gay Sweatshop: Four Plays and a Company*. London: Methuen, 1989.

Oxford English Dictionary (OED). Online edition. http://www.oed.com.

Pelias, Ronald J. "Empathy and the Ethics of Entitlement." *Theatre Research International* 16.2 (1991): 142–52.

Penfold, Merimeri, translator. *Nga Waiata Aroha a Hekepia: Love Sonnets by Shakespeare; Nine Sonnets*, by William Shakespeare. Auckland: Holloway Press, University of Auckland, 2000.

Phelan, Peggy. *Mourning Sex: Performing Public Memories*. London: Routledge, 1997.

Potter, Lois. "English and American Richards, Edwards, and Henries." *Shakespeare Quarterly* 55.4 (2004): 450–61.

Pryor, Judith. *Constitutions: Writing Nations, Reading Difference*. Abingdon: Birkbeck Law Press, 2008.

Radstone, Susannah, ed. "Special Debate: Trauma and Screen Studies." *Screen* 42.2 (2001): 188–216.

Richardson, Niall. *The Queer Cinema of Derek Jarman: Critical and Cultural Readings*. London: Tauris, 2009.

Rimmon-Kenan, Shlomith. *Narrative Fiction: Contemporary Poetics*. 2nd ed. London: Routledge, 2002.

Salmond, Anne. *The Trial of the Cannibal Dog: Captain Cook in the South Seas*. London: Penguin, 2004.

Sanders, Mark. "Ambiguities of Mourning: Law, Custom, and Testimony of Women before South Africa's Truth and Reconciliation Commission." In *Loss: The Politics of Mourning*, edited by David L. Eng and David Kazanjian, 77–98. Berkeley: University of California Press, 2003.

Schülting, Sabine. "'I am not bound to please thee with my answers': *The Merchant of Venice* on the Post-war German Stage." In Massai, *World-Wide Shakespeares*, 65–71.

Scott-Douglass, Amy. *Shakespeare Inside: The Bard Behind Bars*. London: Continuum, 2007.

Shakespeare in Love. DVD. Directed by John Madden. Culver City, C.A.: Columbia TriStar Home Video, 1999.

Shakespeare, William. *The Norton Shakespeare*. Edited by Stephen Greenblatt *et al*. New York: Norton, 1997.

Sher, Antony and Gregory Doran. *Woza Shakespeare! "Titus Andronicus" in South Africa*. London: Methuen, 1997.

Silverstone, Catherine. "'Honour the real thing': Shakespeare, Trauma and *Titus Andronicus* in South Africa." *Shakespeare Survey* 62 (2009): 46–57.

———. "*Othello*'s Travels in New Zealand: Shakespeare, Race and National Identity." In *Remaking Shakespeare: Performance Across Media, Genres and Cultures*, edited by Pascale Aebischer, Edward J. Esche and Nigel Wheale, 74–92. Basingstoke: Palgrave, 2003.

———. "Speaking Māori Shakespeare: *The Maori Merchant of Venice* and the Legacy of Colonisation." In *Screening Shakespeare in the Twenty-First Century*, edited by Mark Thornton Burnett and Ramona Wray, 127–45. Edinburgh: Edinburgh University Press, 2006.

Sinfield, Alan. "How to Read *The Merchant of Venice* without Being Heterosexist." In *Alternative Shakespeares Volume 2*, edited by Terence Hawkes, 122–39. London: Routledge, 1996.

———. "Introduction: Reproductions, Interventions." In Dollimore and Sinfield, *Political Shakespeare*, 154–57.

———. *Out on Stage: Lesbian and Gay Theatre in the Twentieth Century*. New Haven: Yale University Press, 1999.

Solga, Kim. *Violence Against Women in Early Modern Performance: Invisible Acts*. Basingstoke: Palgrave, 2009.

Sontag, Susan. "Notes on 'Camp'." In *Against Interpretation and Other Essays*, 275–92. New York: Octagon, 1982.

———. *On Photography*. London: Penguin, 2002.

———. *Regarding the Pain of Others*. London: Penguin, 2004.

Stacey, Jackie. "Promoting Normality: Section 28 and the Regulation of Sexuality." In *Off-Centre: Feminism and Cultural Studies*, edited by Sarah Franklin, Celia Lury and Jackie Stacey, 284–304. London: Harper Collins Academic, 1991.

Stannard, David E. *American Holocaust: The Conquest of the New World*. New York: Oxford University Press, 1992.

Stasiulis, Daiva and Nira Yuval-Davis. "Introduction: Beyond Dichotomies—Gender, Race, Ethnicity and Class in Settler Societies." In *Unsettling Settler Societies: Articulations of Gender, Race, Ethnicity and Class*, edited by Daiva Stasiulis and Nira Yuval-Davis, 1–38. Sage Series on Race and Ethnic Relations 11. London: Sage, 1995.

Stonewall. *Section 28—Draft Briefing.* London: Stonewall, [1988].

Taymor, Julie. *Titus: The Illustrated Screenplay, Adapted from the Play by William Shakespeare.* New York: Newmarket Press, 2000.

Taymor, Julie, co-authored with Eileen Blumenthal and Antonio Monda. *Playing with Fire: Theater, Opera, Film.* 3rd ed. New York: Abrams, 1999.

Tempest, The. DVD. Directed by Derek Jarman. London: Second Sight Films, 2004.

Te Po Uriuri (The Enveloping Night). Digital video file. Directed by Toby Mills. Auckland: Tawera Productions and Independent and General Productions, 2001 http://www.nzonscreen.com/title/te-po-uriuri-2001 (accessed: 1 October 2010).

Te Tangata Whai Rawa O Wēniti. Resource Kit. [Written and compiled by the Ministry of Education]. Te Whanganui-a-Tara, Aotearoa [New Zealand]: Te Pou Taki Kōrero, 2004.

Thomas, Philip and Ruth Costigan. *Promoting Homosexuality: Section 28 of the Local Government Act 1988.* Cardiff: Cardiff Law School, 1990.

Thurman, Christopher. "Sher and Doran's *Titus Andronicus* (1995): Importing Shakespeare, Exporting South Africa." *Shakespeare in Southern Africa* 18 (2006): 29–36.

Titus. DVD. Directed by Julie Taymor. Los Angeles: Twentieth Century Fox Home Entertainment, 2000.

Titus Andronicus. Directed by Gregory Doran, 1995. Archives, National Theatre, London.

Tomlinson, Richard, Robert A. Beauregard, Lindsay Bremner and Xolela Mangcu. "The Postapartheid Struggle for an Integrated Johannesburg." In Tomlinson *et al.*, *Emerging Johannesburg*, 3–20.

Tomlinson, Richard, *et al.*, eds. *Emerging Johannesburg: Perspectives on the Post-apartheid City.* New York: Routledge, 2003.

Trauma Industry, The. Panorama. Presented by Allan Little. Produced by Kevin Toolis. BBC 1. 27 July 2009.

Venuti, Lawrence. *The Scandals of Translation: Towards an Ethics of Difference.* London: Routledge, 1998.

Vickers, Brian. *Shakespeare, Co-Author: A Historical Study of Five Collaborative Plays.* Oxford: Oxford University Press, 2002.

Virahsawmy, Dev. *Toufann: A Mauritian Fantasy.* Translated by Nisha Walling and Michael Walling. London: Border Crossings, 2003.

———. *Toufann: A Mauritian Fantasy.* Translated by Nisha Walling and Michael Walling. In Banham, Gibbs and Osofisan, *African Theatre: Playwrights and Politics*, 217–54.

Viswanathan, Gauri. *Masks of Conquest: Literary Study and British Rule in India.* London: Faber, 1990.

Wald, Christina. *Hysteria, Trauma and Melancholia: Performative Maladies in Contemporary Anglophone Drama.* Basingstoke: Palgrave, 2007.

Wandor, Michelene. *Carry On, Understudies: Theatre and Sexual Politics.* 2nd ed. London: Routledge, 1986.

Warner, Michael. "Introduction: Fear of a Queer Planet." *Social Text* 29 (1991): 3–17.

Wayne, Valerie. Review of *Te Tangata Whai Rawa O Weniti/The Māori Merchant of Venice. The Contemporary Pacific* 16.2 (2004): 425–29.

Wesker, Arnold. *Shylock*. In *The Journalists, The Wedding Feast, Shylock*, 171–261. London: Penguin, 1990.

Wilkinson, Jane. Interview with Michael Walling. "Staging Shakespeare Across Borders, 12 December 1999." In Banham, Gibbs and Osofisan, *African Theatre: Playwrights and Politics*, 115–24.

Willis, Deborah. "'The gnawing vulture': Revenge, Trauma Theory, and *Titus Andronicus*." *Shakespeare Quarterly* 53.1 (2002): 21–52.

Wolfenden, John, Chairman, Committee on Homosexual Offences and Prostitution. *Report of the Committee on Homosexual Offences and Prostitution. Presented to Parliament by the Secretary of State for the Home Department and the Secretary of State for Scotland, etc.* London, 1957.

Worthen, W. B. *Shakespeare and the Force of Modern Performance*. Cambridge: Cambridge University Press, 2003.

Wray, Ramona and Mark Thornton Burnett. "From the Horse's Mouth: Branagh on the Bard." In *Shakespeare, Film and Fin-de-Siècle*, edited by Mark Thornton Burnett and Ramona Wray, 165–78. Basingstoke: Macmillan, 2000.

Zarrilli, Phillip B. "For Whom Is the King a King? Issues of Intercultural Production, Perception, and Reception in a *Kathakali King Lear*." In *Critical Theory and Performance*, edited by Janelle G. Reinelt and Joseph R. Roach, 2nd ed., 108–33. Ann Arbor: University of Michigan Press, 2007.

About the Author

Catherine Silverstone is Lecturer in Drama, Theatre and Performance Studies in the School of English and Drama at Queen Mary University of London.

Index

Page numbers in *italic* refer to illustrations. References to performances can usually be found under the title of the play, film or television programme; otherwise they can be found under the name of the director or company.